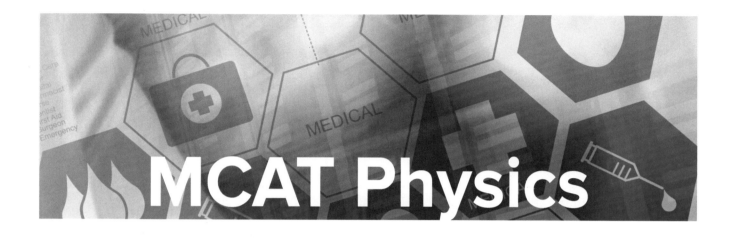

MCAT Physics

CONTENT REVIEW AND PRACTICE PASSAGES

NextStep
TEST PREP nextsteptestprep.com

Printed in the United States of America

Second Printing, 2018

ISBN 978-1-944-935-20-7

Next Step Test Prep, LLC
4256 N Ravenswood Ave
Suite 207
Chicago IL 60613

www.nextsteptestprep.com

MCAT is a registered trademark of the American Association of Medical Colleges (AAMC). The AAMC has neither reviewed nor endorsed this work in any way.

Revision Number: 1.2 (2018-04-01)

FREE ONLINE FULL LENGTH MCAT

Want to see how you would do on the MCAT
and understand where you need to focus your prep?

TAKE OUR FREE MCAT DIAGNOSTIC EXAM
and **FREE FULL LENGTH**
Timed practice that simulates Test Day and provides
comprehensive analysis, reporting, and in-depth explanations.

Included with this free account is the first lesson
in Next Step's online course, a free sample
from our science QBank, and more!

All of these resources are provided free to students who have
purchased a Next Step book. Register for your free account at:

http://nextsteptestprep.com/mcat-diagnostic

Group → 1 2 3 4 5 6 7 8 9 10 11 12 13 14 15 16 17 18
↓ Period

Group→	1	2	3	4	5	6	7	8	9	10	11	12	13	14	15	16	17	18
1	1 H																	2 He
2	3 Li	4 Be											5 B	6 C	7 N	8 O	9 F	10 Ne
3	11 Na	12 Mg											13 Al	14 Si	15 P	16 S	17 Cl	18 Ar
4	19 K	20 Ca	21 Sc	22 Ti	23 V	24 Cr	25 Mn	26 Fe	27 Co	28 Ni	29 Cu	30 Zn	31 Ga	32 Ge	33 As	34 Se	35 Br	36 Kr
5	37 Rb	38 Sr	39 Y	40 Zr	41 Nb	42 Mo	43 Tc	44 Ru	45 Rh	46 Pd	47 Ag	48 Cd	49 In	50 Sn	51 Sb	52 Te	53 I	54 Xe
6	55 Cs	56 Ba	57 La	72 Hf	73 Ta	74 W	75 Re	76 Os	77 Ir	78 Pt	79 Au	80 Hg	81 Tl	82 Pb	83 Bi	84 Po	85 At	86 Rn
7	87 Fr	88 Ra	89 Ac	104 Rf	105 Db	106 Sg	107 Bh	108 Hs	109 Mt	110 Ds	111 Rg	112 Cn	113 Nh	114 Fl	115 Mc	116 Lv	117 Ts	118 Og

*	58 Ce	59 Pr	60 Nd	61 Pm	62 Sm	63 Eu	64 Gd	65 Tb	66 Dy	67 Ho	68 Er	69 Tm	70 Yb	71 Lu
**	90 Th	91 Pa	92 U	93 Np	94 Pu	95 Am	96 Cm	97 Bk	98 Cf	99 Es	100 Fm	101 Md	102 No	103 Lr

STOP! READ ME FIRST!

The book you're holding is one of Next Step's six MCAT review books and contains both concise content review and questions to practice applying your content knowledge. In order to get the most out of this book, we strongly recommend that you follow a few simple steps:

1. Register for a free MCAT bundle at http://nextsteptestprep.com/mcat-diagnostic and begin your prep by taking the MCAT Diagnostic and Science Content Diagnostic to assess your strengths and weaknesses.

2. Begin working through the Next Step Review set starting with the Verbal, Quantitative, and Research Methods book. Complete this entire book at the start of your prep.

3. Use the Study Plan generator in your free account at nextstepmcat.com to generate a day-by-day study plan to take you through the rest of the Next Step Books.

4. Begin working through the rest of the Next Step MCAT review books, including this one. To get the most value out of these books, use spaced repetition to ensure complete mastery of the material. A spaced repetition approach would look something like this:

I. Begin by skimming through the chapter to familiarize yourself with the key terms and content in the book. Then go back and read the chapter carefully.

II. Sleep on it! Solidifying those long term memories requires sleep.

III. Come back to the chapter *the next day*, re-skim it and then ***complete the questions at the end of the chapter***. Carefully read all of the explanations, even for the questions you got right.

IV. Take notes in your Lessons Learned Journal from the chapter. For a full explanation on what a Lessons Learned Journal is, watch Lesson 1 included in the free online bundle at nextstepmcat.com.

IV. Sleep on it!

V. Two days later, come back, briefly re-skim the chapter, re-do the questions at the end of the chapter, and review your Lessons Learned Journal.

Mastering the MCAT requires more than just a good set of books. You'll want to continue your prep with the most representative practice tests available. Your free bundle includes Next Step Full Length #1. After you've completed that, you can upgrade your account to include additional practice exams.

Finally, if you would like more extensive help, including daily live office hours with Next Step's senior faculty, contact us for more information about our online course. You can reach us at 888-530-NEXT or mcat@nextsteptestprep.com.

This page left intentionally blank.

TABLE OF CONTENTS

This page left intentionally blank.

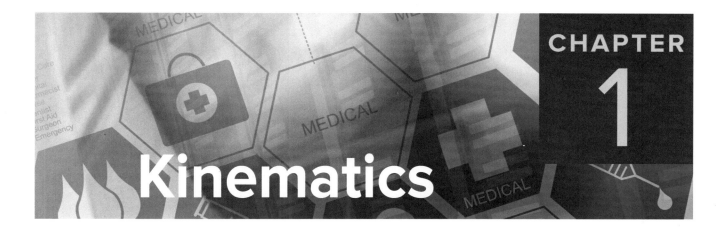

Kinematics

CHAPTER 1

0. Introduction

Kinematics is the study of objects in motion without direct reference to the forces acting upon those objects. It involves a foundational set of concepts in physics, and plays an important role in your MCAT study because it provides you the opportunity to hone crucial physics skills—such as applying units, vectors, and dimensional analysis, as well as setting up and solving physics problems in a time-efficient manner—on a set of concepts that are generally relatively intuitive and relatable.

1. Units and Vectors

A high-level conceptual distinction can be drawn between dimensions and units. Dimensions can be thought of as properties with physical reality, including basic concepts such as distance, mass, volume, and time, as well as more specific concepts such as density or velocity that can be defined in terms of more basic properties (density is mass divided by volume, velocity is distance divided by time). Units, in contrast, are arbitrary measuring tools that we use to keep track of dimensions. For example, distance can be measured in meters, kilometers, miles, inches, yards, or any other unit that comes to mind—we can even somewhat jokingly say that if something is twice the size of our friend named Amber, it is two Ambers high, although this unit of distance would be pretty useless and not make any sense outside of a specific conversational context.

In scientific contexts, the International System of Units (SI units, also known as the metric system) is generally used. The MCAT may ask you to work with non-SI units such as miles or yards, but you are not expected to memorize the conversion factors—if needed, they will be provided to you. The metric system includes base units and prefixes that indicate different orders of 10: for instance, a kilometer is 10^3 meters. The SI base units relevant for the MCAT are provided below in Table 1, and Table 2 presents a list of the prefixes used to indicate magnitude.

DIMENSION	NAME	ABBREVIATION	NOTES
Length	Meter	m	You do not *have* to know that a meter is 3.28 feet, but having a rough sense of this relationship may be useful to help visualize problems if you are not used to reasoning in meters.
Mass	Kilogram	kg	The base unit is technically not the gram, although grams (g) are commonly used in chemistry. In physics problems, it is crucial to remember that the base unit is the kilogram.
Time	Second	s	Minutes, hours, days, weeks, and years are used, and the MCAT expects you to know that there are 60 seconds in a minute, 60 minutes in an hour, 7 days in a week, and approximately 365 days in a year. You are extremely unlikely to encounter units such as kiloseconds.
Electric current	Ampere	A	
Temperature	Kelvin	K	Degrees Celsius (°C) are also acceptable, with 0°C corresponding to 273.15 K.
Amount of substance	Mole	mol	This is more relevant for chemistry than physics, but a mole contains 6.02×10^{23} atoms/molecules.

Table 1. Base SI units.

MULTIPLES			FRACTIONS		
Prefix name	Prefix abbreviation	Factor of 10	Prefix name	Prefix abbreviation	Factor of 10
Deca	da	10^1	**Deci**	**d**	$\mathbf{10^{-1}}$
Hecto	h	10^2	**Centi**	**c**	$\mathbf{10^{-2}}$
Kilo	**k**	$\mathbf{10^3}$	**Milli**	**m**	$\mathbf{10^{-3}}$
Mega	**M**	$\mathbf{10^6}$	**Micro**	**μ**	$\mathbf{10^{-6}}$
Giga	**G**	$\mathbf{10^9}$	**Nano**	**n**	$\mathbf{10^{-9}}$
Tera	**T**	$\mathbf{10^{12}}$	**Pico**	**p**	$\mathbf{10^{-12}}$
Peta	P	10^{15}	Femto	f	10^{-15}
Exa	E	10^{18}	Atto	a	10^{-18}
Zetta	Z	10^{21}	Zepto	z	10^{-21}
Yotta	Y	10^{24}	Yocto	y	10^{-24}

Table 2. SI prefixes, with essential prefixes bolded.

Practicing with SI prefixes and how they interact with scientific notation will help you tremendously on Test Day by improving your speed and accuracy with unit conversions. Skillful conversion between units is slightly different than simply practicing with scientific notation from a mathematical point of view, because you may have to select between answer choices that are not expressed in terms of scientific notation (for instance, wavelengths of visible light are conventionally expressed as hundreds of nanometers). There are two basic strategies for accomplishing this: (1) take a value expressed in some set of units, convert it into scientific notation, and then convert that into the units required by the question; and (2) become familiar with doing quick conversions between units of a more or less similar scale.

Let's consider how to implement these strategies by answering a simple question: The wavelength of a ray of red light is 700 nm. How can this be expressed in terms of: (a) scientific notation, (b) micrometers, and (c) picometers?

a) We know that a nanometer is 10^{-9} meters. Therefore, 700 nm = 700×10^{-9} m. However, this is not correct scientific notation. To convert this to proper scientific notation, we need to move the decimal point on 700 to the left by 2 places, which means that we need to increase the exponent by 2. Therefore, 700×10^{-9} m is equivalent to 7×10^{-7} m. Another way of doing this would be to recognize that $700 = 7 \times 10^2$, allowing us to rewrite 700×10^{-9} m as $(7 \times 10^2) \times 10^{-9}$ m, which works out to 7×10^{-7} m.

b) We can approach (b) in multiple ways. If we start by converting 700 nm into scientific notation (7×10^{-7} m), we then know that we need to increase the exponent by 1 to obtain a quantity expressible in micrometers (10^{-6} m). This means we need to move the decimal point to the left, resulting in 0.7×10^{-6} m, or 0.7 μm. It would also be possible to solve this by applying dimensional analysis along the following lines: 7×10^{-7} m $\times 1$ μm/10^{-6} m = $7 \times 10^{-7} / 10^{-6}$ μm = 7×10^{-1} μm = 0.7 μm. If you're comfortable with the fact that 1 μm = 10^3 or 1000 nm, then it may be intuitively straightforward that 700 nm is almost 1 μm but not quite, making it 0.7 μm.

c) Picometers are much smaller than nanometers, so we know that 700 nm must be a very large number of picometers. In fact, picometers are smaller by an order of 10^3, which means that we need to add 3 zeros to get the desired result: 700,000 pm. This reasoning is identical to the reasoning that you would apply to determine that 700 kg = 700,000 g (say this out loud if it doesn't seem intuitive: seven hundred *kilo*grams equals seven hundred *thousand* grams). This can also be solved by moving the decimal point to the right by 3 places as we decrease the exponent of 10 by 3, or by dimensional analysis as was demonstrated for (b). If you apply dimensional analysis, note that you can start with either 700 nm, if you work with the equivalence ratio of 1 nm = 1×10^3 pm, or with the result of (a), 7×10^{-7} m, if you apply the equivalence ratio of 1 pm = 1×10^{-12} m. You can pick whichever approach you like from a mathematical standpoint; what matters is that you choose a strategy and apply it consistently and correctly.

Derived units can be expressed as combinations of base units. For instance, a newton (N) is defined as a kilogram times a meter divided by seconds squared (kg·m/s²). Table 3 presents a list of MCAT-relevant derived units. Note that many derived units can be expressed in terms of other derived units more usefully than in terms of SI base units; for instance, it is much more helpful to think of watts (power) in terms of joules (energy) per second than it is to think of watts as kilograms times meters squared divided by seconds cubed.

$$N = \frac{kg \cdot m}{s^2}$$

> ## MCAT STRATEGY > > >
>
> There are multiple approaches that can lead to correct solutions of conversion problems like this. Which approach you choose doesn't particularly matter—remember that for the MCAT, results are the only thing that count, so you don't have to justify your technique to a math or physics professor as long as it gets good results. What does matter is that you put in practice ahead of time to become very comfortable with doing conversions like this quickly so that you can implement your chosen method under time pressure.

NAME	ABBREVIATION	QUANTITY	EXPRESSION IN TERMS OF OTHER SI DERIVED UNITS	EXPRESSION IN TERMS OF SI BASE UNITS
Hertz	Hz	Frequency		s^{-1}
Newton	N	Force		$kg \cdot m \cdot s^{-2}$
Pascal	Pa	Pressure	N/m^2	$kg \cdot m^{-1} \cdot s^{-2}$
Joule	J	Energy, work, heat	$N \cdot m$	$kg \cdot m^2 \cdot s^{-2}$
Newton-meter	$N \cdot m$	Torque	$N \cdot m$	$kg \cdot m^2 \cdot s^{-2}$
Watt	W	Power	J/s	$kg \cdot m^2 \cdot s^{-3}$
Coulomb	C	Electric charge		$s \cdot A$
Volt	V	Voltage	W/A	$kg \cdot m^2 \cdot s^{-3} \cdot A^{-1}$
Farad	F	Electric capacitance	C/V	$kg^{-1} \cdot m^{-2} \cdot s^4 \cdot A^2$
Ohm	Ω	Electric resistance	V/A	$kg \cdot m^2 \cdot s^{-3} \cdot A^{-2}$
Weber	Wb	Magnetic flux	$V \cdot s$	$kg \cdot m^2 \cdot s^{-2} \cdot A^{-1}$
Tesla	T	Magnetic field strength	Wb/m^2	$kg \cdot s^{-2} \cdot A^{-1}$
Henry	H	Inductance	Wb/A	$kg \cdot m^2 \cdot s^{-2} \cdot A^{-2}$
Becquerel	Bq	Radioactivity		s^{-1}
Gray	Gy	Absorbed dose of ionizing radiation	J/kg	$m^2 \cdot s^{-2}$
Sievert	Sv	Equivalent dose of ionizing radiation	J/kg	$m^2 \cdot s^{-2}$

Table 3. Derived SI units relevant for the MCAT.

[handwritten annotation: Scalar = no direction]

For physics on the MCAT, it is crucial to be able to distinguish between vector and scalar quantities, and to know how to perform basic mathematical manipulations of vectors. Vectors are quantities that incorporate both magnitude and distance, whereas scalars are quantities that only refer to magnitude. A simple example of a vector is "50 miles northeast," and a simple example of a scalar is temperature. What about just the quantity of 50 miles? No direction is specified, so 50 miles by itself must be a scalar. Many important quantities in physics, such as displacement, velocity, acceleration, and force, are vectors.

Vectors are generally defined in terms of a two-dimensional x-y plane or a three-dimensional space consisting of x, y, and z axes. For the MCAT, it is extremely unlikely that you will need to apply vector analysis to three-dimensional coordinate systems, so the rest of this discussion will focus on two-dimensional vectors with x-components and y-components. However, all of the points made can also be extended to spaces with three or more dimensions.

Vectors as functions are often referred to in bold and/or with arrows above the letter of the function, such as v or $\vec{v}$. They also can be drawn as arrows in a coordinate axis system or specified as x and y coordinates in parentheses; e.g., the vector (3, 4) on a standard coordinate graph refers to the arrow drawn from the origin to a point +3 units on the x-axis and +4 units on the y-axis. This formulation is deceptively simple, though; while this is obviously enough to specify a point on a graph, we may now ask: what is the magnitude of this vector and what is its direction? Consider Figure 1, which illustrates the problem at hand.

MCAT STRATEGY > > >

When you study physics concepts, study units too! They can help out because the units provided in answer choices can essentially tell you how to solve a problem. To take a simple example, knowing that the units of torque are N·m essentially *tells us* that we can find torque by multiplying force times distance (although we have to keep track of cos(θ) too, as part of determining the force correctly). Studying units also helps you to study physics equations by thinking about them as statements about real-world relationships, not just letters on the page.

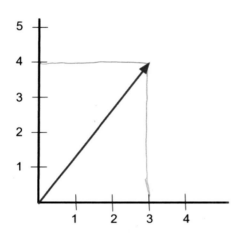

Figure 1. A simple vector, $\vec{v}$.

The magnitude of the vector (3, 4) is the length of the arrow drawn from the origin to reach the point defined by x = 3, y = 4. As can be seen in Figure 1, this arrow forms a right triangle with sides formed by a line of +3 units on the x-axis and +4 units on the y-axis. In order to find its length, we must use the Pythagorean theorem:

Equation 1. Pythagorean theorem. $a^2 + b^2 = c^2; c = \sqrt{a^2 + b^2}$

As applied to this problem, the magnitude of the vector works out to be 5. What about its direction? In order to figure this out, we need to specify the angle of the arrow, for which we need to use trigonometry. From a formal mathematical point of view, this results in what is known as a polar vector, but luckily, for the MCAT we can just reason about this problem intuitively in terms of determining the angles in the triangle relative to some axis. Let's align the bottom of this triangle with the x-axis, as shown in Figure 2. If we know the lengths of all the sides of a right triangle, we can use a very important set of trigonometric relationships to determine the angles:

Equation 2.   SOHCAHTOA
> Sine = opposite/hypotenuse
> Cosine = adjacent/hypotenuse
> Tangent = opposite/adjacent.

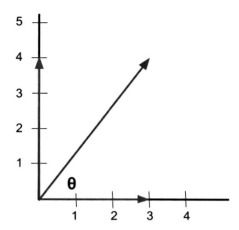

Figure 2. Simple vector broken down into its x- and y-components, with θ indicating the angle with the x-axis.

Let's consider θ, the angle formed with the origin in Figure 2. We know the hypotenuse is 5 units in length, and the opposite side of this angle is 4 units in length. Therefore, $\sin(\theta) = 4/5 = 0.8$. You certainly don't need to know exactly what angle has a sine of 0.8 (the MCAT would provide you this information if it were to come up in a problem), but you should be able to recognize that it must be closer to 90° than 0°. It turns out that θ is approximately 53°. The MCAT is unlikely to give you such a simple problem, but understanding these basics is crucial for recognizing how to deal with a situation that does occur frequently: what if we know the magnitude of a vector and its angle with the x- and y-axes, but need to break it down into its x- and y-components? This is illustrated in Figure 3, where the vector has a magnitude of 5 and forms a 30° angle with the x-axis.

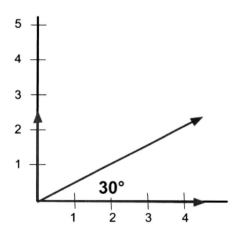

Figure 3. Vector with magnitude and angles.

What are the x- and y-components of this vector? We can answer this using the following formulas:

Equation 3.$\qquad\qquad\qquad\vec{v}_x = \vec{v}\cos\theta$, where θ is the angle formed with the x-axis.

Equation 4.$\qquad\qquad\qquad\vec{v}_y = \vec{v}\sin\theta$, where θ is the angle formed with the x-axis.

Given that $\cos(30°) = \sqrt{3}/2$ (or 0.87) and $\sin(30°) = 1/2$, the x- and y-components of the vector in Figure 3 are 4.35 and 2.5, respectively.

Next, let's consider how to perform basic mathematical operations on vectors. For the MCAT, the most important skill to master is how to add and subtract vectors, especially when they are perpendicular. Interestingly, it turns out that working the example illustrated in Figure 3 in reverse actually illustrates how to add and subtract vectors. Keeping in mind that subtracting is the same thing as adding negative quantities (graphically, you can just flip the head and tail of a vector), the rest of this discussion will only discuss addition. The most general way to think about adding vectors is that you simply add their x- and y-coordinates, as shown in Equation 5.

Equation 5.   If $\vec{u} = (x_u, y_u)$ and $\vec{v} = (x_v, y_v)$, $\vec{u} + \vec{v} = (x_u + x_v, y_u + y_v)$

Graphically, vectors can be added by connecting the "tail" of one vector to the "head" of another and drawing a line that connects the beginning of one vector with the end of the second. Figure 4 illustrates this for one pair of perpendicular vectors and one pair of nonperpendicular vectors.

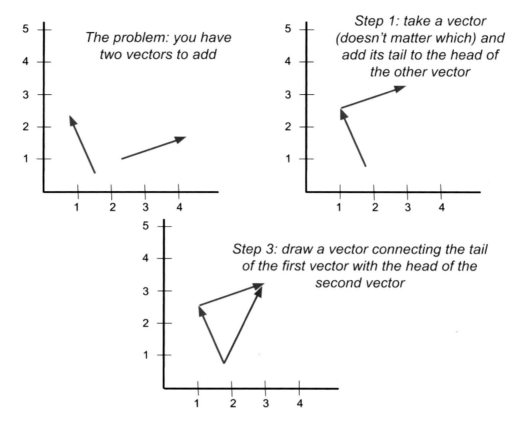

Figure 4. Graphical addition of vectors. (One pair perpendicular starting at origin with same values as obtained for vector in Fig. 3, one pair non-perpendicular not starting at origin).

Note that the vectors in Figure 4 are exactly the x- and y-components of the vector in Figure 3. By adding them together graphically, we obtain a hypotenuse that corresponds to the vector in Figure 3. The generalization here is that a vector at some angle in a two-dimensional plane can be broken down into its x- and y-components, and that the x- and y-components can be added together to form a vector at some other angle.

Vectors can also be multiplied. You may remember the terms "dot product" and "cross product" from physics classes; these terms describe different ways of multiplying vectors. You are not responsible for dot products and cross products of vectors for the MCAT. Instead, you should approach vector multiplication by being very careful to only multiply vectors within a single dimension by resolving vectors into their x- and y-components as needed. Let's illustrate this by working through a simple kinematics problem based on the principle that given a constant velocity, distance = velocity × time (these terms are defined more precisely in Section 2).

MCAT STRATEGY > > >

The concept of breaking down vectors into x- and y-components and of adding x- and y-components to obtain the total magnitude of a vector is extremely common in kinematics in particular, and in MCAT physics in general. Practice until this becomes a reflex.

Imagine that a ball is moving at a velocity of 10 m/s at an angle of 60° to the ground. How far will it travel horizontally in 2 seconds?

In order to solve this, we have to determine the ball's horizontal velocity—that is, its x-component. We do so by multiplying the overall velocity by the cosine of its angle with the horizontal: 10 m/s × cos(60°) = 10 m/s × 0.5 = 5 m/s in the horizontal direction. Now that we have the horizontal velocity, we can solve for distance: horizontal distance = 5 m/s (horizontally) × 2 s = 10 m. This example is illustrated in Figure 5.

Figure 5. Schematic of above example.

2. Displacement, Velocity, and Acceleration

The crucial concepts involved in kinematics are displacement, velocity, and acceleration.

Displacement is a vector quantity referring to change in location. It is the vector equivalent of distance, which is a scalar. What this means concretely is that displacement refers to the distance between where something starts and where it ends up, regardless of the path that it took to get there—that is, it is a path-independent quantity. Distance, on the other hand, refers to how far something traveled along its path, and does not incorporate any reference to direction. For instance, if you walked in a circle with a circumference of 10 m and returned to your starting point, you have walked a *distance* of 10 m, but your *displacement* was 0 m because your ending point was the same as your starting point.

Figure 6. Displacement vs. distance.

Velocity is a vector quantity describing change in displacement over time, with common units including meters per second and miles per hour. Its scalar equivalent is speed.

Acceleration is a vector quantity referring to change in velocity over time, and is generally given in units of meters per second squared (m/s²). If this seems counterintuitive, reflect that this is the algebraic equivalent of meters per second (velocity) per second: $\frac{\frac{m}{s}}{s} = \frac{m}{s} \times \frac{1}{s} = \frac{m}{s^2}$.

$$a = \frac{\Delta v}{t} = \frac{m}{s^2}$$

Because displacement, velocity, and acceleration are vector quantities, they can have positive or negative values depending on the coordinate system that you set up for a given problem. For instance, it is common to consider upwards motion to be positive and downwards motion to be negative. A common misconception is that the sign of one of these quantities can predict the sign of another quantity, but in reality, they are completely independent of each other, as shown in Table 4.

VELOCITY	ACCELERATION	PHYSICAL INTERPRETATION
Positive (upwards)	Positive (upwards)	Object is moving upwards faster and faster
	Zero	Object is moving upwards at a constant velocity
	Negative (downwards)	Object is moving upwards but slowing down
Zero	Positive (upwards)	Object is just beginning to move upwards from rest or is instantaneously transitioning from downwards to upwards motion
	Zero	Object is stationary
	Negative (downwards)	Object is just beginning to move downwards from rest or is instantaneously transitioning from upwards to downwards motion
Negative (downwards)	Positive (upwards)	Object is moving downwards but slowing down
	Zero	Object is moving downwards at a constant velocity
	Negative (downwards)	Object is moving downwards faster and faster

Table 4. Velocity and acceleration with various signs.

Graphs of displacement, velocity, and acceleration versus time can be analyzed to obtain useful information. On a linear graph of displacement over time, the slope of the line is equivalent to velocity. On a linear graph of velocity over time, the slope of the line is acceleration. The MCAT will only expect you to be able to carry out graphical analysis of this type if the graph is linear; doing this with non-linear graphs requires differential calculus, which is beyond the scope of the math that you need to know for the MCAT.

To understand why the slope of a graph of displacement over time indicates velocity, just consider the units. Recall that to determine the slope of a line on a graph, you pick two points and calculate the change in y (Δy) divided by the change in x (Δx). In a graph of displacement over time, the y values have units of distance and the x values have units of time, so determining the slope means dividing distance by time—which corresponds exactly to the definition of velocity! Using similar reasoning, determining the slope of a linear graph of velocity would involve dividing m/s (the units on the y-axis) by s (the units on the x axis), resulting in m/s² or acceleration.

The area under the curve of a graph of acceleration versus time is change in velocity, and the area under the curve of a graph of velocity versus time is displacement. Again, dimensional analysis can help clarify this point. Consider the graph of acceleration versus time in Figure 7. How would we determine the change in velocity from 0 to 4 s?

MCAT STRATEGY > > >

The material in Table 4 is often a source of confusion for students, especially for people who may be returning to physics after some time off. Misconceptions about this material can cause points to be lost on Test Day, so work on making this knowledge a reflex. One way to do this is to take an object from your surroundings—a pen or something, it doesn't need to be fancy—and act out all the scenarios described in Table 4. This way, your knowledge won't just be theoretical.

Figure 7. Acceleration versus time. Line starts from origin and then reaches the value of 4 m/s² at 4 s.

The area under this curve is a triangle whose area can be calculated as area = $\frac{1}{2}(b \times h)$, where b corresponds to x = 4 and h corresponds to y = 4. However, in physics, we should always pay attention to units, so we can calculate the area as follows: area = $\frac{1}{2}(x \times y) = \frac{1}{2}\left(4s \times 4\frac{m}{s^2}\right) = \frac{1}{2}\left(16\frac{m}{s}\right) = 8\frac{m}{s}$. Similar reasoning can confirm that the area under the curve of a graph of velocity versus time (that is, with velocity on the y-axis and time on the x-axis) must have units of distance. Again, for the MCAT, you will only be expected to carry out these calculations as applied to linear graphs, because calculus is not required. What about the area under the curve of a graph of displacement versus time? This would yield units of distance × time, such as m·s, and it turns out that this is not a physically meaningful concept.

Table 5 summarizes the crucial concepts you should be familiar with for displacement, velocity, and acceleration, and Table 6 summarizes how to interpret these units graphically.

	DEFINITION	COMMON UNITS	SCALAR EQUIVALENT
Displacement	Change in location	Meters (m), miles	Distance
Velocity	Change in location over time	Meters per second (m/s), miles per hour	Speed
Acceleration	Change in velocity over time	Meters per second squared (m/s^2)	None

Table 5. Displacement, velocity, and acceleration.

GRAPH TYPE	PHYSICAL MEANING OF SLOPE OF THE GRAPH	SLOPE IS:			PHYSICAL MEANING OF AREA UNDER THE CURVE
		POSITIVE AND LINEAR	ZERO	NEGATIVE	
Displacement vs. time	Velocity	Object is moving in (+) direction at a constant rate	Object is stationary	Object is moving in (−) direction at a constant rate	[Not meaningful]
Velocity vs. time	Acceleration	Velocity is increasing (becoming more positive or less negative)	Object is moving at a constant velocity	Velocity is decreasing (becoming less positive or more negative)	Displacement
Acceleration vs. time	[No special name; change in acceleration over time]	Acceleration is increasing (becoming more positive or less negative)	Object is speeding up or slowing down at a constant rate	Acceleration is decreasing (becoming less positive or more negative)	Change in velocity

Table 6. Graphical interpretation of displacement vs. time, velocity vs. time, and acceleration vs. time.

MCAT STRATEGY > > >

Draw out the scenarios described in Tables 4 and 6. Make your own graphs and simple diagrams. This will help you learn the content more actively, which is necessary because all of these facts are must-knows on Test Day. It is unlikely that you will encounter very many questions on these topics, but they are fair game, and they are very "gettable points." Make sure you master this material so that you do not have to spend too much time reasoning through these principles on Test Day.

3. Major Kinematics Equations

There are four crucial kinematics equations you must remember and be able to apply in problem-solving. They each assume constant acceleration. They are provided in Table 7, along with any useful ways of rewriting the equation and notes about when to use them.

EQUATION	REWRITTEN FORM	MISSING VARIABLE	NOTES
$d = v_{avg}t$	$d = \frac{\Delta v}{2}t$	Acceleration	Displacement = velocity × time
$v_f = v_i + at$	$\Delta v = at$	Displacement	Change in velocity = acceleration × time
$d = v_i t + \frac{1}{2}at^2$	$\Delta x = v_i t + \frac{1}{2}at^2$	Final velocity	Displacement = (velocity × time) + 1/2 (acceleration × time squared) [in the $\frac{1}{2}at^2$ term, note that t is squared in order to cancel out seconds squared in the units of acceleration (m/s^2)].
$v_f^2 = v_i^2 + 2ad$	$v_f^2 = v_i^2 + 2a\Delta x$	Time	Units on each side work out to (m^2/s^2).

Table 7. Big Four kinematics equations.

4. Special Case #1: Free Fall

It is useful to prepare for a few special cases of kinematics that are especially likely ways that the MCAT could test projectile motion. Free fall is probably the simplest of these, and can be thought of something falling downwards under constant acceleration from gravity (g) (-9.8 m/s^2, which you can generally round to -10 m/s^2 to make calculations simple) without experiencing any air resistance and therefore not attaining terminal velocity. We can analyze this situation using the Big Four kinematics equations, with $v_i = 0$ m/s, $y_i = 0$ m, $a = g$ (-9.8 m/s^2), and the convention that downward motion is negative along the y-axis. This leads to the following special cases:

> **MCAT STRATEGY > > >**
>
> The art of solving kinematics problems is visualizing them correctly and then applying the correct equation—that is, the equation that corresponds to all the variables you're given in the question. For this reason, you should be sure to incorporate a review of the variable missing from each formula into your study process.

EQUATION	SPECIAL CASE FOR FREE FALL	MISSING VARIABLE	NOTES WHEN USED FOR FREE FALL
$d = v_{avg}t$	$y = \frac{v_f}{2}t$	Acceleration	This is somewhat less likely to be useful for free fall because it contains no term for g, but is still good to have in your tool kit.
$v_f = v_i + at$	$v_f = gt$	Displacement	This is a very simple way to solve for impact velocity or time to impact, given appropriate input.
$d = v_i t + \frac{1}{2}at^2$	$y = \frac{1}{2}gt^2$ or $t = \sqrt{\frac{2y}{g}}$	Final velocity	The form of this equation written to solve for t is a very useful way of determining time to impact.
$v_f^2 = v_i^2 + 2ad$	$v_f^2 = 2gy$	Time	This equation is your best option if you don't have any information about time.

Table 8. Kinematics equations for free fall.

MCAT STRATEGY > > >

Whether you memorize the free fall equations separately—or the equations for other special cases—is up to you. On one hand, doing so creates more of a burden of things to memorize, but on the other hand, it can help save time on Test Day. If you do choose to memorize them, you should still study how they are derived because that will help you consolidate your knowledge. If you choose not to memorize them, make sure to do ample practice problems and to keep your algebra skills sharp.

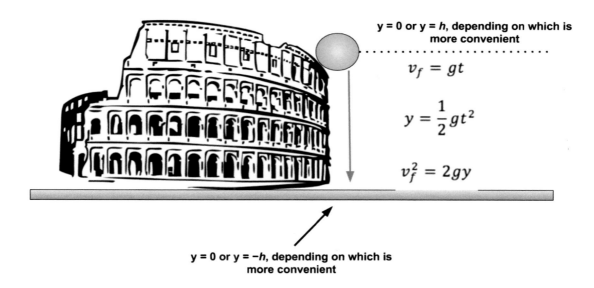

y = 0 or y = h, depending on which is more convenient

$$v_f = gt$$

$$y = \frac{1}{2}gt^2$$

$$v_f^2 = 2gy$$

y = 0 or y = −h, depending on which is more convenient

Figure 8. Diagram of free fall.

5. Special Case #2: Projectile Motion

Projectile motion is more complicated than free fall because it involves horizontal motion and the initial motion in the y-direction is upward, as shown in Figure 9.

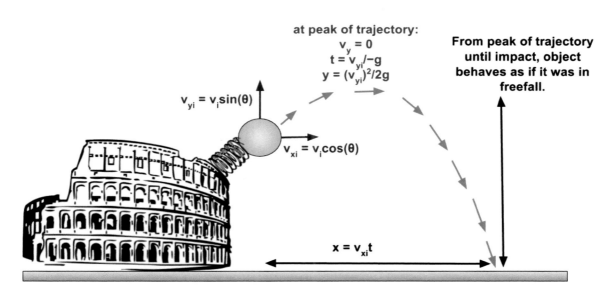

at peak of trajectory:
$v_y = 0$
$t = v_{yi}/-g$
$y = (v_{yi})^2/2g$

From peak of trajectory until impact, object behaves as if it was in freefall.

$v_{yi} = v_i \sin(\theta)$

$v_{xi} = v_i \cos(\theta)$

$x = v_{xi}t$

Figure 9. Diagram of projectile motion.

As with free fall, we assume no air resistance, and the only acceleration experienced by the projectile is downward acceleration due to gravity (g).

The key to solving projectile motion problems is breaking down the initial velocity of the projectile into its x- and y-components and using those components to analyze horizontal and vertical movement, respectively. Equation 6 illustrates how to resolve the initial velocity (v_i) of the projectile, where θ is the angle formed with the horizontal (x-axis).

Equation 6.   Given v_i for some projectile released at angle θ, $v_{xi} = v_i\cos(\theta)$ and $v_{yi} = v_i\sin(\theta)$.

Modeling the horizontal motion of a projectile is simple. We have a constant forward velocity, which only leaves us able to solve for horizontal displacement and time. Modeling the vertical motion of a projectile is more complicated, though, because we have acceleration due to gravity to contend with, as well as the fact that the projectile first goes up and then goes down, so velocity goes from positive to negative in the y direction. The crucial insight here is that at the top of its trajectory, the y-component of the projectile's velocity is 0, as it instantaneously transitions from the positive to the negative direction (note that the acceleration remains constant: g or −9.8 m/s²). The following tips can be used to tackle projectile motion problems:

Always resolve the initial velocity into $v_{xi} = v_i\cos(\theta)$ and $v_{yi} = v_i\sin(\theta)$.

Since v_x is constant, $x = v_x t$.

The peak height of a projectile is given by $h = \frac{v_{yi}^2}{2g}$. The time to reach that height is $t = \frac{v_{yi}}{-g}$. If these formulas seem counterintuitive, check the units and verify that they can be derived from two of the Big Four kinematics equations.

Due to the lack of air resistance, it takes a projectile as long to return from its peak height to its initial height as it does to reach its peak height.

When using the Big Four kinematics equations to analyze the vertical motion of a projectile, it is *essential* to remember that the initial vertical motion is in the *opposite* direction as the acceleration (the projectile goes *up*, acceleration pulls it *down*).

6. Special Case #3: Motion on an Inclined Plane

Motion on an inclined plane is another special case in kinematics where it is important to break down certain vectors into their components. In projectile motion, we had to split up a projectile's initial velocity into x- and y-components, but in motion on an inclined plane, it is generally most useful to split up acceleration into components parallel to the inclined plane and perpendicular to the inclined plane. For a full discussion of why this is the case, consult Chapter 2, where forces and free-body diagrams are discussed in more detail.

> > **CONNECTIONS** < <

Physics chapter 2

The principle of splitting acceleration due to gravity into parallel and perpendicular components is the same as we've discussed before, but the alignment of angles is slightly different, because θ is usually given in terms of the incline of the plane with regard to the ground. In this scenario, we can break up g, the acceleration due to gravity, into its perpendicular-to-the-plane component $g_\perp$ and its parallel-to-the-plane component $g_\parallel$ as follows:

Equation 7.
$$g_\perp = g\cos(\theta), \; g_\parallel = g\sin(\theta)$$

If you find it difficult to remember the trigonometry of inclined planes, you can use intuitive reasoning to help you choose between sine and cosine. Consider extreme cases: what would happen at angles of 1° and 89°—that is, right around 0° and right around 90°? For this example, consider what would happen if the inclined plane had an angle of 89° to the horizontal. An object on that plane would essentially be in free-fall; therefore, the acceleration parallel to the plane at this angle should be almost 1 g. Sin(89°) is almost equal to sin(90°), which equals 1, so that tells us that we should use sine for $g_\parallel$. To confirm this, let's consider a plane at an angle of 1° to the horizontal—that is, a plane that is barely inclined at all. An object on such a plane would experience very little acceleration due to gravity. That tells us that the trigonometric term modifying the acceleration vector should be minimized at $\theta = 0°$—again, sine fits the bill, because sin(0°) = 0.

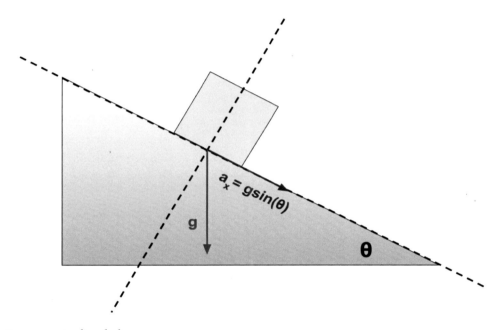

Figure 10. Motion on an inclined plane.

7. Must-Knows

> Key SI base units: meter, kilogram, second.
> SI prefixes: kilo (10^3), mega (10^6), giga (10^9), tera (10^{12}), deci (10^{-1}), centi (10^{-2}), milli (10^{-3}), micro (μ; 10^{-6}), nano (10^{-9}), pico (10^{-12}).
> Methods of converting among units:
> – Dimensional analysis
> – Conversion of given values to scientific notation and back
> – Shorthand tricks that you may develop with experience
> SOHCAHTOA: sine = opposite/hypotenuse, cosine = adjacent/hypotenuse, tangent = opposite/adjacent.
> Vectors have magnitude and direction.

MCAT STRATEGY > > >

One and only one thing counts for the MCAT: picking the right answer. Your way of getting the correct answer must be reliable, but it does not have to be something you would find in a physics textbook or something you think your physics instructor would approve of. It can be extremely helpful to incorporate simple, common-sense checkpoints into your approach to problem-solving, especially for errors where students commonly make mistakes, such as the choice of sine versus cosine to resolve vectors in complicated physical setups.

> Where θ is the angle formed with the x-axis, $\vec{v}_x = \vec{v}\cos\theta$ and $\vec{v}_y = \vec{v}\sin\theta$.
> If $\vec{u} = (x_u, y_u)$ and $\vec{v} = (x_v, y_v)$, $\vec{u} + \vec{v} = (x_u + x_v, y_u + y_v)$.
> Key kinematics concepts:
>   – Displacement = change in location; is a vector quantity (scalar equivalent is distance).
>   – Velocity = change in displacement over time; is a vector quantity (scalar equivalent is speed); area under the curve of a velocity vs. time graph is displacement.
>   – Acceleration = change in velocity over time; is a vector quantity; area under the curve of an acceleration vs. time graph is change in velocity.
>   – If one quantity is zero, that does *not* mean that other quantities are zero too! Zero displacement can co-occur with non-zero velocity and/or acceleration, zero velocity can co-occur with non-zero acceleration, and zero acceleration can occur with non-zero velocity. Make sure that you can conceptualize these situations!
> Big Four kinematics equations:
>   – $d = v_{avg}t$ or $d = \frac{\Delta v}{2} t$; missing acceleration
>   – $v_f = v_i + at$ or $\Delta v = at$; missing displacement
>   – $d = v_i t + \frac{1}{2}at^2$ or $\Delta x = v_i t + \frac{1}{2}at^2$; missing final velocity
>   – $v_f^2 = v_i^2 + 2ad$ or $v_f^2 = v_i^2 + 2a\Delta x$; missing time
> Free fall: object falls downward under constant acceleration of -9.8 m/s^2.
> Projectile motion:
>   – Split initial velocity into v_x and v_y.
>   – v_x is constant; v_y changes due to constant acceleration of -9.8 m/s^2.
>   – $v_y = 0$ at top of projectile's trajectory.
> Motion on an inclined plane:
>   – $g_\perp = g\cos(\theta)$, $g_\parallel = g\sin(\theta)$

This page left intentionally blank.

Practice Passage

Motor recovery after surgery is a major challenge to orthopedic patients, as use of the affected joints and muscles during healing is necessary, but painful. Optimal post-surgical treatment of scaphoid (wrist) ligament tears and distal forearm fractures should stabilize a tear or fracture site while still allowing for early wrist motion along multiple axes. A research group proposed that patients should utilize a dart-throwing pattern of motion following wrist surgery for torn scaphoid ligaments.

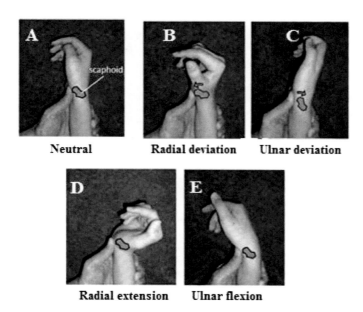

Figure 1. Movement axes for wrist and location of the scaphoid bone

Data collection involved recording scaphoid motion during 9 separate movements: a pure flexion-extension motion from 30 degrees of flexion to 30 degrees of extension and a pure radioulnar deviation motion from 20 degrees of ulnar deviation to 10 degrees of radial deviation and 7 additional motions (Figure 1) reflecting variations of a dart-throwing motion.

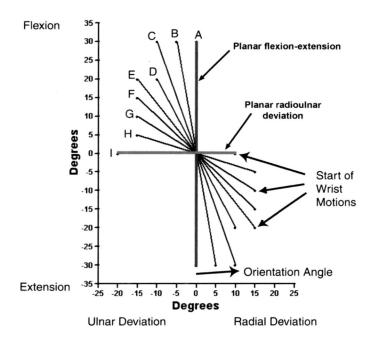

Figure 2. Nine dart-throwing wrist motions studied as viewed in the transverse plane

Analyses involved scaphoid and lunate kinematic data from 29 (average 47.8 years, range 29 to 58; 14 female, 15 male) wrists. Each wrist was cyclically moved through flexion-extension, radioulnar deviation and dart-throwing motions. Colles fractures are among the most common arm/wrist joint injuries and typically occur as the result of a fall onto an outstretched hand.

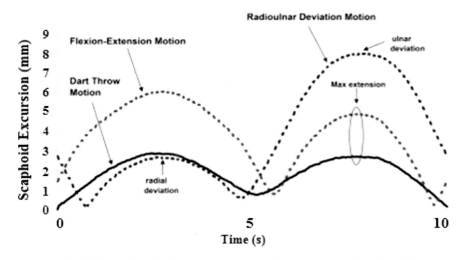

Figure 3. Absolute magnitude of 3D scaphoid tuberosity excursion during one cycle of dart-throwing motions

Adapted from Werner, F. St-Amand, H. (2016). Scaphoid Tuberosity Excursion is Minimized during a Dart-Throwing Motion: A Biomechanical Study. Journal of Hand Therapy : Official Journal of the American Society of Hand Therapists, 29(2), 175–182. under CCBY

1. What is the slope of the data plotted in Figure 3?
   A. Position
   B. Velocity
   C. Acceleration
   D. Force

2. If a subject is asked to trace a path of wrist movement along vector A for 5 seconds and then along vector H for 4.9 seconds (as seen in Figure 2), what will be the net movement vector for their wrist?
   A. C
   B. E
   C. F
   D. G

3. If the radius bone of the forearm can take up to 1150 N of force along its axis before fracturing, which of the following is likely to cause a Colles fracture in a 60 kg man?
   A. Falling on an arm that makes a 60° angle with the ground.
   B. Falling on an arm that makes a 45° angle with the ground.
   C. Falling on an arm that makes a 60° angle with the vertical.
   D. Falling on an arm that makes a 45° angle with the vertical.

4. What is the most likely reason the researchers chose the motions depicted in Figure 2?
   A. To determine the peak scaphoid excursion during wrist motion.
   B. To minimize the magnitude of force exerted on the scaphoid.
   C. To address most possible variations of a dart-throwing motion.
   D. To maximize the magnitude of force exerted on the scaphoid.

5. What is the net excursion of the scaphoid during one complete rotation of the wrist?
   A. 0 N
   B. 0 J
   C. 0 W
   D. 0 mm

6. A patient is asked to throw a dart in order to hit the bullseye in the center of a target 5 m away. If the initial velocity of the dart is 10 m/s at 45° with the horizontal, from a height level with the bullseye, where will the dart hit the target?
   A. 2.5 m below the bullseye
   B. 1.0 m below the bullseye
   C. 0.0 m above the bullseye
   D. 2.5 m above the bullseye

7. A patient experiences a tear injury of his or her wrist. The diagram below shows the tension in two remaining ligaments holding up the scaphoid bone against gravity at maximum radial extension.

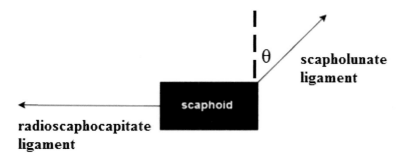

If the wrist is held in this position and θ = 30°, which of the following is most likely to be true?

A. There is no acceleration of the scaphoid as a result of the scapholunate ligament.
B. There is no acceleration of the scaphoid as a result of the radioscaphocapitate ligament.
C. Tension in the scapholunate ligament is twice as large as the tension in the radioscaphocapitate ligament
D. The vector sum of the two ligamental tensions is 0 N.

Practice Passage Explanations

Motor recovery after surgery is a major challenge to orthopedic patients, as use of the affected joints and muscles during healing is necessary, but painful. Optimal post-surgical treatment of scaphoid (wrist) ligament tears and distal forearm fractures should stabilize a tear or fracture site while still allowing for early wrist motion along multiple axes. A research group proposed that patients should utilize a dart-throwing pattern of motion following wrist surgery for torn scaphoid ligaments.

Key terms: stabilize tear, dart-throwing motion, scaphoid ligaments

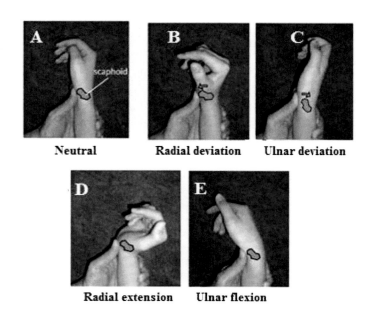

Figure 1. Movement axes for wrist and location of the scaphoid bone

Figure 1 shows the exact definition of wrist movements, not much MCAT testable material here so move on quickly

Data collection involved recording scaphoid motion during 9 separate movements: a pure flexion-extension motion from 30 degrees of flexion to 30 degrees of extension and a pure radioulnar deviation motion from 20 degrees of ulnar deviation to 10 degrees of radial deviation and 7 additional motions (Figure 1) reflecting variations of a dart-throwing motion.

Key terms: deviation, radioulnar

Cause and effect: wrist was flexed/extended across a range of 60°; movement recorded

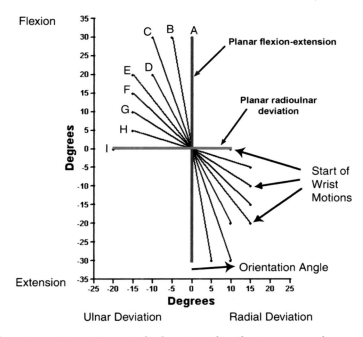

Figure 2. Nine dart-throwing wrist motions studied as viewed in the transverse plane

Figure 2 axes shows the 9 vectors of wrist movement tested, anticipate vector math questions

Analyses involved scaphoid and lunate kinematic data from 29 (average 47.8 years, range 29 to 58; 14 female, 15 male) wrists. Each wrist was cyclically moved through flexion-extension, radioulnar deviation and dart-throwing motions. Colles fractures are among the most common arm/wrist joint injuries and typically occur as the result of a fall onto an outstretched hand.

Key terms: kinematic data, Colles fracture

Cause and effect: excessive F on the arm from fall → bone fracture

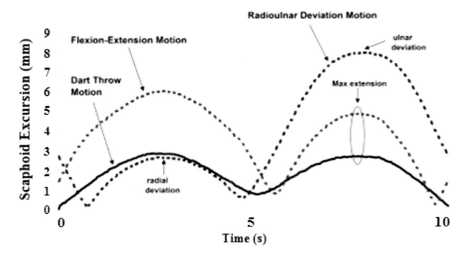

Figure 3. Absolute magnitude of 3D scaphoid tuberosity excursion during one cycle of dart-throwing motions

Figure 3 shows that radial deviation was in sync with flexion/extension of the wrist, suggesting these movements are coordinated when throwing a dart; largest movement is ulnar deviation (8 mm)

Adapted from Werner, F. St-Amand, H. (2016). Scaphoid Tuberosity Excursion is Minimized during a Dart-Throwing Motion: A Biomechanical Study. Journal of Hand Therapy : Official Journal of the American Society of Hand Therapists, 29(2), 175–182. under CCBY

1. B is correct. Examining Figure 3 we can see that the units of the slope are distance (mm) / time (s), which is a measurement of velocity.
    A. Position is measured in distance.
    C. Acceleration is measured in distance per time squared.
    D. Force is measured in mass•distance per time squared.

2. B is correct. The answers indicate we will need to use Figure 2 and find the sum of two or more vectors. To sum vectors, we trace a path from one vector to the next and then map the path from the origin to the endpoint of the vector sum. The closest approximation to this vector sum is vector E. We can also see that we have a completely vertical vector (A) and a minimally left-leaning vector (H), which will result in a mostly vertical vector that is less than 45° from vector A.

3. C is correct. In order to fracture the bone, the fall must generate 1150 N of force or more along the bone. Since the man is falling on his outstretched arm, we must calculate the force of his fall along the arm. Set up a free body diagram.

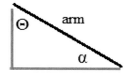

Θ angle between arm and vertical

α angle between arm and ground

    We can now see that the $\cos \theta$ = adjacent/hypotenuse = $F_{vertical}/F_{along\,arm}$. Solving for the force along the arm we get $F_{along\,arm} = F_{vertical}/\cos \theta$. The man's weight (mg) will be the vertical component of his force and is equal to (60 kg) (10 m/s^2) = 600 N. Thus, we need

$$600 \text{ N}/\cos \theta \geq 1150 \text{ N} \rightarrow 600/1150 \geq \cos \theta$$
$$0.5 \geq \cos \theta$$

Only angles equal to or greater than 60° will yield cosine values ≤ 0.5 (since cosine decrease as the angle increases).

    A: An arm angle of 60° with the vertical corresponds to 30° between the arm and the ground
    B, D: Both sin 45° and cosine 45° are equal to √2/2.

4. C is correct. The study was designed to analyze wrist movement in the context of post-surgical recovery. Thus, the correct answer should take this goal into account.
    A. This choice is tempting, as it may offer the researchers insight into the abilities of the joint during recovery, but this would not explain the large variety of motions chosen by the study designers.
    B, D: Given the rehabilitative nature of the study, and the ideas stated in the first paragraph, it is unlike the researchers would want to place too much (D) or too little (A) stress on the joint.

5. D is true. The net work or movement as a result of a cyclical process is 0, since the system is right back where it started at the end of the cycle. Thus the excursion should be 0 and in units of distance. Choice C is tempting, since work = Fdcosθ and W_{net} = ΔKE and is always measured in joules (aka N•m), but the question asked for net excursion, which Figure 3 shows us is measured in distance.

6. D is correct. This question requires us to use equations of kinematics and projectile motion. First we need to find the time it will take the dart to travel the 5 m to the target, then we can find out the height of the dart at that time. To do this we need the horizontal velocity.

v_x of the dart = $v_0 \cos 45 = 10\sqrt{2}/2$ m/s   Time to travel 5 m = $(5 \text{ m})/(10\sqrt{2}/2) = 1/\sqrt{2}$ s

v_y of the dart = $v_0 \sin 45 = 10\sqrt{2}/2$ m/s

Now we can use one of our kinematics equations to find out the height of the dart at that exact time.

$\Delta y = v_y t + \frac{1}{2} at^2$ $\Delta y = 10\sqrt{2}/2 \,(1/\sqrt{2}) + \frac{1}{2} (-10)(1/\sqrt{2})^2 = 5 + (-5)(1/2) = 5 - 5/2 = +2.5$ m

Thus, the dart will impact the target 2.5 m above the bullseye.

7. C is correct. If the bone is at rest (aka in equilibrium) in this position, we can assume that the net force acting on the bone is 0 N. The radioscaphocapitate acts in the horizontal direction while the scapholunate acts in the horizontal and vertical direction (opposing gravity). The components of the tension in the scapholunate require a total tension that is twice that in radioscaphocapitate such that the tensions in the horizontal are equal and opposite for the two ligaments.

A, B: No net acceleration does not mean there are no forces acting on the scaphoid bone, only that they add up to 0 N.

D. This answer forgets the effects of gravity, which will act to oppose the vertical component of the tension in the scapholunate ligament.

Independent Questions

1. Which of the following is the SI base unit for mass?
   A. The kilogram, one of which is equal to 10^3 grams
   B. The kilogram, one of which is equal to 10^{-3} grams
   C. The gram, one of which is equal to 10^3 kilograms
   D. The gram, one of which is equal to 10^{-3} kilograms

2. All of the following are examples of vector quantities EXCEPT:
   A. displacement.
   B. acceleration.
   C. velocity.
   D. distance.

3. A soccer forward kicks the ball high in the air, at a 60° angle to the ground. If the ball is kicked with an initial total velocity of 14 m/s, what is its approximate initial vertical velocity? Note the following approximate values: sin 30° = 0.5, sin 60° = 0.87, cos 30° = 0.87, and cos 60° = 0.5.
   A. 7 m/s
   B. 10.5 m/s
   C. 12.1 m/s
   D. 28 m/s

4. An object is moving forward along a track. At time = 1 s, the speed of the object is 7 m/s. At time t = 2 s, its speed is 6 m/s, and at time t = 3 s, its speed is 4 m/s. According to typical convention regarding velocity and acceleration, which of the following is true?
   A. The object has a positive velocity and a positive acceleration.
   B. The object has a positive velocity and a negative acceleration.
   C. The object has a negative velocity and a positive acceleration.
   D. The object has a negative velocity and a negative acceleration.

5. Which of the following statements are true?
   I. On a linear graph of distance traveled vs. time, the slope denotes the velocity.
   II. On a linear graph of acceleration vs. time, the area under the curve has the units of velocity.
   III. On a linear graph of velocity vs. time, the slope denotes the acceleration.
   A. I only
   B. III only
   C. II and III only
   D. I, II, and III

6. A car is traveling due west with a constant velocity of 30 m/s. In this situation:
   A. the acceleration of the car is zero.
   B. the acceleration of the car is constant.
   C. neither A nor B is true.
   D. both A and B are true.

7. A freight train accelerates at a constant rate of 2 m/s^2 for 75 meters. If its velocity at the end of this acceleration is 20 m/s, what must its initial velocity have been?
   A. 10 m/s
   B. 14 m/s
   C. 15.9 m/s
   D. 18 m/s

8. In a fit of anger, a man unfortunately throws his new phone horizontally out his window with an initial velocity of 16 m/s. If his window is 45 meters high, what horizontal distance will the phone travel before hitting the ground? Assume no air resistance.
   A. 20 m
   B. 45 m
   C. 48 m
   D. 144 m

Independent Question Explanations

1. A is correct. The SI base unit for mass is the kilogram, not the gram (eliminate choices C and D). One kilogram is equivalent to 1000, or 10^3, grams. (Do not fall for choice B; it attempts to confuse you with the true statement that one gram is equivalent to 10^{-3} kilograms.)

2. D is correct. Remember, vectors are quantities that include a component of both magnitude and direction. Displacement, velocity, and acceleration are all vectors. In contrast, distance is a scalar quantity. (Think of it this way—a distance might be something like "25 miles." This does *not* tell us anything about the direction of travel, so it must not be a vector.)

3. C is correct. The question states that the ball is kicked at a 60° angle to the ground. A diagram of this situation is shown below.

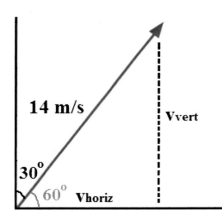

As shown here, the vertical component of the ball's velocity is represented by the line opposite to the 60° angle. Remember, sine = opposite/hypotenuse. Here, then, sin 60° = (v_{vert})/(14 m/s). Since sin 60° is approximately equal to 0.87, we can rewrite this equation as 0.87 = (v_{vert})/(14 m/s), or v_{vert} = (0.87)(14 m/s). You do not need to be able to find the exact value of this amount, as you will not be given a calculator on the MCAT. However, you should be able to discern that, since (0.5)(14) is equal to 7 and (0.75)(14) is equal to 10.5 then (0.87)(14) must be even larger. Choice C is the only logical answer as choice D is greater than the initial velocity. Note that choice A represents the horizontal component of the ball's initial velocity.

4. B is correct. Conventionally, an object moving forward has a positive velocity, while an object moving backwards has a negative velocity. Since our object is traveling forward, we can eliminate choices C and D. The sign of an object's acceleration relates to whether the object is speeding up or slowing down relative to the forward direction. Here, the object is slowing down in the forward direction, so our acceleration must be negative. (In contrast, acceleration would be positive if our object was continually speeding up.)

5. C is correct. The area under an acceleration vs. time graph has the same units as velocity (m/s), so Roman numeral (RN) II is accurate. Regarding RN III, this statement is also correct, because the slope of a velocity vs. time graph does denote the acceleration (as acceleration is the derivative of velocity). Finally, RN I is false, because it is the slope of a *displacement* vs. time graph that denotes velocity.

6. D is correct. Don't get tripped up here—an acceleration that remains steady at 0 m/s is a constant acceleration! Here, the car has a positive velocity, but its velocity is not changing over time. Since acceleration represents the change in velocity over time, the car's acceleration is zero. Since this acceleration value is not changing, we can also say that the car is experiencing constant acceleration. Thus, both choices A and B are true.

7. A is correct. Here we are given acceleration, distance, and final velocity. Since we are looking for initial velocity, we can use the equation $v_f^2 = v_i^2 + 2a\Delta x$. Plugging in numbers yields (20 m/s)^2 = v_i^2 + 2(2 m/s^2)(75 m). This simplifies to 400 m^2/s^2 = v_i^2 + 300 m^2/s^2. We can conclude that v_i^2 = 100 m^2/s^2 and therefore v_i = 10 m/s.

8. C is correct. Since the phone has only horizontal velocity at the time when it is thrown, we can treat this as a free fall problem. (Remember, free fall refers to situations where an object has no initial vertical velocity and experiences constant acceleration due to gravity.) We cannot find horizontal range directly; instead, we must first find time. Luckily, we can use our simplified free fall equation: $t = \sqrt{\frac{2y}{g}}$, where y is the distance fallen (which should be negative, as our object is moving downward) and where g can be rounded to −10 m/s^2. Plugging in values, we get $t = \sqrt{\frac{2(-45 \text{ m})}{-10 \text{ m/s}^2}} = \sqrt{9 \text{ s}^2}$ = 3 s. Next, we can use the equation $x = v_x t$ to find the horizontal distance traveled (x). We get x = (16 m/s)(3 s), or x = 48 m.

This page left intentionally blank.

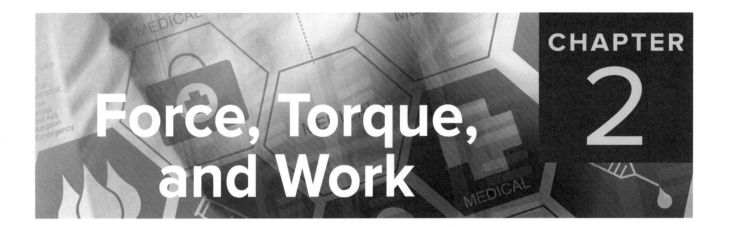

Force, Torque, and Work

0. Introduction

We briefly mentioned force in the discussion of kinematics in Chapter 1, because it was necessary to talk at least a little bit about why things accelerate. In this chapter, we'll focus more directly on force, explore how the basic laws of force are used to model various situations that might come up in MCAT questions, and then explore the related topics of torque, work, and power. We'll also return to work and power in Chapter 3, which focuses on energy, but it's useful to see how these concepts are applied both in the contexts of mechanical setups and in a more general theoretical context.

This chapter is important for the MCAT both because you could directly be asked questions asking you to construct a free-body diagram, solve a static equilibrium problem, or calculate the torque or work in a given situation, and because it deals with fundamental concepts that can appear in questions or passages that initially seem to be about something else entirely. However, the MCAT tends not to give you extremely elaborate equilibrium setups that take three or more equations to solve, like you may have seen in physics classes. Therefore, study this chapter carefully, but remember that how physics is tested on the MCAT is not quite the same as how you may have been tested in Physics 101, and keep in mind that kinematics and force are only part of the puzzle of MCAT physics—make sure to also save energy for high-yield topics to come, like waves and electromagnetism.

1. Units and Definitions

So, what is force, anyway? On the most basic level, you can think about it as an interaction of some sort that can cause an object to accelerate. This may not be a very satisfying answer on a mechanical level, but that is often the case for fundamental properties of physics: asking what force *is*, or what mass *is*, can lead to very deep questions that, in some cases, research physicists are still working on fully understanding.

However, we can also approach this question by examining the units that we use to express force. The SI unit for force is the newton (N), named after the 17th-century English physicist and mathematician Isaac Newton, who was responsible for formulating the fundamental laws of motion, codifying our understanding of gravity in a way that lasted until Einstein's adjustments in the early 20th century, and developing differential and integral calculus, among other accomplishments. A newton is defined as follows: $N = \frac{kg \cdot m}{s^2}$, or kilograms times meters divided by seconds squared. This might initially seem completely opaque, and we might ask what on earth it means to multiply a kilogram (mass) by meters (distance) and divide by time. Nonetheless, it turns out that this is actually a fairly intuitive definition, if we just look at it right. Let's start with the simple core of this definition: meters per second (m/s). This is velocity. If we divide velocity by time, we get meters per second per second, or meters per second squared (m/s²). This is acceleration. The kilogram term means that a newton is the amount of force necessary to accelerate one kilogram by one meter per second squared.

MCAT STRATEGY > > >

You may want to use the list given below as a checklist: before moving on, verify your level of understanding and preparedness to handle all of these types of scenarios. A rule of thumb is that you should be able to explain to someone else how to tackle a given type of problem.

On a fundamental level, there are only four kinds of forces in nature: the gravitational force, which acts on mass, the electromagnetic force, which acts on charge, and the strong and weak nuclear forces, which act on subatomic particles and are beyond the scope of the MCAT. At this point, you might say: OK, well, gravity and electromagnetism are all well and good, but what about the force that I exert on something when I push it? It turns out that so-called contact forces are actually special cases of electromagnetism, although this fact has no real practical ramification for the MCAT.

It is helpful to have some big-picture understanding of what force is, if only to avoid misconceptions, but the MCAT is much less interested in your ability to analyze forces on the level of basic principles of nature than it is in your ability to problem-solve. With this in mind, it can be helpful to classify forces into different "types" that correspond to different physical situations and problem-solving setups. The following types of forces, in this sense, occur on the MCAT:

> Gravitational force. This force acts on mass at a distance.
> Electromagnetic force. This category of force is most likely to appear in electrostatics problems.
> Contact/pushing force. Think of this as the kind of force you can exert on an object by pushing it horizontally.
> Normal force. This is the force that surfaces exert in response to gravity (i.e., if you're standing on the floor, the floor pushes back up at you in response to the force that you exert on it).
> Friction. This is the force that pushes back against horizontal movement.
> Tension. This is the force exerted by an ideal string. It basically allows contact/pushing forces to be exerted at a distance, and the inclusion of an ideal pulley into the problem setup allows that force to be transmitted along paths more complicated than straight lines.
> Centripetal force. This refers to any force that makes an object follow a curved path. It is often associated with tension (such as if an object on a swing is being swung in a circle), but centripetal forces can also be exerted by gravity, in the case of planets orbiting the sun, or magnetic fields in mass spectrometry machines.
> Force applied to springs. A special law, known as Hooke's law (F = kx) applies to this case.

Over the course of this chapter, we will cover how to handle all of these "types" of forces in more depth.

2. Newton's Laws

Newton's three laws of motion were published in 1687, in a work entitled *Principia Mathematica*, and revolutionized the world of science, setting the groundwork for classical mechanics. Prior to Newton, many scientists had expressed interest in concepts of force and motion, but had generally failed to grasp some important points about inertia.

Newton's first law is a statement about inertia. It states that within a reference frame, an object remains at rest or at a constant velocity unless an external force acts upon it. This law is easy to skip over, but it was historically transformative, especially for the part of it that says "or at a constant velocity." If you compare Newton's first law with everyday experience, the part about an object remaining at rest unless acted on by an external force is intuitively clear, but the part about remaining at a constant velocity is much less so. In real-world contexts, we see objects slow down all the time. This led the Greek philosopher Aristotle, and philosophers that followed in his footsteps for nearly 2,000 years, to posit that objects would keep moving only as long as a force continued to be applied to them. Newton had the insight to reformulate inertia and recognize that forces of resistance and friction were responsible for the observations that objects slow down and stop.

Newton's second law defines force. It states that the total sum of forces acting on an object is equivalent to its mass times its acceleration.

Newton's third law is about how forces come in pairs. It states that when body A exerts a force on body B, body B exerts an equal and opposite force on body A. *Body A = Body B*

To summarize in equation form:

> **MCAT STRATEGY > > >**
>
> To some extent, Newton's laws are an exception to the rule that the MCAT cares more about application than theory. Newton's laws are testable content, so you should take the time to understand them carefully and be able to explain which is which.

> **MCAT STRATEGY > > >**
>
> There are a couple misconceptions about Newton's laws that you should be careful to avoid. First, remember that an object can be at equilibrium and have a non-zero velocity—that is, "at equilibrium" and "at rest" are *not* the same things. Second, regarding Newton's third law, remember that a pair of forces that operate according to this law operate on *different objects*.

Equation 1.   Newton's first law: $\vec{F}_{net} = 0$ at equilibrium.

Equation 2.   Newton's second law: $\vec{F}_{net} = m\vec{a}$.

Equation 3.   Newton's third law: $\vec{F}_{AB} = -\vec{F}_{BA}$.

3. Applications of Force

Next, let's turn to problem-solving with forces, using the principles of Newton's laws and our classification of the general types and arrangements of forces that you may encounter.

The basic skill that you need to master to solve equilibrium problems with forces is drawing free-body diagrams quickly and accurately. A free-body diagram is simply a representation of all the forces acting on an object. Consider Figure 1, which illustrates the relatively simple scenario of a man pulling a box along the ground.

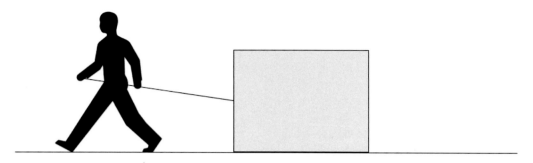

Figure 1. Man pulling a box along the ground.

As a first step in drawing a free-body diagram, let's focus on the box and figure out which forces apply to it. We'll need to account for the "pulling" force exerted by the man (technically, this is an example of a tension force), the friction force opposing that movement, the force of gravity pulling the box towards the earth, and the normal force exerted by the ground on the box (i.e., the force of the ground pushing back up against the box). This is shown in Figure 2.

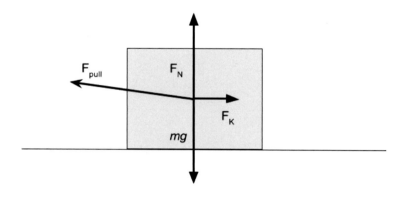

Figure 2. Free-body diagram of the box being pulled by the man.

In Figure 2, F_{pull} is the pulling force exerted by the man. Note that it is drawn at the same angle that we see in Figure 1. If this was an actual problem that we had to solve, we would probably get specific information about the angle, but we don't have to worry about it at this point. F_N is the normal force, and mg indicates the force of gravity on the box. Finally, F_K is the force of kinetic friction opposing the motion of the box. Note that its magnitude is smaller than that of F_{pull}. In free-body diagrams, it is generally best to draw the arrows such that their magnitude more or less corresponds to the magnitudes of the forces in question. There's no need to be perfectionistic about this, especially on the MCAT, but you ideally want a rough sense of what's bigger than what.

An important point about free-body diagrams is that it's important to work with the center of mass of the objects being modeled, as shown in Figure 2. This is relatively trivial when you're working with a single mass, but can become more complicated if you're modeling the forces that operate on a single system composed of multiple masses. To analyze such a system, you need to set up a reference point. If you have a set of masses m_1, m_2, ..., m_k at distances x_1, x_2, ..., x_k from the reference point, the center of mass can be calculated as follows:

Equation 4.
$$x_{center} = \frac{m_1 x_1 + m_2 x_2 + ... + m_k x_k}{m_1 + m_2 + ... + m_k}$$

Once you have the free-body diagram set up, you can proceed to resolve forces that are non-perpendicular to each other. In principle, you can choose the axes however you want, but for the MCAT you want to keep things simple. For a diagram like Figure 2, you'll probably just want to have the x-axis run horizontally and the y-axis vertically. Once you do that, you can resolve F_{pull} into its two components: $F_{pull}(x)$ and $F_{pull}(y)$. $F_{pull}(x)$ can be calculated as $F_{pull} \cdot \cos(\theta)$ and $F_{pull}(y)$ is $F_{pull} \cdot \sin(\theta)$. Since in this case θ is quite small, we'll expect that most of the magnitude of F_{pull} should be reflected in $F_{pull}(x)$. This may seem obvious here, but incorporating reality checks like this into your process can pay off in more involved setups. The breakdown of F_{pull} is presented in Figure 3.

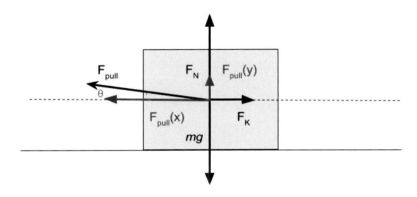

Figure 3. Free-body diagram of box being pulled, with non-perpendicular forces resolved.

At this point, you're now ready to go and solve whatever problem is posed to you. Now, you might object at this point: what about Newton's third law? Haven't we forgotten about the equal and opposing forces? On one hand, yes—our free-body diagram *does* not account for (1) the force exerted by the box on the man pulling it, (2) the downwards force exerted by the box on the ground, (3) the horizontal force exerted by the box on the ground in response to friction, and (4) the gravitational force exerted by the box on the earth. The reason for this is, to put it bluntly, *we don't care*. The point of a free-body diagram is not to account for every force that's present in the setup of a problem, but to isolate the forces that act on the object of interest. This may be different from what you have been taught to do in physics classes. However, the MCAT isn't physics class: you won't have picky professors grading you on the elegance and completeness of your free-body diagrams, and you definitely won't get any partial credit for labeling all of the forces correctly. Your goal is to get the answer in a reasonable amount of time. Although it may indeed be helpful to practice identifying all of the forces in a frame of reference and then isolating the ones you want to focus on in a free-body diagram, the end goal should be for you to draw free-body diagrams quickly, without accounting for irrelevant forces.

In Figures 2 and 3, we saw that the horizontal motion of the box across the ground was opposed by the force of friction. This is worth exploring in more depth, because static and kinetic friction have specifically been identified as topics to know for the MCAT. Figure 4 presents an overview of static and kinetic friction, but let's start by thinking about it on a conceptual level. Imagine that you have a moderately heavy box on a hardwood or linoleum floor (not carpet)—say, a small box of books, or a moving box, or something like that. If you gently push it, nothing will happen. However, if you keep increasing the force with which you push it, it will eventually start sliding across the floor. If you give it a single intense push, it will travel for a certain length, but it will slow down and eventually stop on its own.

The concepts of static and kinetic friction give us technical language that we can deploy to describe these everyday, familiar events. Static friction applies when we are pushing on an object and it doesn't move; the force of static friction is opposite in direction to the applied force, and its magnitude is greater (this is necessary to overcome the applied force and prevent movement). We can formalize this by saying that $|F_{applied}| < |F_{static}|$. Note that we used absolute value bars to make it very clear that we're talking about *magnitude* here, not direction, but this convention is not commonly followed when discussing friction. The next question we might ask is how we go about determining the specific magnitude of the static force. Upon some reflection, we might notice that the force of static friction differs depending on the material—after all, it takes much less force to send something sliding across ice than it would across a rough wooden surface. We can condense these observations by noting that $F_{static} = \mu_s N$, where μ_s is the coefficient of static friction and N is the applied force.

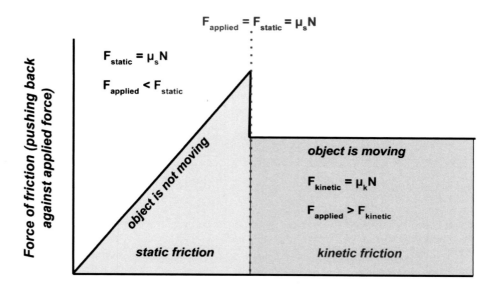

Figure 4. Static versus kinetic friction.

Eventually, if you keep pushing harder and harder, the object will dislodge and start sliding. At this moment, we can still say that $F_{static} = \mu_s N$, but now $|F_{applied}| = |F_{static}|$, and the object is put into motion. Once the object is in motion, it is subject to a force of kinetic friction. The force of kinetic friction is similar in that it is a property of the surface an object is sliding across. However, it remains constant as the applied force increases (and is even present if the applied force suddenly drops to zero); therefore, we can define it as $F_{kinetic} = \mu_k N$, where N is the normal force of the object and μ_k is the coefficient of kinetic friction.

MCAT STRATEGY > > >

A key point about static and kinetic friction is the idea that more force is needed to push an object into motion than is needed to overcome kinetic friction once an object is in motion.

These equations are summarized below:

Equation 5. Static friction: $F_{static} = \mu_s N$, $|F_{applied}| < |F_{static}|$

Equation 6. Kinetic friction: $F_{kinetic} = \mu_k N$, $|F_{applied}| > |F_{static}|$

Next, let's turn to how the concepts of force and free body diagrams can be used to analyze projectile motion. We covered projectile motion previously in Chapter 1 on kinematics, where our main goal was to predict the outcomes of projectile motion in terms of distance traveled, the time needed for the projectile to hit the ground, and so on. In the context of this chapter, the most important thing is for us to correctly understand which forces are acting on the projectile.

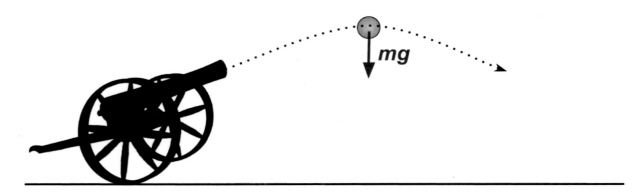

Figure 5. Projectile motion.

Figure 5 shows a simple free-body diagram of a projectile at the height of its trajectory, neglecting air resistance. Under such assumptions—which usually apply for MCAT problem-solving—the *only* force acting on the projectile is gravity. What if we do need to account for air resistance? The details are somewhat complex, but the idea is fairly simple. Air resistance, also known as drag, opposes the direction of the object's motion. Its magnitude is affected by four factors: (1) the density of the air (or, more generally, the density of the medium through which an object is moving); (2) the velocity of the object (in fact, by v^2); (3) the cross-sectional area of the object; and (4) a drag coefficient that reflects specific properties of the object. The fact that the force of drag increases with the *square* of the velocity means that eventually drag will equal the force of gravity, meaning that the object can no longer accelerate. This point is known as the terminal velocity.

> **MCAT STRATEGY > > >**
>
> The MCAT is unlikely to ask you to perform detailed calculations relating to drag, and if so, it would almost certainly come up in the context of a passage. Therefore, you should be aware of drag and terminal velocity on a conceptual level. If it does show up, don't let Test Day be the first time you've thought about it.

Masses on inclined planes are another setup commonly encountered in introductory physics. Similarly to projectile motion, we've already covered inclined planes from the point of view of kinematics, but it's nonetheless worth reviewing the forces at work in this setup. In Figure 6, with a box on an inclined plane, there are three forces that need to be considered: the normal force, the force of friction, and the force of gravity. Note that without further information, we don't know whether the force of friction is static or kinetic. The normal force points up perpendicularly from the box resting on the surface of the plane, the frictional force is pointed in a way that would oppose the motion of the box down the plane, and the force of gravity points down towards the bottom of the frame of reference as shown in the figure. The main challenge posed by inclined plane setups is that the forces are not all perpendicular/parallel to each other. The way to address this problem is to set up a system with an x-axis and a y-axis, and then resolve whichever force is not parallel to one of those axes into its x- and y-components. This is shown below in Figure 6, with the original forces in blue and the x- and y-components of gravity shown in red.

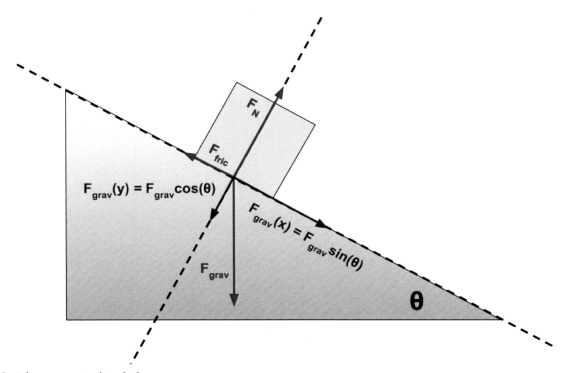

Figure 6. A box on an inclined plane.

One potentially counterintuitive aspect of this setup is that sin(θ) is used to calculate the x-component of F_{grav}, although we're used to associating the sine with vertical components of a vector. There are two basic approaches you can take to this difficulty. One is just to memorize it. However, although brute-force memorization *can* allow you to solve similar problems, it's better to understand the reasons underlying this fact, so that you can still solve the problem if the setup gets tweaked or changed somehow. The second approach is to carefully note that in this setup, θ refers to the angle that the plane forms with the ground, *not* the angle that F_{grav} makes with F_N. The latter angle is the one we care about. If we work through the trigonometry carefully, we'll note that θ corresponds to the angle formed by F_{grav} with the vertical line formed by extending F_N downwards. The sine is the opposite side divided by the hypotenuse, and here that corresponds to motion down the plane.

Pulleys are another common setup used in physics problem. The basic idea of pulleys is that they allow the angle through which a force is transmitted to be changed. The term "tension" is used to refer to the force exerted by an ideal string on an object. Let's explore how this plays out in the setup provided in Figure 7, where a box on an inclined plane is attached via a pulley to another box that is hanging down without any support. Note that in this setup, frictional forces are neglected. One seemingly simple question we might ask would be: which box will go downwards and which will go upwards? On an intuitive level, we might say that it depends on how heavy the boxes are relative to each other; this is correct, but let's try to answer more specifically.

In order to answer this question, we need to draw free-body diagrams for each of the masses. There are two forces we care about here: the force exerted by gravity on each mass and the tension force exerted by the string. For m_1, the mass on the inclined plane, we can actually omit the normal force for the purposes of this discussion because we're not accounting for friction (if you were doing this in physics class, you'd get in trouble for this omission, but in the world of MCAT physics, informed shortcuts are OK).

The mass on the plane (m_1) and the dangling mass (m_2) are both being pulled down by gravity, but the pulley transmits those forces such that each mass is also being pulled up by the other mass. Let's first look at the forces exerted directly by gravity on each mass, and then consider how the masses interact with each other in this system. The action of gravity on m_2 is extremely simple: it pulls it down directly. Therefore, $F_{grav \rightarrow m2} = m_2 g$. Turning to m_1, we have a situation very similar to the inclined plane scenario we saw in Figure 6, so $F_{grav \rightarrow m1} = m_1 g\sin(\theta)$.

So far, this is pretty straightforward. However, we have to account for the pulley. Let's first consider the effect that m_2 has on m_1. Intuitively—leaving aside the reciprocal effect here—we can see that applying force to m_2 downwards would cause it to drag m_1 up the inclined plane. In the absence of any other forces, we just have to account for gravity. The effect of the ideal pulley is to transfer the downward force exerted by gravity on m_2 ($F_{grav \rightarrow m2}$) to m_1. This means that $|F_{grav \rightarrow m2}| = |F_{m2 \rightarrow m1}|$, but the two forces are exerted in different directions. Therefore, $F_{grav \rightarrow m1} = m_2 g$, but in the direction formed by the intersection of the ideal string with m_1, which for the purposes of this exercise we can consider as being parallel with the inclined plane. Using similar reasoning, we can conclude that m_1 is pulling m_2 upwards exactly to the extent to which m_1 is being pulled downwards by gravity; that is, $|F_{grav \rightarrow m1}| = |F_{m1 \rightarrow m2}|$. Therefore, m_2 is being pulled upwards by $F_{m1 \rightarrow m2} = m_1 g\sin(\theta)$. We could also denote the forces that the masses exert on each other as F_T to indicate more specifically that they are examples of a tension force.

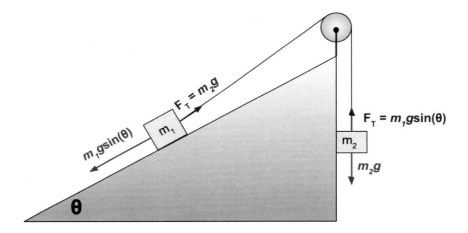

Figure 7. Pulleys and inclined planes.

Now we're in the position to give a more informed answer to which block will go down and which will go up. Let's consider m_2; taking the downwards direction as positive, we can observe that $F_{net} = F_{grav} - F_T$. If $F_{net} > 0$, the mass will accelerate downwards, if $F_{net} = 0$ it will remain stationary, and if $F_{net} < 0$, it will move upwards. Table 1 summarizes how these possibilities relate to the magnitudes of the masses in question.

MCAT STRATEGY > > >

While studying these setups, you may need to *slow down!* Subconsciously, it's very easy to fall into the trap of skimming through the details because you may remember having done similar problems in physics classes. Don't let yourself fall for that trap, though. The golden rule of physics is that you get out of physics studying what you put into physics studying. Put in the effort to make sure you understand every step.

MOVEMENT OF M_2	F_{NET}	INEQUALITY THAT MUST BE SATISFIED	MAGNITUDES OF F_{GRAV} AND F_T	RELATIONSHIPS OF M_1 AND M_2	SUMMARY
Downwards	> 0	$F_{grav} - F_T > 0$	$F_{grav} > F_T$	$m_2 > m_1\sin\theta$	Details depend on θ and magnitude of differences between the masses
None	0	$F_{grav} - F_T = 0$	$F_{grav} = F_T$	$m_2 = m_1\sin\theta$	$m_1 > m_2$ (since $\sin\theta < 1$ for non-90° angles)
Upwards	< 0	$F_{grav} - F_T < 0$	$F_{grav} < F_T$	$m_2 < m_1\sin\theta$	Masses cannot be equal

Table 1. Outcomes of Figure 7 for m_2.

You don't need to memorize Table 1. Instead, you should walk through the reasoning in Table 1 carefully and make sure you understand the principles of how pulleys work and how ideal strings transmit forces via tension.

Sometimes the application of a force results in an object moving in a circle. This is known as rotational motion, and there are two basic setups in which you can encounter rotational motion: gravity and a mass on a string. Let's consider each of these in turn.

MCAT STRATEGY > > >

It is difficult to predict exactly which setups could be asked about on the MCAT, so you should focus on understanding the principles rather than memorizing the details of specific examples.

As mentioned above, gravitation is one of the four physically foundational types of forces. A distinctive fact about gravity is that it is relatively weak, but acts at a potentially infinite distance, in contrast to the strong and weak nuclear forces, which only operate on the scale of the nucleus. The electromagnetic force likewise can operate at long distances, but objects on the scale of planets, solar systems, or galaxies tend to have small charge differentials, so we tend to actually see the electromagnetic force on a more medium scale (e.g., between molecules, within circuits and electronic devices).

Gravity is defined as an attraction between objects that have mass. This is characteristic of all objects; for instance, as you sit reading this book, gravitational attraction is present between you and the book. However, this gravitational attraction is negligible compared to the effect of Earth on both you and the book. The force of gravity between two objects can be calculated using the following equation:

Equation 7.
$$F_{grav} = G\frac{m_1 m_2}{r^2}$$

In this equation, m_1 and m_2 refer to the masses of the two objects, r is the distance between them, and G is the gravitational constant, which has a value of 6.67×10^{-11} m^3/kg·s^2. There is absolutely no need to memorize G, but you should be aware of the overall structure of this equation, because the MCAT could conceivably ask you to reason proportionally about it by presenting a situation in which mass and radius vary. Another point to note regarding this equation is that the force of gravity decreases exponentially as the distance between two objects increases. In a nutshell, this is why we are affected by the gravitational field of the Earth in daily life, but not by the Sun.

We've already casually used the term g to refer to the acceleration caused by gravity, but at this point it's worth noting that it refers to acceleration caused by gravity on objects close to the surface of the earth; that is, it corresponds to $G\frac{m_1}{r^2}$ in the equation $F_{grav} = G\frac{m_1 m_2}{r^2}$, where m_1 is the mass of the Earth and the distance between the object and Earth is considered to be relatively constant. The idea here is that although it is *technically* true, for instance, that the gravitational force exerted on a person at sea level is greater than that exerted on an airplane cruising at 40,000 feet, such variation is negligible, given that the radius of the Earth itself is nearly 4,000 miles. The value of g is approximately 9.8 m/s², although for the purposes of the MCAT, you can usually use the rough estimation of 10 m/s².

If an object is placed at rest in a location where it is affected by gravity, the outcome is simple: it falls. This is as true if you drop a cup of water in the kitchen as if that cup of water were to be released from space. However, remember that force is proportional to acceleration, or change in velocity. Recall from above that if an object is thrown or expelled from a cannon, the force of gravity causes it to trace a curved path as it falls to the ground. Extending this, it turns out that if an object is traveling at the correct velocity at the correct distance from the Earth, the force of gravity will cause its velocity to "curve" inwards to the Earth, but not to the extent that it will actually fall. This scenario is illustrated below in Figure 8. At any given moment, the instantaneous velocity of the satellite is perpendicular to the force of gravity.

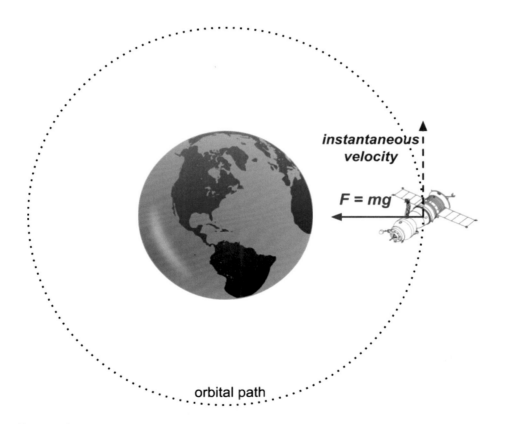

Figure 8. A satellite in orbit.

A force that causes rotational motion is referred to as a centripetal force, and the change in acceleration that it causes is known as centripetal acceleration. The topic of angular (rotational) velocity and acceleration is quite complex, and the details go beyond the scope of the MCAT. However, you should be aware that centripetal acceleration is defined as follows:

Equation 8.
$$a = \frac{v^2}{r}$$

This is a useful fact because it can be applied directly to problem-solving relating to rotational motion. If we have an expression for the centripetal force itself, we can combine the equations, as illustrated below for gravity:

Equation 9.
$$F_c = mg = \frac{mv^2}{r}$$

Equation 10.
$$g = \frac{v^2}{r}$$

This final formula, $g = \frac{v^2}{r}$, can be used to calculate the orbital velocity if the radius is known, or the orbital radius associated with a given velocity. Note that the mass term cancels out on both sides of the equation, indicating that this relationship is actually mass-independent.

Another application of centripetal force is if a mass is tied to a string and swung around. In this case, the centripetal force is the force of tension that the string exerts on the mass, as shown below in Figure 9.

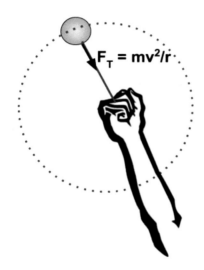

Figure 9. Mass on a string in circular motion.

The details of the electromagnetic force remain beyond the scope of this chapter, but it is also worth mentioning that magnetic fields cause moving charged particles to engage in circular motion. The basic principles of centripetal force analysis apply regardless of the specific force in question.

A final special case of force that you should be aware of is how force can be used to produce a deformation (extension or compression) of a spring. A specific law describes this situation; it is known as Hooke's law. The name Hooke may be familiar to you from cell biology, as Hooke was the first scientist to make observations of cellular structure in samples of cork. Hooke was a remarkable experimentalist who also made foundational contributions to physics. Hooke's law states that the force needed to deform a spring by a certain amount is proportional to the distance of the deformation multiplied by a constant k, or $F_{spring} = kx$. The spring constant k is unique for each spring, and can be thought of a rough measure of the stiffness of the spring. It has units of newtons per meter (N/m). Greater values of k mean that more force is necessary to deform a spring by a certain amount, which indicates that it is stiffer.

Equation 11.
$$F_{spring} = kx$$

The basic principle of Hooke's law is illustrated in Figure 10, in which we see that if a weight of mass m (thereby exerting a force of mg due to gravity) is needed to extend a spring by x, then two such weights are needed to extend the spring by $2x$.

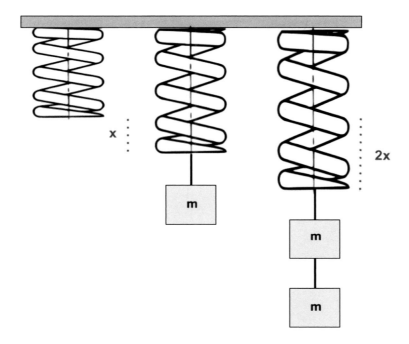

Figure 10. Hooke's law.

More generally, Hooke's law can be applied to compressible/elastic materials, but for the purposes of the MCAT, you're most likely to encounter it as applied to ideal springs. As we'll see in Chapter 8, which discusses waves, springs are important because they are a classic example of oscillating motion, which underpins our understanding of waves.

4. Torque

The physical quantity of torque refers to rotational force; more specifically, it is caused by force applied to a lever arm at a certain distance from an object capable of rotating. The point around which an object rotates is known as the fulcrum. The basic formula for torque is:

Equation 12.
$$\tau = F \bullet d \bullet \sin(\theta)$$

In this equation, τ is torque, F is the force applied, d is the distance between the fulcrum and the point at which the force is applied, and θ is the angle between the lever arm and the force that is applied. You may have seen other ways of articulating torque, such as the equation $\vec{\tau} = \vec{F} \times \vec{d}$, in which torque is defined as the cross product of two vectors, but for the purposes of the MCAT, it is much more straightforward to just think about the absolute magnitude of the force involved modified by $\sin(\theta)$.

MCAT STRATEGY > > >

Torque is often a challenging subject for students; if you have bad memories of torque from Physics 101, try your best to switch into MCAT physics mode. Sometimes university-level coursework in physics can emphasize solving complex and theoretically interesting setups, whereas MCAT physics tends to reward a solid understanding of core concepts and the ability to quickly apply them in novel situations. Therefore, your goal should be to focus first on torque at the level presented here and make sure that you really understand the basics.

Given the equation $\tau = F \bullet d \bullet \sin(\theta)$, there are three ways that torque can be increased: increased force, increased distance from the fulcrum, and ensuring that the force is applied as close to perpendicular as possible to the lever arm. Figure 11 illustrates the importance of distance for optimizing torque, showing that if a constant force is applied, doubling the distance at which the force is applied doubles the torque. This should be relatively intuitive based on your experience using tools such as wrenches; applying force closer to the fulcrum point is less effective.

Figure 11. Torque and distance from the fulcrum.

In contrast, Figure 12 illustrates how torque varies with the angle at which the force is applied. In Figure 12, imagine that a string is connected to the end of the wrench, acting as a mobile handle of sorts that allows you to easily vary the angle at which the force is applied. Even on an intuitive level, it is clear that applying force parallel to the lever arm (at an angle of 0°) would be extremely ineffective, and that a perpendicular approach would be more effective. As shown in Figure 12, applying the same quantity of force at an angle of 30° would reduce the effectiveness by half.

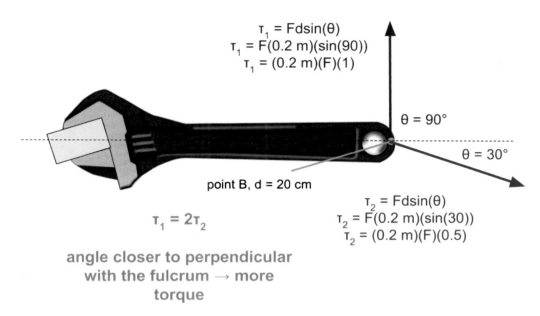

$\tau_1 = Fd\sin(\theta)$
$\tau_1 = F(0.2 \text{ m})(\sin(90))$
$\tau_1 = (0.2 \text{ m})(F)(1)$

$\theta = 90°$

$\theta = 30°$

point B, d = 20 cm

$\tau_2 = Fd\sin(\theta)$
$\tau_2 = F(0.2 \text{ m})(\sin(30))$
$\tau_2 = (0.2 \text{ m})(F)(0.5)$

$\tau_1 = 2\tau_2$

angle closer to perpendicular
with the fulcrum → more
torque

Figure 12. Torque and angle.

Sometimes torque is applicable in situations that do not obviously seem to involve rotation. This is particularly likely to be the case when the rotation is *potential*, but may be balanced out by other torques. Such a situation is presented in Figure 13. Imagine what would happen if the box was too heavy for the board to support, and it collapsed, while remaining attached to the wall. The far edge of the board would trace a circular path as it collapsed toward the wall, as illustrated by the blue arrow. In reality, the situation would probably be more complicated, but this thought experiment is enough to demonstrate that this scenario involves potential rotation.

We can therefore calculate the torque that the box exerts on the fulcrum composed of the attachment point between the board and the wall: $\tau = F \cdot d \cdot \sin(\theta) = mg \cdot d \cdot \sin(90°) = mg \cdot d$. In situations like this, it is useful to think of torque as being clockwise or counterclockwise: in this case, the torque exerted by the box is clockwise. If this physical setup is in equilibrium, some aspects of the attachment point between the board and the wall must exert counterclockwise torque sufficient to prevent rotation.

Figure 13. Torque and gravity.

In an equilibrium situation like that illustrated in Figure 12, you may be required to balance both force and torque. In general, the MCAT is unlikely to give you super-elaborate equilibrium setups, but you should certainly be aware of the possibility that you may need to deploy torque to solve problems, even if no rotation actually happens.

5. Work

In this section, we'll discuss energy for the first time in the textbook by introducing the concept of work. Since the MCAT does not really reward a deep theoretical understanding of physics, it suffices to think of energy as being what accomplishes work. Work is defined in units of joules (J), and 1 J = 1 N·m—that is, 1 newton of force applied across 1 meter. If we recall that a newton is defined as 1 N = 1 kg·m/s², it follows that 1 J = 1 kg·m²/s². It turns out that these SI base units can be expressed in terms of other derived SI units, such as W·s or C·V, but we will handle those definitions as they come up. For the time being, it suffices to understand that work is a very general concept relating to energy transfer, and that one approachable definition of work is force applied over a distance.

This definition of work is illustrated in Figure 14. As was the case with torque, we need to remember that because force is a vector quantity, we need to carefully account for the relevant components of the force that is applied. In Figure 14, we see a constant force being applied at an angle of 30° to the horizontal to accelerate a box horizontally across a surface. Let's assume that the force is applied for a distance d, and that the surface is frictionless. We can calculate the work that is done in this scenario using the following equation:

Equation 13.
$$W = \vec{F} \cdot d = |F| \cdot d \cdot \cos(\theta)$$

As always, there are two ways that you can approach studying the equation for work: either remember that force is a vector, so you may have to resolve it into its components, or memorize the equation that pre-includes the trigonometric transformation necessary to do so. However, if you memorize the equation that contains the trigonometric term, remember that if you are presented with a physical setup that is radically different from the context in which you learned the equation, you may have to adjust accordingly—that is, you may have to use sine rather than cosine.

$$W = F \cdot d = F_x \cdot d = F \cos(30) \cdot d = 0.87 \cdot F \cdot d$$

$= 30°$

F_y

F_x

distance = d

box accelerates for distance d

Figure 14. Work as force times distance.

Work can be used to illustrate an important property of forces; namely, the fact that forces can be divided into conservative and non-conservative forces. Conservative forces are path-independent, meaning that the amount of work done by a conservative force does not depend on its path; another way of phrasing this would be to say that for conservative forces, we care about *displacement*, not *distance*. Conservative forces include gravitation, electromagnetic forces, and spring forces. Non-conservative forces are exemplified by friction and air resistance, and can be thought of as exacting a certain energetic cost per distance.

It is important to note that Equation 13, which states that work equals force times distance, only works for constant forces. More generally, work is the area under the curve in a graph of force as a function of displacement, similarly to how change in velocity is the area under the curve in a graph of acceleration over time. You may have to use graphical analysis of this type to solve a problem with a non-constant force on Test Day.

Figure 15 illustrates some of the ways that the concept of conservative forces can be applied. In this setup, let's imagine that we have a highly idealized model of the force exerted by the biceps in which no friction takes place; that is, we're modeling the biceps as being something akin to an ideal pulley, so that it is simply working against gravity. Nonzero work is accomplished by F_{biceps} as it pulls the barbell up, and nonzero work is accomplished by gravity as it pulls the barbell back down to earth. However, if we look at the system as a whole, no net work is accomplished. We can see this as being either because the work performed by the biceps and gravity cancels out, or because the term d = 0 in the net work equation.

$$W = F_{biceps} \cdot d \qquad W = F_{gravity} \cdot -d$$

$$W = F \cdot d; \; d = 0 \rightarrow W = F \cdot 0 \rightarrow W = 0$$

Figure 15. Example of a conservative force.

You might look at this example and find it very counterintuitive that no net work is accomplished here. This is because it only holds if we make some very strict assumptions about the absence of non-conservative forces. In reality, the anatomy and physiology of weightlifting is much more complicated, so this example also points to the necessity of being very attentive to the assumptions that are embedded in a problem setup.

Now that we have covered the concept of work, we can explore an important concept known as mechanical advantage. The basic idea of mechanical advantage is that by cleverly constructing an apparatus, we can apply less force than would otherwise be necessary to perform a certain amount of work. One of the simplest applications of mechanical advantage is a seesaw, as shown in Figure 16.

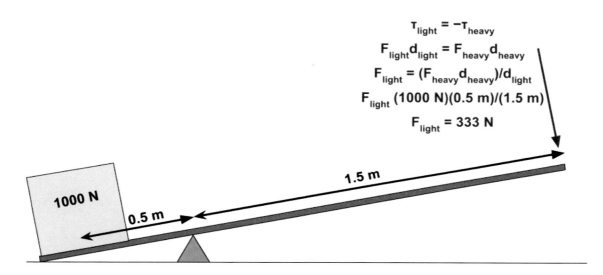

$$\tau_{light} = -\tau_{heavy}$$
$$F_{light}d_{light} = F_{heavy}d_{heavy}$$
$$F_{light} = (F_{heavy}d_{heavy})/d_{light}$$
$$F_{light} (1000 \text{ N})(0.5 \text{ m})/(1.5 \text{ m})$$
$$F_{light} = 333 \text{ N}$$

Figure 16. Mechanical advantage in a seesaw.

The key to understanding mechanical advantage in the setup presented in Figure 16—in which τ_{light}, F_{light}, and d_{light} refer to the side on which a ligher weight is used, and τ_{light}, F_{light}, and d_{light} refer to the side with the 1000 N weight —is balancing the torques. By balancing the torques and solving for F_{light}, we see that any force greater than 333 N would be sufficient to displace the 1000 N box on the other side of the seesaw.

An important point about mechanical advantage is that it allows us to deploy less *force*, but it does not allow us to do less *work*. This can be clearly seen in Figure 17, which depicts how ramps can be used to obtain mechanical advantage. As in other examples we've worked through, in Figure 17, we'll assume that friction is negligible.

pushing up a ramp:

$$F_{parallel} = mg \cdot \sin(\theta) = mg \cdot \sin(22.6) = 0.38mg$$
$$W = F_{parallel} \cdot d$$
$$W = (0.38mg) \cdot 13m$$
$$W = mg \cdot 5m$$

pulling directly up:

$$F_y = mg$$
$$W = F_y d$$
$$W = mg \cdot 5m$$

13 m

5 m

θ = 22.6°

mechanical advantage with a ramp: same W, less F

Figure 17. Mechanical advantage with a ramp.

In Figure 17, we can see that pushing the box up a ramp with a 22.6° angle means that it is only necessary to exert 38% of the force that would be needed to haul the same box up vertically. However, this is compensated for by the fact that the force must be exerted over a much longer distance. In fact, these two factors compensate for each other exactly. As shown in the calculations in Figure 17, the work done is exactly the same regardless of whether the ramp is used. This also follows from the fact that gravity is a conservative force. For ramps, the ideal mechanical advantage can be calculated as follows: mechanical advantage = length of incline / height of incline. In this case, the mechanical advantage would be 2.6, indicating that the force needed to lift up the box vertically would be 2.6 times the force needed to move the box up the incline.

$$\frac{13}{5} = 2.6$$

Equation 14.   mechanical advantage = length of incline / height of incline

6. Power

The final topic covered in this chapter is power. Power is a fairly simple concept; it is defined as work divided by time. Its units are watts (W), and 1 W = 1 J/s. The idea of power is essentially that a given amount of work could be expended either quickly or slowly, and that a system capable of doing so quickly is more "powerful" than a system in which the energy represented by a given amount of work is dissipated slowly.

Equation 15. $P = \frac{W}{t}$

A clear and intuitive example of power is provided by a comparison of firewood and TNT, a common type of explosive. Perhaps somewhat surprisingly, firewood actually contains more energy per unit mass than TNT. However, burning firewood releases that energy fairly slowly, whereas the energy contained in TNT is released almost instantaneously. Therefore, TNT generates more power than firewood.

Firewood:
- more energy per unit mass
- slower
- → less power

TNT (explosives):
- less energy per unit mass
- faster
- → more power

Figure 18. Firewood, TNT, and power.

Although the definition of power (work divided by time) is fairly straightforward, it is important to develop a sensitivity for the clues in a question that can push you towards thinking about work. Since work can be defined as force times distance (for a constant force), if a question gives you force, distance, and time, that may be an indication that you should think about power. As we will see in

7. Must-Knows

> Force: something that causes an object with mass to accelerate. Units = newtons, $N = \frac{kg \cdot m}{s^2}$.
> Newton's 3 laws:
  - Newton's first law: $\vec{F}_{net} = 0$ at equilibrium.
  - Newton's second law: $\vec{F}_{net} = m\vec{a}$.
  - Newton's third law: $\vec{F}_{AB} = -\vec{F}_{BA}$.
> Free-body diagrams: work with center of mass and draw out all forces acting on an object.
  - Center of mass: $x_{center} = \frac{m_1 x_1 + m_2 x_2 + ... + m_k x_k}{m_1 + m_2 + ... + m_k}$
  - Resolve non-perpendicular angles using trigonometry.
  - Solve using Newton's laws (usually first and second laws)
> Friction:
  - Static friction: when object isn't moving; $F_{static} = \mu_s N$, where μ_s is the coefficient of static friction and N is the applied force.
  - Kinetic friction: when object is moving; $F_{kinetic} = \mu_k N$, where μ_k is the coefficient of kinetic friction and N is the applied force.
  - More force is needed to overcome static friction than to overcome kinetic friction.
> Gravitation: a force of attraction between objects with mass.
  - $F_{grav} = G\frac{m_1 m_2}{r^2}$; note that F_{grav} is proportional to mass and inversely proportional to the *square* of the distance between the objects.
> Centripetal forces cause rotational motion; common examples are gravity (e.g., satellites in orbit) and tension force (mass on a string):
  - Centripetal acceleration: $a = \frac{v^2}{r}$; $F_{cent} = \frac{mv^2}{r}$, can be applied to problem-solving if you need to solve for F_{cent} or have an expression for it (e.g., $F = mg$ for gravity).

> Hooke's law: force needed to compress/stretch a spring by x is $F = kx$, where k is a constant unique to each spring that represents its stiffness.
> Torque: can be thought of as rotational force; $\tau = F \bullet d \bullet \sin(\theta)$, where d = distance from the fulcrum to the point where the force is applied and θ = angle formed by the force and the axis parallel to the lever arm.
>   – Be aware of static equilibrium with torque: you may need to balance clockwise and counterclockwise forces.
> Work = defined in units of energy (joules; $1\ J = 1\ N{\cdot}m = kg{\cdot}m^2/s^2$)
>   – $W = \vec{F} \cdot d = |F| \cdot d \cdot \cos(\theta)$, where θ is angle formed between force vector and the horizontal.
> Conservative forces, such as gravity: work is path-independent. Non-conservative forces are path-dependent, and include friction and air resistance.
> Mechanical advantage: less force → same work. For ramps: mechanical advantage = length of incline / height of incline.
> Power: work divided by time; units are watts; $1\ W = 1\ J/s$.

Practice Passage

Students in a biophysics class used a hinged beam setup (Figure 1) in order to simulate forces present in the human arm. A horizontal beam (L = 0.5 m) with a mass (M_b) of 2.0 kg, was attached to a frictionless hinge. The hinge was also attached to a vertical beam which has a frictionless wheel at its top.

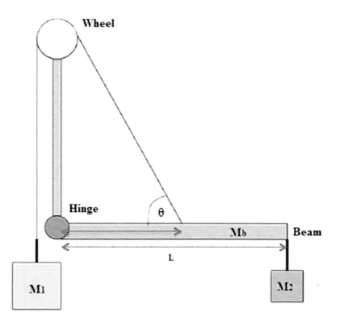

Figure 1. Schematic diagram of simulated human arm

Experiment 1

A massless string was attached to the center of the horizontal beam on one end and the string was draped over the wheel and then attached to mass (M_1) its opposite end. The angle formed between the string and the horizontal beam was measured. The angle the string formed with the horizontal beam was measured to be 57°.

Experiment 2

A second mass (M_2, 1.0 kg) was attached at the end of the horizontal beam and the angle at the hinge was measured. Next, the weight of M_1 was adjusted until the two beams formed a right angle and remained motionless. At this position, the measured angle between the string and the horizontal beam was 60°.

(Note: cos 30° = 0.86, tan 30° = 0.57, tan 60° = 1.73; drawing is not to scale)

1. At the conclusion of experiment 2, what is the length of the string between where it is attached to the horizontal beam and the point where it comes in contact with the wheel?
   A. 0.3 m
   B. 0.5 m
   C. 0.7 m
   D. 1.0 m

2. What is the weight of M_1 when the system is at equilibrium at the end of experiment 2?
   A. 2.3 kg
   B. 4.6 kg
   C. 23 N
   D. 46 N

3. What is the approximate horizontal force that the beam exerts on the hinge during experiment 2?
   A. 9.8 N
   B. 17 N
   C. 23 N
   D. 34 N

4. What is the approximate tension in the string when the system is at equilibrium in experiment 2?
   A. 5 N
   B. 15 N
   C. 30 N
   D. 45 N

5. Which of the following anatomical parts of the human body is NOT simulated in the experimental setup described in the passage?
   A. Ligaments
   B. Triceps
   C. Humerus
   D. Radius

6. If the string is cut, releasing M_1, what will happen to the horizontal beam?
   A. Rotation, while the center of mass of the beam translates
   B. Neither rotation nor translation
   C. Rotation, while the center of mass of the beam does not translate
   D. Translation, while the center of mass of the beam rotates

7. In the simulation of the human arm, M_1 most closely simulates which anatomical structure?
   A. Ligament
   B. Tendon
   C. Bone
   D. Muscle

Practice Passage Explanations

Students in a biophysics class used a hinged beam setup (Figure 1) in order to simulate forces present in the human arm. A horizontal beam (L = 0.5 m) with a mass (M_b) of 2.0 kg, was attached to a frictionless hinge. The hinge was also attached to a vertical beam which has a frictionless wheel at its top.

Key terms: hinge, forces, human arm

Cause and effect: arm functions much like two beams connected by a hinge (elbow) so expect Qs on torque

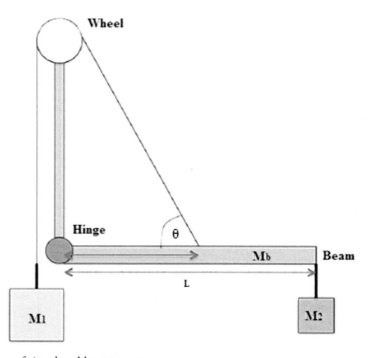

Figure 1. Schematic diagram of simulated human arm

Figure 1 shows an equilibrium between the clockwise and counter clockwise torques around the pivot point of the "elbow"; when we see right triangles and trigonometric relationships on the exam, anticipate using them to calculate

Experiment 1

A massless string was attached to the center of the horizontal beam on one end and the string was draped over the wheel and then attached to mass (M_1) its opposite end. The angle formed between the string and the horizontal beam was measured. The angle the string formed with the horizontal beam was measured to be 57°.

Key terms: M_1, string angle

Cause and effect: mass altered the angle at the hinge and at the beam/string point, but only beam/string angle is given

Experiment 2

A second mass (M$_2$, 1.0 kg) was attached at the end of the horizontal beam and the angle at the hinge was measured. Next, the weight of M$_1$ was adjusted until the two beams formed a right angle and remained motionless. At this position, the measured angle between the string and the horizontal beam was 60°.

Key terms: M$_2$, right angle, measured angle

Cause and effect: new mass is added to rotate beam CW, M1 increased until equilibrium is reached at hinge = 90°, string/beam = 60°, string/wheel = 30°

(Note: cos 30° = 0.86, tan 30° = 0.57, tan 60° = 1.73; drawing is not to scale)

1. B is correct. The state of the system at the end of experiment 2 is rotational equilibrium with the hinge set at 90°. The system forms a right triangle at the "elbow" in which the string is the hypotenuse and the horizontal beam is the side adjacent to the 60° angle. Since this is a special right triangle (30°, 60° and 90°), the length of the side of the triangle adjacent to the 60° angle is x and the length of the hypotenuse is 2x, where x = 0.25 m (we know this because we are told the string is attached to the center of the 0.5 m beam).

2. D is correct. This question asks for weight, not mass, so we can eliminate choices A and B immediately. The sum of the torques acting on the horizontal beam must be zero to have the system be at equilibrium. Torque (τ) is a twisting force (F) applied at some distance from the center of rotation, which in this case is the hinge. The equation for torque is τ = rFsinθ. First determine the clockwise (downward) torque acting on the horizontal beam. The center of mass of the beam is located at the center of the beam, 0.25 m from the pivot point. The force of gravity acting on the beam is 2.0 kg (-9.8 m/s^2) ~ -20 N. Thus, rFsinθ = 0.25(-20 N)(sin 90°) = 0.25(-20)(1) = -5 N•m. The clockwise torque is the mass hung at the end of the horizontal beam, which creates a torque of 1.0 kg (-9.8 m/s^2) x 0.5 m which is a torque of -5 N•m. The total clockwise torque is -10 N•m. Therefore, the counterclockwise torque (up) must be 10 = T(0.25)→T = 10/0.25 = 40 N•m, which is provided by the vertical component of the tension in the string. The tension in the string is T = 40/sin 60° = 40/0.86 = 46 N. Thus, M$_1$ = 46/9.8 = 4.6 kg and its weight will be 4.6(10) = 46 N.

3. C is correct. The force the beam exerts on the hinge is simply the x component of the tension in the rope (since the other forces on the beam are gravity due to the mass of the beam and gravity due to M$_2$ and are both vertical). As shown in the previous questions, we can calculate the tension in the string is 46 N and the horizontal component of the tension will be F$_x$ = (46 N)(cos 60°) = 46(0.5) = 23 N.

4. D is correct. First, you must determine the clockwise (downward) torque acting on the horizontal beam. The center of mass of the beam is located at the center of the beam, d = 0.25 m, from the pivot point. The force of gravity acting on the beam is 2.0 kg(-9.8 m/s^2) ~ -20 N, which is a torque of -5 N•m. The other torque acting in the clockwise direction is the mass hung at the end of the horizontal beam, which creates a torque of 1.0 kg(-9.8 m/s^2)(0.5 m) = -5 N•m. The total clockwise torque is -10 N•m. Therefore, the counterclockwise torque (up) must be 10 and T = 10/(0.25) = 40 N•m, which is provided by the vertical component of the tension in the string. We are told that the angle between the string and the horizontal board is 57°, so the angle the string makes with the wheel is 180 – 90 – 57 = 33 ~ 30°. Since cos 30° = 40/T, we calculate that T = 40/0.86 = 46 N.

5. B is correct. The biceps are the muscles on the front side of the humerus that apply a force that reduces the angle between the lower and upper portion of the arm. The biceps are attached by tendons to the humerus near the shoulder and attached to the radius, in the forearm close to the elbow. The tension in the string is what exerts the force on the beams and simulates the biceps, not the triceps. The triceps are the muscles on the back of the humerus, opposing the biceps, providing a force (when the biceps relax) that extends the arm, and increasing the angle of the arm.

A, C, D: The ligaments connecting the humerus and radius at the elbow are simulated in the experimental setup by the hinge, and choice A can be eliminated. The vertical and horizontal beams simulate the humerus and radius (and ulna as well). Choices C and D can be eliminated.

6. A is correct. If the string is cut, the net torque on the board will be negative (clockwise). Torques cause rotation of an object. The board will rotate around its hinge, and its center of mass will move down and to the left as the board rotates around the pivot point of the "elbow." This is translation of the center of mass.

7. D is correct. Examining the figure, we can see that the weight of M_1 provides the force that generates torque on the "forearm" beam counterclockwise. The force-generating tissue in the body are the muscles.

A, B, C: These structures do not generate force during joint movement, they are connective or support structures.

Independent Questions

1. A box is sliding across a frictionless floor at 8 m/s. Which of Newton's laws most supports the fact that the box will continue to slide in the same direction at 8 m/s unless acted upon by an external force?
   A. Newton's first law
   B. Newton's second law
   C. Newton's third law
   D. None of the above; the given statement is not in accordance with any of Newton's laws.

2. All of the following are examples of the four fundamental forces EXCEPT:
   A. gravitational force.
   B. pressure.
   C. electromagnetic force.
   D. the strong nuclear force.

3. A sled sits on a flat, rough surface. The coefficient of static friction is 0.4, and the mass of the sled is 8 kg. A child attempts to push the sled forward with a horizontal force of 10 N. What magnitude of static frictional force will the sled experience in response?
   A. 3.2 N
   B. 10 N
   C. 32 N
   D. 80 N

4. When a projectile is in the air, assuming no non-conservative forces are present, which of the following is true?
   A. The projectile will slow down in the horizontal direction over time.
   B. The projectile will eventually reach terminal velocity.
   C. The projectile experiences only gravitational force.
   D. The projectile experiences both gravitational force and the horizontal force pushing it forward.

5. A medical gurney is on a frictionless inclined plane. If the plane has an incline greater than 0° but less than 90°, the magnitude of acceleration of the gurney down the plane: (Assume that gravitational acceleration has a magnitude of 10 m/s^2.)

   A. can be 0 m/s^2.
   B. can be any value greater than 0 m/s^2.
   C. can be greater than 10 m/s^2.
   D. must fall between 0 and 10 m/s^2.

6. If the mass of the earth were doubled while the distance between the earth and the sun were quadrupled, how would the gravitational force exerted on the earth by the sun change?
   A. The new gravitational force would be one-eighth the previous force.
   B. The new gravitational force would be one-half the previous force.
   C. The new gravitational force would be the same as the previous force.
   D. The new gravitational force would be twice the previous force.

7. A simplified model of a mammalian forelimb is shown below. The forelimb has a uniformly-distributed mass of 2 kg and a length of 30 cm. A downward force of 10 N is exerted at the end of the limb, 30 cm from the point of rotation.

   What is the magnitude of the upward force that must be exerted 10 cm from the point of rotation to prevent the forelimb from moving?

   A. 3.3 N
   B. 10 N
   C. 30 N
   D. 60 N

8. For maximum torque, a force should be exerted at a _____ angle to the lever arm. For maximum work, a force should be exerted at a _____ angle to the desired displacement.
   A. 90°; 90°
   B. 0°; 0°
   C. 90°; 0°
   D. 0°; 90°

Independent Question Explanations

1. A is correct. Newton's first law states that an object will remain at rest or at constant velocity unless acted upon by an external force. Here, since our object is already traveling at 8 m/s, it will continue to move at 8 m/s unless some force acts to change this. Choice B, in contrast, is incorrect; Newton's second law gives us the equation F_{net} = ma, but neither net force nor mass are discussed here. Newton's third law (choice C) states that if one object exerts a force on another, the second object will also exert an equal and opposite force on the first.

2. B is correct. The four fundamental forces in physics are the gravitational force, the electromagnetic force, and the strong and weak nuclear forces. Pressure, which has SI units of newtons per square meter, is not an example of such a force.

3. B is correct. The formula for static frictional force is F_{static} = μ_sN. Here, the normal force (N) is (8 kg)(10 m/s^2) = 80 N, and μ_s = 0.4. F_{static}, then, should be equal to (80 N)(0.4), or 32 N. However, note that this value is the *maximum* value of the static frictional force. If a force smaller than this amount is acting on the object, the static frictional force will simply be equal and opposite to that force. Here, a 10-N force is attempting to push the object, so static friction will oppose this force with an equal value of 10 N.

4. C is correct. The question stem stipulates that no non-conservative forces (friction, air resistance, etc.) are present. When this is the case, a projectile will experience only gravitational force. The projectile will continue to move forward, but with no horizontal force acting upon it; as a result, its horizontal velocity will not change over time. Terminal velocity is only relevant in cases where air resistance *is* present.

5. D is correct. The only force acting parallel to the plane is the relevant component of the gravitational force (the x-component). This force is equal to $F_{grav}\sin(\theta)$, or mgsinθ. Since this is the only force that will drag the gurney along the plane, it is also our net force. From Newton's second law, remember that F_{net} = ma. Substituting in our equation yields mgsinθ = ma, or gsinθ = a. The

values for sin θ between 0° and 90° range from 0 to 1, so gsinθ will range from 0 to g. This is best stated by choice D. Alternatively, you could use reasoning; the gurney would have an acceleration of 0 m/s^2 if the plane were entirely horizontal, and it would have a magnitude of acceleration of g (or 10 m/s^2) if the plane were positioned at a 90° angle. Thus, in this scenario, its magnitude of acceleration must fall between these two values.

6. A is correct. The formula for gravitational force is $F_{grav} = \frac{Gm_1m_2}{r^2}$. If m_1 were doubled while r was quadrupled, this would alter F_{grav} by a factor of $\frac{2}{4^2}$, which simplifies to one-eighth. In other words, the new gravitational force would be one-eighth the previous force.

7. D is correct. We are asked what upward force is required to place the system in rotational equilibrium. For this to occur, the sum of the downward (counterclockwise) torques must equal the sum of the upward (clockwise) torques. We have two downward torques: that of the 10-N applied force and that of the weight of the board (20 N), which is exerted at the board's center of mass, 15 cm from the point of rotation.

$$\tau_{total\ downward} = (10\ N)(0.3\ m)(\sin 90°) + (20\ N)(0.15\ m)(\sin 90°)$$

$$\tau_{total\ downward} = 3\ N{\cdot}m + 3\ N{\cdot}m = 6\ N{\cdot}m$$

The upward torque, then, must also be equal to 6 N·m. We are told that the upward force is exerted 10 cm from the point of rotation, meaning that we can calculate it as follows:

$$\tau_{upward} = F \cdot d \cdot \sin (\theta)$$
$$6\ N{\cdot}m = (F)(0.1\ m)(\sin 90°)$$
$$6\ N{\cdot}m = 0.1F$$
$$F = 60\ N$$

8. C is correct. Remember, the torque equation contains a term for sin (θ). This value has a maximum at θ = 90°, since sin (90°) = 1. In contrast, the work equation includes a term for cos (θ). This value has a maximum at θ = 0°, since cos (0°) = 1.

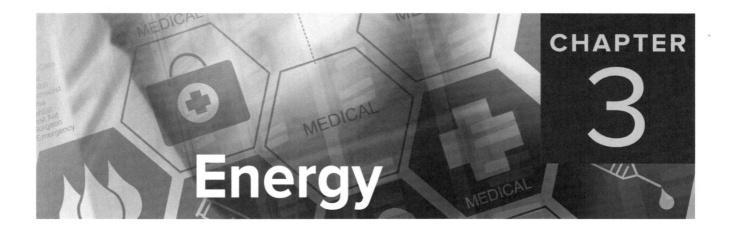

Energy

0. Introduction

In the previous chapter, we introduced energy by discussing work and power; in particular, we discussed work as resulting from a force exerted over a distance. In this chapter, we'll explore energy in more depth, as well as the connection between energy and work. As we'll see, an understanding of these principles can allow us to solve many MCAT physics problems effectively.

1. Kinetic Energy and Potential Energy

Objects in motion have energy. This energy is referred to as kinetic energy, and is defined as follows:

Equation 1.

$$KE = \tfrac{1}{2}mv^2$$

This equation is simple and may be familiar from physics classes, but there are a few points worth noting, including the fact that kinetic energy is proportional to mass. Additionally, the fact that the velocity term is squared has some important implications. First, it indicates that kinetic energy increases exponentially with velocity, which is a relationship that you should be ready to deploy when problem-solving. Second, it indicates that kinetic energy is not a vector quantity, because squaring the velocity term means that sign differences go away.

Let's take a quick look at the units involved in kinetic energy, because it's always a good habit to analyze the units when presented with a new equation. Our units are mass times velocity squared, or $kg \cdot (\tfrac{m}{s})^2$, which equals $\frac{kg \cdot m^2}{s^2}$, or $\frac{kg \cdot m}{s^2} \cdot m$, which is the same as a N·m, which corresponds to the unit of joules that we introduced for work in the previous chapter. This suggests that kinetic energy and work are two ways of talking about the same underlying phenomenon, which is a core point of this chapter that we'll return to several times.

> ### MCAT STRATEGY > > >
>
> It's always worth taking a minute or two to crunch through the units and convince yourself that everything adds up. Developing a sense for how units work out is useful both because it can help you figure out how to solve problems that are otherwise unclear and because it can provide a useful way of checking your work.

Another important form of energy is potential energy. Potential energy refers to the energy that an object has stored within itself, and can occur in multiple forms: gravitational, elastic, electric, and magnetic. In this chapter, we'll focus primarily on gravitational and elastic potential energy, but you should be aware of the existence of electric and magnetic potential energy as well.

Gravitational potential energy is defined as follows:

Equation 2.
$$PE_{grav} = mgh$$

Like kinetic energy, gravitational potential energy is proportional to mass. In this equation, g refers to the acceleration due to gravity, and h refers to height defined with regard to some arbitrary reference scheme. This point is worth reinforcing. As will become clearer as we work through examples later in the chapter, when we work with gravitational potential energy, we're primarily concerned with *change* in energy, so we can feel free to define the referential framework in whatever way makes our lives easier.

For example, you might ask: if we're modeling the potential energy of a ball flying through the air, why should we set the ground as $y = 0$? Why not use the center of the earth as a more absolute frame of reference? Sure, we could, but it would be pointless because the ball isn't going to fall beneath the ground. The takeaway point for this for the MCAT is that if you're presented with a problem that defines a system of axes, you should feel free to work with that, whereas if you have to define your own axes, remember that you need to focus on *change* in height, so pick whichever reference points are convenient and don't agonize over it.

Just as we did with kinetic energy, let's do a quick units check with gravitational potential energy. Mass has units of kilograms, height has units of meters, and g has units of m/s^2, so putting them together we have kg$\cdot \left(\frac{m}{s^2}\right) \cdot$ m. Just like for kinetic energy, this works out to $\frac{kg \cdot m^2}{s^2}$, or $\frac{kg \cdot m}{s^2} \cdot$ m, which is the same as a N·m, which is equivalent to a joule.

The other form of potential energy that we'll be interested in in this chapter is elastic potential energy. For MCAT purposes, we can usually think of this as the energy stored in a spring, but more generally it refers to energy stored in objects by compressing them. Elastic potential energy is defined as follows:

Equation 3.
$$PE_{elastic} = \tfrac{1}{2}kx^2$$

In this equation, k is the spring constant, which is specific for each spring and can be thought of as an indicator of how stiff a spring is. Its units are newtons per meter, which indicates that it is a measure of how much force it takes to deform a spring by a certain amount. Working through an analysis of the units involved, we get the following result: $\frac{N}{m} \cdot$ m^2, which easily simplifies to a N·m, which is again the definition of a joule.

Figure 1 shows simple illustrations of these types of energy.

Figure 1. Kinetic energy, gravitational potential energy, and elastic potential energy.

Now that we have these various definitions of ways that energy is manifested, our next question is: so what? To understand how these definitions can be useful, we have to discuss the principle of conservation of energy.

2. Conservation of Energy

Conservation of energy is a fundamental law of nature. This principle states that energy can neither be created nor destroyed, just transferred from one form to another. We can articulate this using the following equation (just as a mathematical refresher, Σ = sum):

Equation 4A.
$$\Sigma E_{initial} = \Sigma E_{final}$$

This simple equation states that the total final energy within a system is equal to the total initial energy. When phrased in such a general way, this is a law of nature with no known exceptions. However, our life does get a little bit more complicated depending on whether we're dealing with only conservative forces (see Chapter 2; examples include gravitation) or if we want to incorporate non-conservative forces, such as friction.

If we neglect non-conservative forces such as friction, we can transform the above equation into one that more specifically states that the sum of kinetic and potential energy remains the same:

Equation 5A.
$$KE_{initial} + PE_{initial} = KE_{final} + PE_{final}$$

This concept frequently appears in the context of gravitation, especially in setups where the force of gravity acts to transform potential energy into kinetic energy. If we're dealing with a combination of kinetic energy and gravitational potential energy (i.e., not elastic potential energy or electric/magnetic potential energy), we can rewrite the above equation as follows:

MCAT STRATEGY > > >

Don't just view equations and physics concepts as things to memorize; instead, work on envisioning them as tools that you can add to your toolkit. Your end goal for the MCAT is to be able to solve problems quickly, and the way to build this skill is to develop a sense for which of your conceptual tools are the best fit for a given problem. In turn, an important part of building this skill is to think about multiple ways of tackling practice problems, and to note what works and what doesn't work. Think on an analogy with cooking: if your goal is to heat your food, you could use a microwave, the stovetop, an oven, a fryer, and so on—but some choices will be better for certain situations than others.

Equation 5B. $\frac{1}{2}mv_i^2 + mgh_i = \frac{1}{2}mv_f^2 + mgh_f$

This equation is especially important because it provides a connection with kinematics. If we're asked to solve a problem in which we need to calculate initial/final velocity or change in the y-dimension due to the action of gravity, we could apply kinematics formulas, but it might be easier and more efficient just to view the scenario in terms of conservation of energy.

For an example of this, consider the setup shown in Figure 2, which is a relatively simple example of how this principle can be applied. In Figure 2, we see that a soccer ball with a radius of 10 cm will be dropped from a ledge measuring 4 m (note that the drawing is not to scale), and we want to know how fast it will be moving at impact. There are two ways we could go about solving this: using kinematics equations and using the interconversion of kinetic and potential energy, based on the insight that in this problem the ball's potential energy will be entirely converted to kinetic energy.

1. <u>Kinematics</u>: the most appropriate kinematics equation would be $v_f^2 = v_i^2 + 2ad$, where v_f is what we want to solve for, $v_i = 0$ m/s, $a = g$ (9.8 m/s²) and $d = 4.1$ m (remembering that we need to account for the radius of the ball to determine how high its center of mass is). Substituting in, we get $v_f^2 = 0 \frac{m^2}{s^2} + 2(9.8\frac{m}{s^2})(4.1$ m$) \rightarrow v_f = \sqrt{2(9.8\frac{m}{s^2})(4.1 \text{ m})}$. At this point, let's make some mathematical simplifications: we can consider gravity to be 10 m/s² and our distance to be 4 m. Now we can solve the problem: $v_f = \sqrt{2(10\frac{m}{s^2})(4 \text{ m})} \rightarrow v_f = \sqrt{80}\frac{m}{s} \approx 9\frac{m}{s}$.

2. <u>Conservation of energy</u>: Our full equation is $\frac{1}{2}mv_i^2 + mgh_i = \frac{1}{2}mv_f^2 + mgh_f$, but we can make some quick simplifications, by recognizing that the initial kinetic energy is zero, the final potential energy will be zero, and that we can cancel out mass because the mass of the ball is constant. This gives us the simplified equation $gh_i = \frac{1}{2}v_f^2$, and we can then solve for v_f as follows: $v_f = \sqrt{2gh}$. Using the same simplications we used in (1), we get the same solution: $v_f = \sqrt{2(10\frac{m}{s^2})(4 \text{ m})} \rightarrow v_f = \sqrt{80}\frac{m}{s} \approx 9\frac{m}{s}$.

Figure 2. Simple example of interconversion of kinetic and potential energy.

For the problem we solved in Figure 2, the choice between using kinematics or conservation of energy is mostly just a question of preference. As we saw, both strategies get you the same answer, so if you encounter a problem like this on the MCAT, what you need to do is to quickly pick a strategy and execute it. However, sometimes you do have to pick one strategy or the other. For example, note that conservation of energy doesn't directly tell you anything about time, so if you have to solve for time, you'll need to bring in kinematics equations at some point.

There are also some problems for which you essentially *have* to use conservation of energy, at least within the scope of MCAT physics. Note that one aspect of the setup in Figure 2 that made it easy to solve using kinematics equations is that we didn't have to worry about resolving gravity, or any of the velocity terms, into x- and y-components. Consider Figure 3, in which we model what happens if a ball with an initial velocity of 20 m/s traverses something akin to a roller coaster.

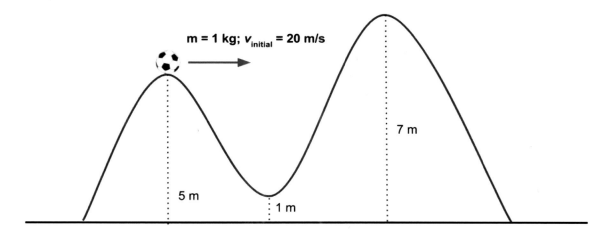

Figure 3. Interconversion of kinetic and potential energy.

Analyzing how the speed of the soccer ball varies across its path depending on height is trivial, albeit somewhat time-consuming. Using the equation $\frac{1}{2}mv_i^2 + mgh_i = \frac{1}{2}mv_f^2 + mgh_p$, and with our knowledge of v_i (20 m/s) and h_i (5 m), we can easily determine how fast the ball will be going at a given height or what height would be necessary to get a certain velocity. However, this problem would be very challenging to tackle using kinematics equations because we'd have to account for the angle of the ramp, similarly to inclined plane problems. However, the path is curved, so we can't use the normal trigonometry that we would apply to solve an inclined plane problem. Within the constraints of the math and physics required for the MCAT, this problem is essentially impossible to solve using kinematics equations.

We'll explore springs in Chapter 8, where we deal with periodic motion and waves in more depth, but the same principle can be applied to analyze the relationship between velocity and location in the context of ideal springs:

Equation 5C. $$\frac{1}{2}mv_i^2 + \frac{1}{2}kx_i^2 = \frac{1}{2}mv_f^2 + \frac{1}{2}kx_f^2$$

The above equations can be extremely useful for problem-solving, but require us to neglect non-conservative forces. What if we need to account for non-conservative forces, such as friction? The principle of conservation of energy still holds; after all, this is a basic law of nature. We just need to make our accounting slightly more complex, as shown in the equation below:

Equation 6.
$$\Sigma E_{initial} - \Sigma E_{nonconservative} = \Sigma E_{final}$$

In this equation, the terms $\Sigma E_{initial}$ and ΣE_{final} refer to conservative forces (and just as a reminder, Σ = sum).

The idea here is simple, and you shouldn't get bogged down in equations. If we ignore non-conservative forces, we can simply say that initial energy equals final energy, while if we have to account for non-conservative forces, we have to recognize that some energy gets dissipated, often in the form of friction/thermal energy.

3. Work-Energy Theorem

The conservation of energy leads us to an elegant and important result known as the work-energy theorem. This theorem states that the work performed on or by an object is equal to the change of its kinetic energy:

Equation 7.
$$W = KE_{final} - KE_{initial}$$

The value of work we can obtain using this theorem can be either positive or negative. As we will see routinely in the context of thermodynamics, the convention when referring to energy is for a positive change in energy to reflect energy put *into* a system and for a negative change to reflect energy taken *out of* a system. Such energy can be harnessed to do other forms of desired work, or can be dissipated into the environment, often in the form of thermal energy.

From the point of view of MCAT problem-solving, the work-energy theorem is a double-edged sword. If your problem fits the specifications of what it's asking for directly, then the work-energy theorem is a beautiful and quick way to solve your problem. However, depending on what the question is asking for, it may not be suitable. To clarify this point, let's look at an example.

Consider what happens when a bowling ball hits some pins, as shown in Figure 4. In this example we'll neglect friction, which is reasonable enough given how smooth a bowling alley can be, and we'll also assume that the ball keeps going after it hits the pins, and doesn't immediately bounce into a wall or anything. What if we find ourselves wondering how much energy was transferred to the pins?

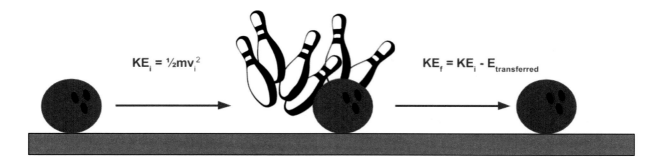

Figure 4. Energy transfer when a bowling ball knocks down pins.

Assessing how much energy is transferred to the pins would initially seem quite challenging, but it turns out to be trivial if we can measure the velocity of the bowling ball before and after impact. If we understand that asking about the energy transferred by the bowling ball is the same thing as asking how much work the bowling ball performs on the pins, we can use our equation $W = KE_{final} - KE_{initial}$, and substitute in the measured v_i and v_f values into the formula $E_{transferred} = \frac{1}{2}mv_f^2 - \frac{1}{2}mv_i^2$. This value will be negative, which indicates that energy was transferred *from* the ball.

4. Pressure-Volume Curves

A basic theme of this chapter has been the ways in which work and energy correspond to different physical quantities. A final way that this is manifested is in the way that pressure and volume are related to work. We'll discuss pressure as applied to fluids in more depth in Chapter 5, which is dedicated to fluids, but for the time being, we can define pressure as a certain force exerted over a certain area:

Equation 8A. $$P = \frac{F}{A}$$

If we multiply through to isolate force, we get:

Equation 8B. $$F = PA$$

Once we have this expression, things get interesting. Let's recall that one definition of work is force multiplied by distance. Let's combine these equations and see what we get:

Equation 9A. $$W = F\Delta x$$

Equation 9B. $$W = PA\Delta x$$

This equation is interesting because it suggests a relationship between work and pressure, but we need to figure out what the $A\Delta x$ term means. If we imagine a cylinder of gas being compressed by a piston, though, we can see that this corresponds to a change of volume: the area of the circular interface between the cylinder of gas and the piston remains constant, but the Δx term corresponding to the length of the cylinder changes. With this in mind, we can rewrite the equation above as follows:

Equation 9C. $$W = P\Delta V$$

This relationship—that pressure times change in volume equals work—is more general, and doesn't only apply to cylindrical volumes of gas being compressed, but the math to prove this more generally goes beyond the scope of the MCAT. A consequence of this is that energy can also be defined in units of liter atmospheres (L·atm), with 1 L·atm equaling approximately 101 J.

Let's next construct a graph of a process in which volume is on the x-axis (making it our independent variable) and pressure is on the y-axis. It may be helpful to continue thinking about this in terms of using a piston to compress gas. By pushing the piston in or out, we can alter the volume of the gas in the cylinder. In turn, the gas itself can push the

> ## MCAT STRATEGY > > >
>
> This formula is best used when you need to relate change in velocity to energy. However, it does not directly provide any information about change in position or about time. Therefore, you should think of the work-energy theorem as being like the physics equivalent of a scalpel: it is the perfect tool for certain tasks, but it is not as widely applicable as a hammer (in our case, the hammer could probably be thought of as the general principle of conservation of energy).

MCAT STRATEGY > > >

The equation $W = P\Delta V$ is worth making a special note of, because it ties together two concepts—pressure and work—that are often studied in different chapters. This fact alone means that students can sometimes have trouble linking them under the stressful, time-limited conditions of Test Day. Work through the derivation until it makes sense to you, and you'll never again forget that these concepts can be linked!

piston out by expanding. By convention, if we're talking about the volume of the *gas* on the x-axis, then an increase of volume means that the gas is doing work by expanding.

Consider the example below in Figure 5, in which a gas expands by a certain volume and the pressure decreases by a certain amount. The area under the line (or area under the curve more generally) corresponds to the amount of work that has been done. This is analogous to how displacement is the area under the curve of a graph of velocity over time. In this case, if we had been given numerical values, the amount of work could be calculated by breaking down the area into a rectangle and a triangle, which have easily calculated areas.

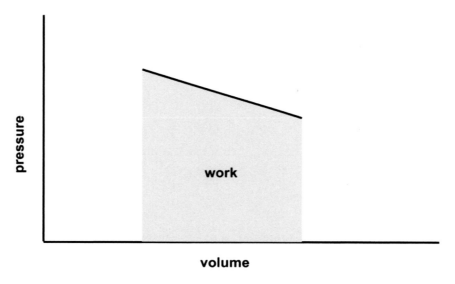

Figure 5. Simple pressure-volume graph.

Some machines involve a cycle in which the system returns to its initial state. In such circumstances, the work done is equivalent to the area encapsulated by the curve. A fairly simple example is shown below in Figure 6.

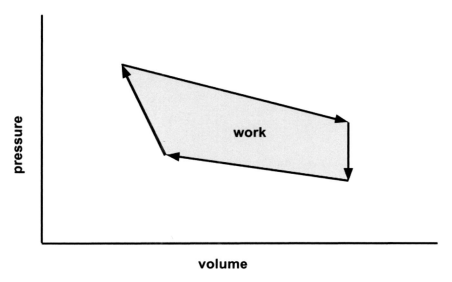

Figure 6. Pressure-volume cycle.

The precise area under the curve may be difficult to calculate, especially if the pressure-volume cycle involves actual curves rather than linear transformations. Doing so would require calculus, which goes beyond the scope of the math required for the MCAT. However, you can be conceptually tested on this knowledge or presented with an area that would be easy to estimate.

4. Must-Knows

> Kinetic energy: energy due to motion.
  - $KE = \frac{1}{2}mv^2$; units equate to $\frac{kg \cdot m}{s^2} \cdot m = N \cdot m = J$.
> Potential energy: energy an object has stored within itself; can be gravitational, elastic, electric, or magnetic.
> Gravitational potential energy: $PE_{grav} = mgh$, where h is defined relative to an arbitrary reference system. We can use arbitrary values of h because we're most interested in *change* of PE.
  - Units equate to $N \cdot m = J$.
> Elastic potential energy: $PE_{elastic} = \frac{1}{2}kx^2$. Units equate to $N \cdot m = J$.
> Conservation of energy: energy can neither be created nor destroyed, just transferred from one form to another. This is a basic law of nature; no exceptions have been found.
> Non-conservative forces like friction may remove energy from a specific system that we're interested in modeling, and it may then be dissipated as thermal energy, but the physical law of conservation of energy is still followed.
> Within a system of conservative forces (i.e., if we neglect non-conservative forces), the sum of kinetic and potential energy is conserved.
  - $KE_{initial} + PE_{initial} = KE_{final} + PE_{final}$

> If focus is on gravitational potential energy:
  - $\frac{1}{2}mv_i^2 + mgh_i = \frac{1}{2}mv_f^2 + mgh_f$
  - Note connection between conservation of energy and the kinematic quantities of v and Δy—this means that conservation of energy can be used to elegantly solve some kinematics problems.
  - For some problems, you can choose between the strategies of kinematics equations or conservation of energy; kinematics equations are needed if you need to account for time, and conservation of energy is needed if the physical setup is too complicated to apply MCAT trigonometry.

> To account for nonconservative forces, apply $\Sigma E_{initial} - \Sigma E_{nonconservative} = \Sigma E_{final}$, where $\Sigma E_{initial}$ and ΣE_{final} refer to conservative forces.

> Work-energy theorem links work and kinetic energy:
  - $W = KE_{final} - KE_{initial}$
  - *Very* elegant way to solve problems where you need to link work/energy with change in velocity.

> $W = P\Delta V$; work = area under the curve of a graph with pressure on y-axis and volume on x-axis.
  - Common application: use of pistons to compress gas.

This page left intentionally blank.

Practice Passage

An engineer is designing a new ramp for an upcoming skateboarding competition. The goal is to minimize friction and ensure maximum energy retention for gravity-defying tricks and audience entertainment. Three variations of the ramp shown in Figure 1 were developed and tested with various objects riding the ramps.

Figure 1. Ramp schematic

Test 1

The curved ramp was coated with a layer of polyethylene. The ramp dimensions were as follows: A = 6 m, B = 8 m, C = 5 m, D = 10 m. A 40 kg skater on a frictionless skateboard was used for the trials.

Test 2

The curved slopes on the ramp were changed to inclined planes while all other ramp dimensions remained the same. The new ramp was coated with a layer of polyethylene and a 30 kg skater on a frictionless skateboard was used for the trials.

Test 3

The ramp was built with 30° inclined planes using material with a rough, irregular surface ($\mu_{kinetic}$ = 0.2) and the following dimensions: A = 14 m, B = 4 m, C = 3 m, D = 8 m. Both skaters took turns riding a sled of negligible mass up and down the ramp.

Test 4

The ramp from test 3 was coated with a layer of calcium phosphate-based enamel to make the entire surface smooth and frictionless. Both skaters took turns riding the sled up and down the ramp.

For tests 1 and 2, each skater started at the top of one side of the ramp and completed 10 laps (from one end of the ramp to the other and back). Skater velocity and acceleration were measured at fixed points along the ramp. The values were used to estimate the various forms of energy in the system.

1. What is the kinetic energy of the 40 kg skater at the bottom of the ramp in test 3?
   A. 2.1 kJ
   B. 3.2 kJ
   C. 4.2 kJ
   D. 6.4 kJ

2. How will the velocity of the skater at the center of the ramp in test 1 compare to their velocity at the center of the ramp in test 2?
   A. Skater velocity during test 1 will be greater than the velocity during test 2.
   B. Skater velocity during test 2 will be greater than the velocity during test 1.
   C. Skater velocity during test 1 will be equal to the velocity during test 2.
   D. There is not enough information to answer this question.

3. Which of the following vectors represents the force of gravity on the skater during test 1 when they are in the position shown below?

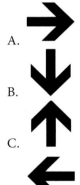

A.

B.

C.

D.

4. During test 2, what is the ratio of total mechanical energy of the skater at the top of the ramp to their total mechanical energy as they enter region B?
   A. 1:2
   B. 4:5
   C. 1:1
   D. 5:4

5. Which formula correctly represents the possible work done by kinetic friction on a skater sliding down the entire length of the inclined plane during test 3?
   A. $(0.2)(30)(9.8)(\cos 30)^2(16)$
   B. $(0.2)(40)(9.8)(\sin 30)(14)$
   C. $(0.2)(30)(9.8)(\cos 30)(16)$
   D. $(0.2)(30)(9.8)(\sin 30)^2(16)$

6. Which of the following forces are acting on the skateboard during test 1 as it rolls along at a constant speed?
   I. Weight of the skater
   II. Gravity
   III. Normal force
   A. I and II only
   B. I and III only
   C. II and III only
   D. I, II and III

7. During test 1, skater 1 rides from the top to the bottom of the ramp where they collide with skater 2, who is initially at rest. If the skaters continue together up the ramp, how far up the ramp will they reach?

   A. A
   B. B
   C. C
   D. D

Practice Passage Explanations

An engineer is designing a new ramp for an upcoming skateboarding competition. The goal is to minimize friction and ensure maximum energy retention for gravity-defying tricks and audience entertainment. Three variations of the ramp shown in Figure 1 were developed and tested with various objects riding the ramps.

Key terms: variations of the ramp

Cause and effect: ramps are designed to maximize energy, reduce friction

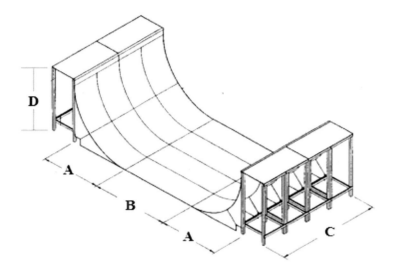

Figure 1. Ramp schematic

Figure 1 shows 2 ramps with a curved surface and a long flat slope in between them; PE_{max} occurs at the top of the ramp, KE_{max} occurs in region B

Test 1

The curved ramp was coated with a layer of polyethylene. The ramp dimensions were as follows: A = 6 m, B = 8 m, C = 5 m, D = 10 m. A 40 kg skater on a frictionless skateboard was used for the trials.

Key terms: dimensions, frictionless skateboard

Test 2

The curved slopes on the ramp were changed to inclined planes while all other ramp dimensions remained the same. The new ramp was coated with a layer of polyethylene and a 30 kg skater on a frictionless skateboard was used for the trials.

Key terms: inclined planes

Contrast: ramps are now linear slopes, lighter skater

Test 3

The ramp was built with 30° inclined planes using material with a rough, irregular surface ($\mu_{kinetic}$ = 0.2) and the following dimensions: A = 14 m, B = 4 m, C = 3 m, D = 8 m. Both skaters took turns riding a sled with negligible mass up and down the ramp.

Key terms: irregular surface, friction, sled

Cause and effect: friction of the ramp will cause E loss from the sleds

Test 4

The ramp from test 3 was coated with a layer of calcium phosphate-based enamel to make the entire surface smooth and frictionless. Both skaters took turns riding the sled up and down the ramp.

Key terms: frictionless enamel

Contrast: ramp is identical to test 3 but with no friction, E will be conserved

For tests 1 and 2, each skater started at the top of one side of the ramp and completed 10 laps (from one end of the ramp to the other and back). Skater velocity and acceleration were measured at fixed points along the ramp. The values were used to estimate the various forms of energy in the system.

Key terms: laps, velocity, acceleration

Cause and effect: kinematic data is collected from the riders but not given.

1. A is correct. The total mechanical energy of the system in test 3 is not conserved due to friction. The initial gravitational potential energy of the skater = mgD = 40(10)(8) = 3.2 kJ so the final kinetic energy will have to be less than this (eliminate choices B, C and D). There is no need to calculate the energy lost to friction, though we can set it up below.

$E_{friction} = F_{friction}(d_{ramp})\cos\theta$ where θ is 180° since kinetic friction directly opposes motion. Full calculations for each of these values is actually needed and shown in the explanations for question 5.

2. C is correct. The differences between tests 1 and 2 that we are told about is that the curved ramp is changed to an inclined plane (a linear ramp) and the skater in test 2 is 10 kg lighter. While the exact lengths of the ramps will be different, the law of conservation of energy states that since both skaters start initial potential energy (mgD), which is all converted to kinetic energy ($\frac{1}{2} mv^2$) at the bottom of the ramp since there is no friction. Since their weight is directly involved in both forms of energy, their weight differences will not factor into their final velocities. We can do the math to confirm.

   Skater 1: $m_1gD = \frac{1}{2} m_1v^2 \rightarrow v^2 = m_1gD / (\frac{1}{2} m_1) \rightarrow v = \sqrt{gD / (\frac{1}{2})}$

   Skater 2: $m_2gD = \frac{1}{2} m_2v^2 \rightarrow v^2 = m_2gD / (\frac{1}{2} m_2) \rightarrow v = \sqrt{gD / (\frac{1}{2})}$

3. B is correct. Since the skater is on earth, gravity will always want to bring him or her straight down towards the center of the earth.

4. C is correct. Since there are only conservative forces acting on the skater (gravity), his or her total mechanical energy will be conserved throughout the time on the ramp.

5. C is correct. Work = Fdcosθ, where θ is the angle between the force and the displacement (θ = 180° as the skater goes down the plane), and d is the distance over which the force acts. The force of kinetic friction on an inclined plane is $\mu_k F_N$ where μ_k is the coefficient of kinetic friction and F_N is the normal force. The normal force is calculated as mgcosθ, where θ is the angle of the inclined plane. Thus, the formula for the kinetic frictional force is (0.2)(m)(9.8)(cos 30), where m could be 30 or 40 kg depending on which skater we use. The distance of the ramp in test 3 can be calculated knowing its base or height distance (14 m, 8 m) and the angle of inclination 30°.

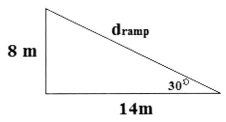

Sin 30° = ½ = opposite/hypotenuse = height/d_{ramp} = 8/d_{ramp} so d_{ramp} = 8 / ½ = 16 m. Finally, we can calculate the work done by kinetic friction, using 30 kg for the mass (we could also have used 40 kg):

(0.2)(30)(9.8)(cos 30)(16 m)(cos 0) = (0.2)(30)(9.8)(cos 30)(16).

6. D is correct. There are three forces acting on the skateboard.

One of these forces is the weight of the rider, shown here with arrow 1. Another is the force of gravity on the board itself, shown with arrow 2. Finally, arrows 3 show the force of the ground pushing up on the skateboard (normal force). These three forces balance out to zero. With no net force, the skateboard doesn't accelerate, but rolls along at a constant speed.

7. B is correct. In test 1 the system is frictionless so the total energy of the skaters must remain the same throughout their movements. At the point of collision, skater 1 and skater 2 now share the total energy skater 1 had at the top of the ramp (mgD = 40×10×10 = 4 kJ). This is the total energy both skaters will have as they continue up the ramp as 1 mass. We can do the math, but on Test Day, save time by estimating and using critical thinking.

$$m_i gh_i = m_f gh_f$$
$$m_i h_i = m_f h_f$$
$$h_f = m_i h_i / m_f$$
$$h_f = 40(h_i) / 70 = 4/7\ h_i$$

Since the new combined mass of the 2 skaters (40 + 30 = 70 kg) is a little less than double the original mass that started at the top of the ramp, the new height they will reach is a little more than half of their original position of 10 m up the ramp, point B.

Independent Questions

1. All of the following are units for energy EXCEPT:
   A. L·atm.
   B. N·m.
   C. kJ.
   D. kg·m·s^{-2}.

2. A 400-kg motorcycle is moving down the street at 40 km/s. How much kinetic energy does this motorcycle have?
   A. 3.2×10^5 J
   B. 8.0×10^6 J
   C. 3.2×10^9 J
   D. 3.2×10^{11} J

3. A 2000-kg boat initially traveling at a rate of 5 m/s speeds up to a rate of 15 m/s. Later, the boat increases its velocity even further, to 25 m/s. How does the work required to go from 5 m/s to 15 m/s compare to the work required to go from 15 m/s to 25 m/s?
   A. The work is the same for both transitions.
   B. The work required to go from 5 m/s to 15 m/s is twice the work required to go from 15 m/s to 25 m/s.
   C. The work required to go from 5 m/s to 15 m/s is half of the work required to go from 15 m/s to 25 m/s.
   D. The work required to go from 5 m/s to 15 m/s is one-quarter of the work required to go from 15 m/s to 25 m/s.

4. A spring is attached to a wall (as shown below) and oscillates horizontally.

   When not stretched or compressed, the spring extends 2 cm from the wall. If the spring is extended as far as possible, then let go, which of the following is true?

   A. The mass at the end of the spring had maximum kinetic energy when fully extended.
   B. The mass at the end of the spring had maximum potential energy when fully extended, and that potential energy will be converted to kinetic as it moves toward its 2-cm-from-the-wall equilibrium position.
   C. The mass at the end of the spring had maximum potential energy when fully extended, and that potential energy will solely be converted to kinetic for the entire duration until the mass comes to a stop.
   D. The mass at the end of the spring will have maximum potential energy when it reaches its 2-cm-from-the-wall equilibrium position.

5. A ball is thrown horizontally from the top of a tall building. Assuming no air resistance, which of the following equations holds true? Note that $v_{f\,vertical}$ refers to the ball's vertical velocity at the instant it hits the ground.
   A. $v_{f\,vertical} = 2gh_i^2$
   B. $v_{f\,vertical} = \sqrt{2gh_i}$
   C. $v_{f\,vertical} = \sqrt{v_{i\,horizontal}^2 + 2gh_i}$
   D. $v_{f\,vertical} = 2gh_i$

6. Non-conservative forces include which of the following?
   A. Friction, air resistance, and the spring force
   B. Friction, air resistance, and gravitational force
   C. Friction and air resistance
   D. Neither friction nor air resistance

7. A gas is held inside a cylindrical apparatus. During an experiment, the pressure of the gas changes from 20 atm to 40 atm while the volume is held constant at 1.5 L. Which of the following statements is true of this transition?
   A. No work is done by the gas.
   B. 30 J of work are done on the gas.
   C. The gas performs 30 J of work on its surroundings.
   D. 60 J of work are done on the gas.

8. A physics student constructs a system that contains a rubber balloon filled with neon gas. The balloon expands to twice its original size. If no heat was added to the system, which of the following options are true?
   I. Work was performed on the neon gas.
   II. Work was performed by the neon gas.
   III. The temperature of the gas inside the balloon decreased.
   IV. The temperature of the gas inside the balloon increased.
   A. I and III only
   B. I and IV only
   C. II and III only
   D. II and IV only

Independent Question Explanations

1. D is correct. The units kg·m·s^{-2} represent force, not energy. Remember, F = ma, so the units for force must be equal to (kg)(m/s^2), which are also termed newtons. The other answer choices are all units for energy.

2. D is correct. Be careful here; the motorcycle's velocity is given in km/s, but the base units for joules include meters, not kilometers. We thus have to convert 40 km/s into m/s:

   (40 km/s)(1000 m/km) = 40,000 m/s = 4 x 10^4 m/s

   Let's also convert 400 kg into scientific notation to make our math easier:

   400 kg = 4 x 10^2 kg

   Finally, let's solve for kinetic energy.

   KE = ½ mv^2 = ½ (4 x 10^2 kg)(4 x 10^4 m/s)^2
   KE = (2 x 10^2 kg)(16 x 10^8 m/s) = 32 x 10^{10} J = 3.2 x 10^{11} J

3. C is correct. For this problem, we can use the work-energy theorem:

   W = KE$_{final}$ − KE$_{initial}$

   To go from 5 m/s to 15 m/s:

   W = ½ (2000 kg)(15 m/s)^2 − ½ (2000 kg)(5 m/s)^2
   W = (1000 kg)(225 m^2/s^2) − (1000 kg)(25 m^2/s^2)

   To make this math easier, we can convert to scientific notation; note also that multiplying the above values gives us units of kg·m^2/s^2, which are equivalent to joules.

   W = (225 x 10^3 J) − (25 x 10^3 J) = 200 x 10^3 J = 2 x 10^5 J

   To go from 15 m/s to 25 m/s:

   W = ½ (2000 kg)(25 m/s)^2 − ½ (2000 kg)(15 m/s)^2
   W = (1000 kg)(625 m^2/s^2) − (1000 kg)(225 m^2/s^2)
   W = (625 x 10^3 J) − (225 x 10^3 J) = 400 x 10^3 J = 4 x 10^5 J

   Since the work required to go from 5 to 15 m/s was 2 x 10^5 J, while that required to go from 15 to 25 m/s was 4 x 10^5 J, choice C is correct. Note that this math is more time-consuming than a typical MCAT question might be, but it is important to understand the process involved.

4. B is correct. Springs have maximum potential energy when fully extended or fully compressed. Once the mass is released, this potential energy will be converted to kinetic until the mass passes its equilibrium position (which represents where it would be if the spring were neither compressed nor extended). Then, kinetic energy will be converted back to potential as the spring compresses. The oscillations of a spring are thus conversions from potential to kinetic energy and back until the mass comes to a stop.

5. B is correct. When no non-conservative forces are acting, the full equation for conservation of energy is as follows:

   $$\frac{1}{2}mv_i^2 + \text{mgh}_i = \frac{1}{2}mv_f^2 + \text{mgh}_f$$

   However, since mass is present in all four terms, it can be canceled out. Additionally, h$_f$ (final height) is zero, since the ball will hit the ground at the end of its arc. Thus, the mgh$_f$ term cancels. The term for initial kinetic energy also cancels, even though the ball does have some initial kinetic energy, because that kinetic energy is due to *horizontal* movement, and the answer choices are dealing with *vertical* velocity. (In a scenario like this, with no friction or air resistance, horizontal kinetic energy is not converted to anything; instead, the ball will simply retain its horizontal velocity when it hits the ground.)

   Our simplified equation is thus:
   $$\text{gh}_i = \frac{1}{2}v_f^2$$

   Rearranging this equation to place v$_f$ by itself results in choice B.

6. C is correct. Friction and air resistance are classic examples of non-conservative forces. These forces are path-dependent, meaning the work done by such a force depends on the distance over which it acts. (You can also think of non-conservative forces as those which make the equation KE$_i$ + PE$_i$ = KE$_f$ + PE$_f$ untrue.) In contrast, the spring force and gravitational force are conservative.

7. A is correct. Remember, the formula for work done by or on a gas is $W = P\Delta V$. Here, the volume does not change at all, making ΔV equal to zero. Regardless of what happens with the pressure, then, our calculated value for work will equal zero as well. If you chose option B or C, you may have incorrectly thought that it was the change in pressure, not the change in volume, that was present in the equation.

8. C is correct. By convention, we conceptualize an expanding gas as performing work on its surroundings. In other words, the gas must perform work on its container to expand. This makes Roman numeral II true, since work was performed by the gas. (In contrast, if work was performed *on* the gas, it would have been compressed.) Performing work requires energy; since the gas is performing work on its surroundings, it is transferring some of its own energy to those surroundings.

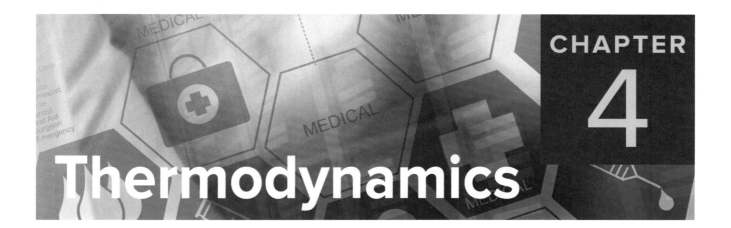

CHAPTER 4

Thermodynamics

0. Introduction

Thermodynamics is a topic that appears in multiple contexts on the MCAT; in this chapter, we discuss the physical foundations of thermodynamics, but many of the applications of thermodynamics that are relevant for the MCAT fall into the category of general chemistry. On a larger scale, thermodynamics is also an important topic for biochemistry. Therefore, we strongly recommend that at some point in your study process you review this chapter together with Chapter 4 from the Chemistry and Organic Chemistry volume and Chapter 12 from the Biochemistry volume, to see how the concepts of thermodynamics fit together on scales ranging from the very nitty-gritty level of physics to the complicated systems of biochemical pathways.

> > **CONNECTIONS** < <

Chapter 4 of Chemistry and Chapter 12 of Biochemistry

Our main focus in this chapter will be explaining thermodynamic systems, the major laws of thermodynamics and ways that they are applied, and heat transfer.

Before we go any further, it's important to avoid any potential confusion by clarifying some terms. Thermodynamics is the study of heat, so our first step should be to clarify what heat is. Misconceptions about heat, temperature, and energy are surprisingly common, and while the MCAT isn't an advanced physics course or a philosophy seminar, understanding the basic differences between these terms can help you study more effectively by avoiding unnecessary confusion.

Heat describes a type of energy transfer. Think of it as being like work in this regard: although we use units of energy to describe work, it doesn't make any sense to say that an object "has" a certain amount of work. Work instead refers to ways that energy—in particular, potential and kinetic energy—is transferred from one object to another. Heat is basically analogous to work, but it involves the transfer of energy through temperature.

MCAT STRATEGY > > >

When studying this, it may be worth investing about 10-20 minutes in convincing yourself on a gut level that heat and temperature are not the same things, and that we need both concepts to describe even everyday thermodynamic events. A simple example, and one that will be helpful to think about throughout this chapter, would be to take objects that have been sitting in a refrigerator for a few days. They all have the same temperature, but no heat will be transferred among them.

Temperature, in turn, is a property of the average kinetic energy of the particles that compose a substance. In the case of ideal gases, in particular, we can envision substances as being made of point-like particles whizzing around at various speeds. Gases are discussed in more detail in Chapter 5 of the Chemistry and Organic Chemistry textbook, but for the purposes of this chapter, it is worth noting that the average kinetic energy of a particle in an ideal gas is defined as $KE = \frac{1}{2}mv_{rms}^2$, where v_{rms}, or the root mean square of velocity, is defined as $\sqrt{\frac{3RT}{M_m}}$, where T is temperature in Kelvin, R is the ideal gas constant, and M_m is the molar mass. These equations are worth knowing in their own right, but it's especially worth noting that combining these equations indicates that temperature is directly proportional to kinetic energy, as shown below:

Equation 1. $$KE = \frac{1}{2}mv_{rms}^2 \text{ and } v_{rms} = \sqrt{\frac{3RT}{M_m}}$$

Equation 2A. $$KE = \frac{1}{2}m \left(\sqrt{\frac{3RT}{M_m}}\right)^2$$

Equation 2B. $$KE = \frac{1}{2}m\left(\frac{3RT}{M_m}\right)$$

Equation 2C. $$KE = \frac{3}{2}T\left(\frac{Rm}{M_m}\right)$$

This version of the equation is sufficient to indicate that kinetic energy is proportional to temperature, but we can make it even better if we recognize that the m/M_m term (mass of a particle divided by molar mass) is equivalent to the ideal gas constant R divided by Avogadro's constant. This, in turn, is defined as the Boltzmann constant (k_B), which has units of joules over Kelvin. This allows us to transform the equation as follows:

Equation 2D. $$KE = \frac{3}{2}k_B T$$

You don't have to memorize this derivation for the MCAT, but you should recognize the following points: first, kinetic energy is proportional to temperature; second, the specific details of this model apply to ideal gases, which are especially straightforward to analyze. The details of accurately modeling solids and liquids are more complicated, but the basic principle still holds that temperature is related to the kinetic energy of the particles in the substance.

With these fundamentals in mind, let's continue to review some other key concepts in thermodynamics, starting with the definitions of thermodynamic systems, and moving on to the laws of thermodynamics.

1. Systems

In the study of thermodynamics, we often talk about systems. A system is essentially just whatever subset of the universe we're interested in modeling at a given time. That's an extremely general, and not particularly helpful, statement, so we can narrow it down a little bit by saying that *usually* (and almost always for MCAT purposes), a thermodynamic system is at thermodynamic equilibrium internally. Thermodynamic equilibrium, in turn, means that no macroscopic transfers of energy or matter are taking place within a system.

Systems can be classified depending on how they can interact with their surroundings. There are three main classes of systems that you should be aware of: open, closed, and isolated.

Open systems do have boundaries, but can exchange both matter and energy with the surroundings. Most of the systems we encounter in our daily lives are open systems, including our own bodies. Another example from a laboratory context might be an open 50-mL centrifuge tube to which you're adding various reagents.

Closed systems, in contrast, can exchange energy with their surroundings, but not matter. A simple example of this would be if you took the 50-mL centrifuge tube we mentioned above and capped it. You now have a system from which no matter will exit and into which no matter will enter, but you're certainly free to heat it and cool it.

Isolated systems can exchange neither energy nor matter with their surroundings. Truly isolated systems are elusive, although they are commonly approximated—in fact, you attempt to approximate an isolated system any time you use an insulator or a Thermos. However, as anyone who's used a commercially available cooler when camping or a Thermos for soup/coffee/tea storage can confirm, attempts to create an isolated system using readily available materials are imperfect. That is, your coffee will eventually get cold, even in the best Thermos. The best example of a true isolated system would be the universe itself, because it has no surroundings.

> ## MCAT STRATEGY > > >
>
> There's no need for you to memorize the examples given in this section. In fact, it would be particularly helpful for you to come up with your own. Coming up with your own examples to illustrate physics concepts is a great way of testing how well you *actually* understand the material, and of diagnosing areas for improvement.

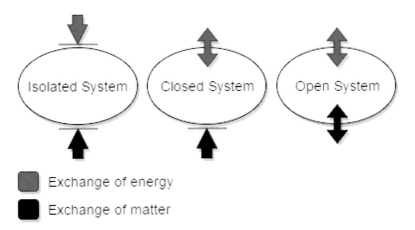

Exchange of energy

Exchange of matter

Figure 1. Open, closed, and isolated systems.

A system at equilibrium can be described in terms of a set of state functions. These include variables that are clearly thermodynamically relevant, such as internal energy, temperature, entropy, Gibbs free energy, and enthalpy, as well as other variables such as pressure, density, and volume. The reason why these are called state functions is that they describe the state of the system without any reference to how the system got that way. They are contrasted to so-called path functions, such as heat and work, which describe how you get from one equilibrium state to another. Conceptually, this distinction is similar to that between conservative and non-conservative forces, although you should be clear on the fact that states and forces are not the same thing.

2. Zeroth Law and Temperature

We'll start our review of the laws of thermodynamics by exploring the zeroth law. The first thing that might strike you about the laws of thermodynamics is the odd convention for numbering them: why start with the *zeroth* law, not the first law? The reason for this is that the zeroth law was formulated after the first and second laws of thermodynamics, but it was felt to be especially fundamental, and therefore it was named the zeroth law.

The zeroth law is primarily of theoretical importance, but you are expected to be aware of it for the MCAT. It establishes the transitivity of thermodynamic equilibrium across systems. More specifically, it states that if system A is in thermal equilibrium with systems B and C, then systems B and C must be in thermal equilibrium with each other. This statement turns out to be important for the mathematical formulation of a definition of temperature that correctly reflects real-world physics, although the details go beyond the scope of the MCAT. For our purposes, we can think of the zeroth law as a piece of theoretical machinery that ensures that temperature makes sense as a concept.

As we discussed in the introduction to this chapter, temperature is a property of a material that is proportional to the kinetic energy of the particles that it contains. Different scales have been developed for measuring temperature. Originally, the Celsius and Fahrenheit scales were both based on the tendency for mercury to expand linearly within the range of temperatures that we encounter in normal circumstances on Earth. The other important temperature scale you should be aware of is the Kelvin scale, which starts at absolute zero. Absolute zero is the temperature at which all motion ceases, and corresponds to the lowest possible temperature. It equals $-273.15°C$ and $-459.67°F$.

The different temperature scales are good for different tasks, and for the MCAT you should be familiar with when to apply each scale.

The Fahrenheit scale is basically good for listening to weather reports and making small talk in the USA and the very few other countries that use this scale. The freezing point of water is 32°F and the boiling point of water is 212°F. Normal body temperature—a clinically relevant temperature that you should know in both Fahrenheit and Celsius—is 98.6°F, although some variation is always present within and among individuals.

The Celsius scale is used in everyday contexts worldwide and in many scientific applications. It is defined based on the melting and boiling points of water: water melts at 0°C and boils at 100°C. Normal body temperature is 37°C. When comparing the Fahrenheit and the Celsius scale, note that the Fahrenheit scale has more narrow increments: it uses a total of 180 degrees to cover the distance between the melting and boiling points of water, whereas the Celsius scale does so in 100 degrees. This means that we can use the following rules to convert between Fahrenheit and Celsius temperatures:

Equation 3A.
$$°C = (°F - 32) \times \frac{5}{9} \quad \text{or} \quad °C = \frac{(°F - 32)}{1.8}$$

Equation 3B.
$$°F = (°C \times \frac{9}{5}) + 32 \quad \text{or} \quad °F = (°C \times 1.8) + 32$$

Two versions are given for the equations above, using a fraction (5/9 or 9/5) or using a decimal expression (1.8), respectively You can use whichever formulation you consider most intuitive. It is recommended that you know these formulas, although on Test Day it will often suffice to use the following simplifications: 5/10 (=1/2) for 5/9, 10/5 (=2) for 9/5, and 2.0 for 1.8. This will produce errors, but generally the answer choices will not be close enough together for this error to cause a problem.

You may also find it useful to simply memorize some general conversion points to give you an intuitive sense of what temperatures in Fahrenheit mean in Celsius and vice-versa, such as: $-40°C = -40°F$ (this is indeed true, although may only be common knowledge to those of you who have lived in Russia, Alaska, Canada, or the far northern Midwest), $0°C = 32°F$, $10°C = 50°F$, $20°C = 68°F$, $37°C = 98.6°F$ (body temperature), $40°C = 104°F$ (a really bad fever), and 100°C = 212°F (boiling point of water). Temperatures outside of the range of −40°C to 100°C can generally be considered as just "really cold" or "really hot" for the MCAT, but you may want to remember that for increasingly higher temperatures, the approximation that °F ≈ 9/5 °C (or even that it is slightly less than double °C) will work increasingly well. Imagine that you're told that a certain chemical process happens at 900°C and you want to convert that into °F. Applying our very quick rule of thumb would say that our answer should be somewhat less than double the value in °C, so something less than 1800°F—let's say 1700°F. It turns out that the actual value is 1652.0°F—so our estimation is off, and your chemistry professor would probably be displeased with you if you took this shortcut on a problem set, but that approximation will almost certainly be good enough for MCAT problem-solving purposes.

The Kelvin scale is used for the absolute measurement of thermodynamic quantities, and its zero point is absolute zero. Therefore, 0 K = −273.15°C = −459.67°F. It is rarely necessary to interconvert between the Kelvin and the Fahrenheit scales, but it is reasonably common to interconvert between the Kelvin and Celsius scales. This is made easier by the fact that the increments in the Kelvin scale are the same as those of the Celsius scale, so we can simply use the easy equations $K = °C + 273$ and $°C = K − 273$, recognizing that the extra 0.15 degree is not going to matter for MCAT purposes.

So, when do you use which temperature scale? To summarize:

> <u>Fahrenheit</u>: Use Fahrenheit to communicate about temperature in an intuitively accessible way with Americans. Don't use it for science. It *might* come up on the MCAT, so you should be prepared to convert it to Celsius if need be.

> <u>Celsius</u>: Use Celsius to communicate about temperature in an everyday way with most people who are not from the United States, and be prepared to recognize it in various scientific contexts, such as chemistry and biochemistry. If you're solving problems quantitatively, you should only use Celsius when you're analyzing ΔT.

> <u>Kelvin</u>: Use Kelvin if you have to solve a quantitative problem using T. The reason for this is that you will never have to worry about negative numbers. Therefore, if you see a term T in an equation, you should think Kelvin automatically. However, if you need to analyze ΔT, you can get away with using Celsius units if doing so is more convenient, because the increments of the Celsius and Kelvin scales are the same.

MCAT STRATEGY > > >

When to use Celsius versus when to use Kelvin is a common point of confusion for students. The trick here is to understand the underlying logic. The beautiful thing about the Kelvin scale is that it's great for math because you never have to worry about negative temperatures. Therefore, it's the default for any equation that incorporates temperature as a term. However, if you only care about *change* in temperature, you can get away with using Celsius as a shortcut. This is why you will often see Celsius units in chemistry equations like $Q = mc\Delta T$. An important point to realize here is that you *could* use the Kelvin scale to solve such problems too, it would just be annoyingly difficult because of the awkward numbers.

3. First Law of Thermodynamics

The first law of thermodynamics reflects our good friend, the principle of conservation of energy, as applied to thermodynamics. Note that this is the second time we've seen conservation of energy so far, and it's not the last: this basic principle is a major thread running through MCAT physics. One way of framing the first law of thermodynamics is the statement that the total energy in an isolated system is constant. However, as we discussed before, truly isolated systems are rare, although they can be simulated.

The first law of thermodynamics can be stated for closed systems by saying that the total energy change of a system (ΔU) is equal to the transfer of energy into the system via heat minus the work performed by the system on its surroundings:

Equation 4.
$$\Delta U = Q - W$$

This is a simple-looking equation but we need to focus on sign conventions to understand what's going on here. The minus sign in the term –W is particularly worth noting. The signs here have to do with the conventions that are used to distinguish energy being added *to* a system (positive) and energy being taken away *from* a system (negative). Therefore, given the fact that we defined this principle specifically with regard to work being done *by the system* on its environment (i.e., negative energy flow from the perspective of the system), we could think of the equation above as $\Delta U = Q + (-W)$, which captures the idea that total energy transfer reflects the joint contributions of heat and work, and that the work term happens to be negative here because of its directionality. If work were to be performed on the system, we could formulate the law as $\Delta U = Q + W$, as long as we were careful to remember that this reflects work performed *by the surroundings* on the system.

MCAT STRATEGY > > >

The first law of thermodynamics is especially important because it is a way to connect work and heat. As we've seen in the last three chapters and will see throughout the rest of this book, work comes up again and again in MCAT physics, such that one of your tasks is to learn all of the concepts linked with work (and the equations that summarize those relationships). If you see heat and work, you should immediately consider applying the first law.

	ΔU	Q	W
(+)	System gaining energy	Heat flow *into* system	Work *by* system
(-)	System losing energy	Heat flow *out* of system	Work *on* system

Table 1. First law of thermodynamics.

Open systems are somewhat more difficult to analyze in a rigorous and quantitative manner because of the need to account for the movement of matter as well as energy and because such systems can be quite complex, but the basic principle of conservation of energy still applies.

4. Second Law of Thermodynamics

The second law of thermodynamics can be phrased in two ways, which are essentially equivalent:

1. If two objects are in thermal contact but not in thermal equilibrium, heat energy will spontaneously flow from the object with the higher temperature to the object with the lower temperature.

2. The entropy of an isolated system will increase over time.

The second law of thermodynamics is a deep principle that has been articulated in many different ways by various researchers over time. In particular, it may seem very surprising that these two statements can be thought of as equivalents. Statement (2) corresponds more closely to how the second law is formulated in more modern sources, but statement (1) provides a more intuitively accessible sense of its mechanism. In order to make sense of how these statements are related, it may be helpful to take a closer look at the concept of entropy.

Entropy is a commonly cited, but somewhat elusive concept. You have probably been taught that entropy is a measure of disorder, and you may remember classic examples like the contrast between a clean (non-entropic) and messy (entropic) bedroom. The idea of entropy as a measure of disorder is useful, but we should be careful to focus primarily on a more rigorous, microscopic version of what we mean by "disorder," because some insight is generally lost when using housekeeping metaphors to make sense of challenging physics concepts.

Entropy can be more rigorously defined using Boltzmann's formula: $S = k_B \ln W$, where S is entropy, k_B is the Boltzmann constant, which we saw above in the introductory section and has units of joules/Kelvin (that is, energy divided by temperature), and W is the number of microstates that correspond to an observable macroscopic state of a substance. Essentially, this refers to the number of specific molecular configurations that an observable substance can have: for instance, we might look at a glass of water and wonder how many specific arrangements of water molecules could be consistent with what we observe. This is sometimes referred to as the degree of freedom of water molecules. We're clearly dealing with very huge numbers here; note that the natural log helps us transform huge numbers into something we can wrap our head around, and this is helped by the fact that the Boltzmann constant is itself very tiny (1.38×10^{-23} J/K).

However, you don't have to know Boltzmann's formula for the MCAT and you certainly don't need to know the Boltzmann constant. So, what's the point of this? There are two basic insights from this discussion that will prove useful.

First, more degrees of freedom equal more entropy, which is the key to understanding how entropy plays out in chemical contexts. The atoms/molecules in solids are more restricted than those in liquids, which are more restricted than in gases, which means that entropy increases as you move from solid to liquid to gas. This is also why entropy decreases as you build larger molecules out of smaller constituents, which is a useful rule of thumb in general chemistry. This is also the sense in which it is best to understand entropy as a measure of disorder.

Second, entropy and energy are connected. Note that the units of the Boltzmann constant imply that the units of entropy are J/K. In fact, the change in entropy due to a reversible process can be defined in terms of heat energy divided by temperature as well: $\Delta S = \frac{Q_{rev}}{T}$, where Q_{rev} is the heat energy due to a reversible process. This provides the key to understanding why the second law of thermodynamics can be articulated either in terms of energy transfer or in terms of entropy change.

> > **CONNECTIONS** < <

Chapters 2 and 11 of Biochemistry and Chapter 1 of Biology

MCAT STRATEGY > > >

Associating entropy with degrees of freedom is very helpful for understanding how entropy is applied in biochemistry, particularly in understanding the critically important fact that hydrophobic substances tend to aggregate together in an aqueous solution. This is discussed at several points in the Biochemistry and Biology textbooks. This is a prototypical instance of how a nitty-gritty physics concept can help set you up for a deeper understanding of biology and biochemistry topics.

Figure 2. The system on the left (disordered, random colors) represents a high entropy state whereas the system on the right (organized, uniform colors) represents a low entropy state.

Note that the second law of thermodynamics doesn't state that you can't reduce entropy, just that you can't do it spontaneously. To appreciate this point, it *is* actually useful to use a macro-scale analogy. If a glass bottle is smashed into pieces, the entropy of its components will drastically increase. Often, the increase of entropy over time is discussed in terms of the linearity of time and irreversible events. It's true enough that the bottle won't reassemble itself and that this is a useful illustration of the second law in action—but it's also useful to remember that we absolutely *can* reassemble the bottle if we are experts in glass-blowing and/or have access to a bottle factory. The issue here is that we would have to invest a considerable amount of energy to do so. Another consequence of the second law of thermodynamics that you should be aware of is that perpetual motion/work machines are impossible. It also predicts that the entropy in the universe as a whole (the only *truly* isolated system) is inevitably increasing over time.

As we've noted before, the MCAT is not an advanced physics class or a philosophy seminar; it's a multiple-choice standardized exam with a focus on problem-solving. Therefore, you should focus on understanding the main predictions of the second law of thermodynamics (spontaneous energy flow from hot to cold objects; increasing entropy over time in isolated systems) and developing an understanding of entropy that you can apply to common chemical and biochemical contexts.

5. Heat Transfer and Applications

Now that we've covered the basic laws governing thermodynamics, we can look at more concrete applications of thermodynamic principles.

As a first step in doing so, let's quickly review the units that we can use to talk about heat transfer. We've stated this before in this chapter but it doesn't hurt to repeat it, because it's a common misconception: *heat and temperature are different things.* Heat is a mechanism of energy transfer and has units of energy, while temperature is a static property proportional to kinetic energy. Largely for historical reasons, multiple units are used in different contexts to refer to heat. The standard SI unit is joules (J), which we have already seen both for heat and for energy in general. In addition, heat can be referred to in terms of calories. A calorie corresponds to the amount of energy needed to heat up 1 g of water by 1°C. This turns out to be 4.184 J; however, complications ensue because this is a very small amount of energy from the point of view of nutrition. For this reason, scientists researching nutrition felt that it would be useful to operate in terms of kilocalories, which are denoted either as kilocalories (kcal) or, somewhat less logically, as "Calories" (with an uppercase C). When you talk about the energy content of food, or the energy expended when exercising for a certain amount of time, you're almost always talking about kilocalories. You may also encounter the BTU, or British thermal unit; this refers to the energy necessary to heat up 1 pound of water by 1°F, and 1 BTU is equal to 1055 J or 0.25 kcal.

We've talked about heat transfer multiple times in this chapter but have yet to discuss the mechanisms. There are three main ways in which heat can be transferred: conduction, convection, and radiation.

> ## MCAT STRATEGY > > >
>
> You certainly don't need to memorize these conversions for the MCAT, although it may be useful to have a rough sense of the magnitudes involved.

Conduction is the most straightforward of these three mechanisms of heat transfer. This term refers to how heat is directly transferred between two substances placed in direct contact with each other, mediated through the transfer of kinetic energy from the particles of one substance to those of the other. Conduction can occur across all phases of matter. Good conductors transmit heat very well, while good insulators are poor conductors of heat. The material in oven mitts, for example, is a good insulator and a poor conductor, which is why you wear them when handling hot metal objects that have been in the oven.

Convection is similar to conduction in that it involves the direct transfer of kinetic energy from one substance to another. However, convection is a little bit more complicated, as it specifically refers to heat transfer that occurs due to the circulation of fluids (i.e., liquids or gases). Convection can occur naturally due to thermally-related differences in the density of fluids, but can also be artificially produced. Natural convection occurs in many circumstances, such as the currents in the world's oceans, but artificial convection is commonly used. The reason why artificial convection is especially useful is because the constant circulation of a fluid ensures that the thermal gradient is maintained. An interesting example of this is a device known as a wine chiller that can be found in some wine/liquor stores. It contains a constantly moving whirlpool of cold water, and is advertised as working up to 25 times as fast as a refrigerator, taking only approximately five minutes to cool a 750-mL bottle from room temperature to being noticeably cold. Note that this is much quicker than the results you could obtain just by placing a bottle in an ice bath. The principle here is convection. Instead of allowing an equilibrium to form between the room-temperature liquid and a static bath of cool water, a constant supply of cool water is constantly in contact with the bottle.

Radiation is the final mechanism of heat transfer, and it is notable for not requiring direct contact between two substances. Electromagnetic waves are generated by all objects with a temperature greater than absolute zero, and these electromagnetic waves carry a certain amount of energy. Thermal radiation can be found more or less everywhere you look, although not all examples are equally important. One of the most common examples we encounter is sunlight, and it is also worth being aware that we lose quite a bit of energy through thermal radiation ourselves.

The stove element heats the kettle and the kettle heats the water by conduction. Water circulating in the kettle transfers heat by convection. Near the stove, air would feel warm due to heat transfer by radiation.

Figure 3. Conduction, convection, and radiation.

MCAT STRATEGY > > >

Don't confuse the term "radiation" as used in thermodynamics (as a form of heat transfer) with the term "radiation" used in atomic physics. Although the wave-particle duality of quantum mechanics could arguably complicate things, as far as we care for the MCAT, these are two different things entirely.

Another important fact about heat transfer is that heating a substance will generally cause it to expand. This is fairly intuitive, because increasing the kinetic energy of the molecules in a substance will mean that they start moving more and therefore separate to some extent. Some exceptions to this exist. The most notable is water, which has a maximum density at about 4°C. This is reflected in the well-known fact that ice is less dense than water; that is, adding kinetic energy to ice to melt it and heat the resulting water up to 4°C will cause it to contract. However, the normal process of thermal expansion takes hold afterwards.

For solids, and for fluids held in a container such that they can only expand in one direction, we can measure expansion in terms of linear expansion (i.e., how much the length L of a solid changes). For fluids in general, it is more useful to think of volume expansion (i.e., how much the volume V of a fluid changes). The equations for both of these are structurally identical, and are given below:

Equation 5A. $$\Delta L = \alpha_L L \Delta T$$

Equation 6A. $$\Delta V = \alpha_V V \Delta T$$

In these equations, L and V represent length and volume, respectively, and ΔL and ΔV represent change in length and change in volume. The constants α_L and α_V are coefficients of thermal expansion that are specific to each substance. Finally, ΔT measures change in temperature. An important thing to note here is not only that ΔL and ΔV are proportional to ΔT, but that they are also proportional to L and V, respectively, so we could also write these equations as follows:

Equation 5B. $$\frac{\Delta L}{L} = \alpha_L \Delta T$$

Equation 6B. $$\frac{\Delta V}{V} = \alpha_V \Delta T$$

Figure 4. A classic example of thermal expansion is seen when the metal making up rails heats up but is held in place by wooden ties. It buckles (bends) as it expands.

These forms of the equations are completely equivalent, but may help to clarify that the change in length/volume that occurs with thermal expansion is *proportional* to the original length or volume of the substance. This is actually completely reasonable when you think about it, because it would actually be pretty strange if a given change in temperature resulted in the same absolute expansion regardless of whether you were dealing with 5 mL of a substance or 500 L.

6. Pressure-Volume Curves and Thermodynamic Conditions

In Chapter 3 on energy, we introduced the idea that pressure times change in volume equals work, and that work can therefore be calculated as the area under the curve on a pressure-volume graph. This concept has relevant echoes in thermodynamics, for two main reasons. First, as we've seen in this chapter, mechanical work is only one way of putting energy into or getting energy out of a system: heat is the other way. Second, note that thermodynamics are inherently at stake in any discussion of pressure and volume in ideal gases, given the ideal gas equation $PV = nRT$, which relates pressure and volume with temperature.

Equation 7. $$PV = nRT$$

In fact, pressure-volume curves like the ones we saw in Chapter 3 often involve changes in temperature. We can see why this is based on the equation $PV = nRT$. If we hold T constant, we get $PV = k$, where k equals some constant (note that this is also known as Boyle's law). The point here is that this fact imposes a very strict constraint on the relationship between pressure and volume. On a pressure-volume graph, this would be expressible as $P = k/V$, which would have a hyperbolic shape.

Various terms are used to describe conditions that may hold for thermodynamic systems. An isothermic system is one in which the temperature is held constant, and isotherms are hyperbolic lines that can be included in a pressure-volume graph that correspond to specific temperatures. An adiabatic system is one in which no heat or matter is transferred between a system and its surroundings. An adiabat is a line similar to an isotherm, except that adiabats correspond to constant entropy values rather than constant temperature values. They look similar to isotherms, but have steeper slopes, and therefore can sometimes be used to "connect" isotherms in pressure-volume graphs of a closed cycle. If the pressure is held constant in a system, it is known as isobaric, and if the volume is held constant, the resulting system is described as isochoric. All four possibilities are shown below in Figure 5.

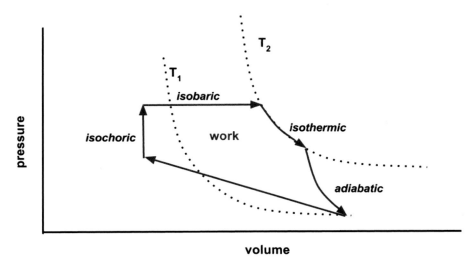

Figure 5. Pressure-volume curve under various conditions.

In Figure 5, the process begins in the upper left with an isobaric change in which the volume of the gas is increased while maintaining the pressure. Note that this increases the temperature. T1 and T2 refer to isotherms, with T2 being hotter than T1. Once T2 is reached, the process becomes isothermic, and the volume increases while pressure decreases, maintaining the temperature at T2. Then an adiabatic process takes place in which the volume is further increased and the pressure is even more sharply decreased, taking us to T1. A linear process then returns the system to the same initial volume but a lower pressure than we started with, and finally, an isochoric process increases the pressure in the system while maintaining the same volume.

7. Must-Knows

> Heat: a form of energy transfer; temperature: a way of measuring the kinetic energy of the particles that make up a substance; *heat and temperature are NOT the same thing.*
> Temperature scales:
  – Fahrenheit: water freezes at 32°F, boils at 212°F, normal body temp. = 98.6°F.
  – Celsius: water freezes at 0°C, boils at 100°C, normal body temp. = 37°C
  – Kelvin: zero point is absolute zero (–273.15°C), increments are same as Celsius.
> Thermodynamic systems:
  – Open systems can exchange matter and energy with their surroundings.
  – Closed systems can only exchange energy with their surroundings.
  – Isolated systems can exchange neither energy nor matter with their surroundings. Arguably the only true example is the universe, although we may try to simulate isolated systems in various contexts.
> State functions: internal energy, temperature, entropy, Gibbs free energy, enthalpy, pressure, density, and volume; path functions: heat and work. Crucial point is that state functions describe the state of a system at a given moment, while path functions describe transitions.
> Zeroth law: if system A is in thermal equilibrium with systems B and C, then systems B and C must be in thermal equilibrium with each other.

- First law: conservation of energy
  - Energy change of a system = transfer of energy into it via heat minus work done by system on surroundings
  - $\Delta U = Q - W$
- Second law: deals with increasing entropy over time.
  - If two objects are in thermal contact but not in thermal equilibrium, heat energy will spontaneously flow from the object with the higher temperature to the object with the lower temperature.
  - The entropy of an isolated system will increase over time.
  - Microscopically, entropy is a measure of how many microstates are compatible with a given macrostate K or a measure of degrees of freedom of the molecules within a state of matter.
- Heat transfer:
  - Conduction: direct transfer between substances in contact with each other.
  - Convection: heat transfer due to circulation of fluids (liquid or gas).
  - Radiation: objects with heat emit EM waves, which transfer energy to objects they hit. Sunlight = thermal radiation.
- Thermal expansion: $\frac{\Delta L}{L} = \alpha_L \Delta T$, $\frac{\Delta V}{V} = \alpha_V \Delta T$
- Thermodynamic conditions relevant for pressure/volume curves:
  - Isobaric: pressure constant
  - Isothermic: temperature constant
  - Adiabatic: no heat or matter transferred
  - Isochoric: same volume

Practice Passage

Thermal strain in humans can be attributed to three main elements: 1) environmental conditions, 2) clothing biophysics, and 3) metabolic heat production. Although body temperature is generally maintained at 37 °C, it can range from 36–40 °C, primarily as a function of physical activity, clothing, environmental conditions, and heat acclimation.

The microenvironment between human skin and clothing is typically 28–30 °C to maintain thermal homeostasis but will change with metabolic heat production and air movement. Thermal injury risk increases when the cooling required to maintain thermal equilibrium exceeds the heat loss to the environment. Skin thickness (d) also impacts the degree of heat conduction to the environment, as illustrated by Equation 1:

$$\frac{Q}{t} = kA \frac{T_{hot} - T_{cold}}{d}$$

Equation 1

where Q is heat lost, t is time, k is the thermal conductivity of air, and A is the area of skin radiating heat.

Researchers placed 20 participants in a room and slowly raised the ambient temperature from 0 °C to 37 °C over the course of 6 hours. The resting metabolic rate of each participant was monitored and the mean group results are plotted in Figure 1. The body eliminates approximately 100 W of heat at an environmental temperature of 37 °C and it increases with ambient temperature. This is achieved through a variety of methods such as radiation, convection, conduction and evaporation of sweat, where the heat of vaporization of water is 590 cal/g. The body loses up to 1.5 L of water per hour at elevated levels of perspiration.

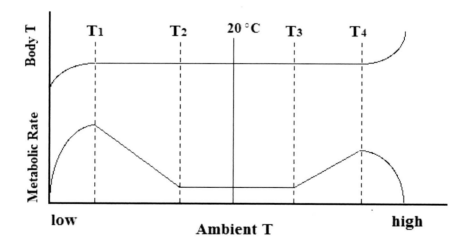

Figure 1. Metabolic rate as a result of ambient temperature

Analysis of the participants' ability to radiate heat power to the environment was analyzed, and found to fit the relationship posited by the Stefan-Boltzmann law:

$$P = e\sigma A(T^4 - T_a^4)$$

where e (emissivity) is the body's effectiveness in emitting energy as thermal radiation, $\sigma = 5.7 \times 10^{-8}$ W/m^{2}K^4, A is the radiating area, T is the temperature of the body, and T_a is the ambient temperature.

Adapted from Potter, AW, Hoyt, RW. (2017). Mathematical prediction of core body temperature from environment, activity, and clothing: The heat strain decision aid (HSDA). J Therm Biol. 2017 Feb;64:78-85 under CCBY 4.0

1. If the average 70 kg male loses 0.6 kg of water per day, what is their rate of heat loss via perspiration (note: 4.18 J = 1 cal)?
   A. 4 W
   B. 8 W
   C. 16 W
   D. 20 W

2. Which of the following would NOT increase the risk of thermal injury?
   A. Increased solar exposure
   B. Decreased skin thickness
   C. Increased air humidity
   D. Increased air temperature

3. According to the data in Figure 1, where will a person most likely experience lethal hyperthermia?
   A. T_1
   B. T_2
   C. T_3
   D. T_4

4. When visiting tropical environments, the human perspiration rate can reach almost 3.8 L/hr. What is the hourly energy loss due to this perspiration?
   A. 2.4 Cal/hr
   B. 24 Cal/hr
   C. 240 Cal/hr
   D. 2400 Cal/hr

5. When the ambient temperature is above 37 °C, by what method can the body most effectively cool itself?
   A. Radiation
   B. Evaporation
   C. Conduction
   D. Convection

6. The upper critical temperature (T_{UC}) represents ambient temperature above which the body must perform cooling processes beyond simple radiation to maintain a safe body temperature. According to Figure 1, the T_{UC} for the study participants is:
   A. T_1.
   B. T_2.
   C. T_3.
   D. T_4.

7. By what factor will the power radiated by a human body (37 °C) change if the ambient temperature were to decrease from 288 K to 272 K?
   A. 0.39
   B. 0.79
   C. 1.00
   D. 1.59

Practice Passage Explanations

Thermal strain in humans can be attributed to three main elements: 1) environmental conditions, 2) clothing biophysics, and 3) metabolic heat production. Although body temperature is generally maintained at 37 °C, it can range from 36–40 °C, primarily as a function of physical activity, clothing, environmental conditions, and heat acclimation.

Key terms: thermal strain, 3 elements, body T

Cause and effect: body T is not constant, but a range effected by internal and external factors

The microenvironment between human skin and clothing is typically 28–30 °C to maintain thermal homeostasis but will change with metabolic heat production and air movement. Thermal injury risk increases when the cooling required to maintain thermal equilibrium exceeds the heat loss to the environment. Skin thickness (d) also impacts the degree of heat conduction to the environment, as illustrated by Equation 1:

$$\frac{Q}{t} = kA \frac{T_{hot} - T_{cold}}{d}$$

Equation 1

where Q is heat lost, t is time, k is the thermal conductivity of air, and A is the area of skin radiating heat.

Key terms: microenvironment, thermal injury risk, skin thickness, heat conduction

Cause and effect: the layer between the skin/clothing acts to cool the body, likely via convection; skin thickness is inversely proportional to heat transfer

Researchers placed 20 participants in a room and slowly raised the ambient temperature from 0 °C to 37 °C over the course of 6 hours. The resting metabolic rate of each participant was monitored and the mean group results are plotted in Figure 1. The body eliminates approximately 100 W of heat at an environmental temperature of 37 °C and it increases with ambient temperature. This is achieved through a variety of methods such as radiation, convection, conduction and evaporation of sweat, where the heat of vaporization of water is 590 cal/g. The body loses up to 1.5 L of water per hour at elevated levels of perspiration.

Key terms: resting metabolic rate, convection, conduction, radiation, evaporation

Cause and effect: increased ambient T caused participants to shed more heat, more water; evaporation of sweat/water is endothermic, draws heat away from body

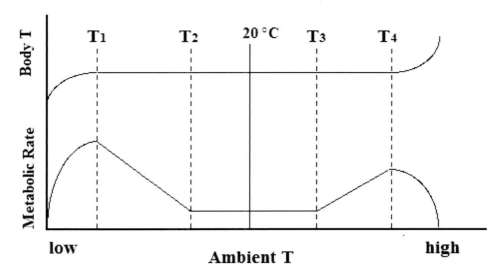

Figure 1. Metabolic rate as a result of ambient temperature

Analysis of the participants' ability to radiate heat power to the environment was analyzed, and found to fit the relationship posited by the Stefan-Boltzmann law:

$$P = e\sigma A(T^4 - T_a^4)$$

where e (emissivity) is the body's effectiveness in emitting energy as thermal radiation, $\sigma = 5.7 \times 10^{-8}$ W/m^{2}K^4, A is the radiating area, T is the temperature of the body, and T_a is the ambient temperature.

Key terms: radiate power, Stefan-Boltzmann

Cause and effect: Power radiation is dependent upon ΔT and emissivity of the body

Adapted from Potter, AW, Hoyt, RW. (2017). Mathematical prediction of core body temperature from environment, activity, and clothing: The heat strain decision aid (HSDA). J Therm Biol. 2017 Feb;64:78-85 under CCBY 4.0

1. C is correct. Since we do not know the environmental T, we cannot use Equation 1 and we must use dimensional analysis here. We are given the mass of water loss (0.59 kg), the heat of vaporization of water (590 cal/g), and we need to find heat loss in watts, or J/s. We are told that 4.18 J = 1 calorie.

   Heat loss $= \dfrac{0.59 \text{ kg}}{1 \text{ day}} \times \dfrac{1000 \text{ g}}{1 \text{ kg}} \times \dfrac{590 \text{ cal}}{1 \text{ g}} \times \dfrac{4.18 \text{ J}}{1 \text{ cal}} \times \dfrac{1 \text{ day}}{24 \text{ hour}} \times \dfrac{1 \text{ hour}}{60 \text{ min}} \times \dfrac{1 \text{ min}}{60 \text{ s}} = \dfrac{0.6(1000)(600)(4)}{24(60)(60)} = 100/6 = 16$ W.

2. B is correct. According to paragraph 2, thermal injury occurs when the cooling required to maintain thermal equilibrium exceeds the heat loss to the environment. According to equation 1, heat loss to the environment is inversely proportional to skin thickness (d).
   A, C, D: These would all increase the heat incident on the body (A, D) or decrease the ability of the body to cool itself (C).

3. D is correct. Hyperthermia, or excessive body temperature, is most likely to be caused when the ambient t is high and/or when the body in unable to effectively eliminate heat. According to Figure 1, both of these events occur beyond T_4.

4. D is correct. We must calculate the total energy lost in the hour. Notice the units in the answer choices are kilocalories, also known as dietary calories (Cal). We are told the person loses about 4 L of water in that hour. Combined with the heat of vaporization of water (round to 600 cal/g) from the passage, and the density of water (1 g/ml) we must know for test day, we can determine the total energy lost.

$$Q = \frac{4\,L}{1\,hour} \times \frac{600\,cal}{1\,g} \times \frac{1\,Cal}{1000\,cal} \times \frac{1\,g}{1\,ml} \times \frac{1000\,ml}{1\,L} = \frac{4(600)(1000)}{1000} = 2400\,Cal$$

5. B is correct. When the ambient temperature is above physiological temperature, then passive processes like radiation, conduction and convection will all transfer heat into the body, not out. In order to cool the body there must be a net outward heat transfer. The only mechanisms left under those conditions are the evaporation of sweat from the skin and the evaporative cooling from exhaled moisture.

6. C is correct. In order for the body to utilize evaporative cooling and other active, non-radiative heat shedding techniques, it must expend energy. We need to find a point on the figure where the metabolic rate goes up with ambient T. Examining the figure, we can see that this occurs at T_3.

7. D is correct. While it may be tempting to jump into calculations using the equation at the end of the passages, the calculations in that equation are way too complicated and large for the test to expect of us. Therefore, there must be an easier way. If the ambient temperature is decreasing, then the body will export heat more efficiently, since $(T^4 - T_a^4)$ will be increasing. Thus, we expect the final power radiation to be higher than the initial power radiation, and the factor change should be greater than 1.

Independent Questions

1. Which of the following statements is always true of an ideal gas?
    A. If two gases are kept at the same temperature, the gas with the higher molecular weight will have a greater average kinetic energy.
    B. Kinetic energy is inversely proportional to temperature.
    C. The higher the molar mass of a gas, the lower the root mean square velocity, assuming other factors are held constant.
    D. Root mean square velocity is proportional to the square of kinetic energy.

2. A student notices that his dinner, as he removes it from the oven, seems to be in thermal equilibrium with the dish that holds it. This dish, in turn, appears to be in thermal equilibrium with the metal oven rack. Which law of thermodynamics posits that, if the student is correct, his dinner must also be in thermal equilibrium with the oven rack?
    A. The zeroth law
    B. The first law
    C. The second law
    D. The third law

3. A block of ice held at −293°C has a Kelvin temperature approximately equal to which of the following?
    A. −566 K
    B. −20 K
    C. 0 K
    D. A temperature of −293°C is impossible for a block of ice.

4. A closed thermodynamic system is best described as:
    A. a system that can exchange matter, but not energy, with its surroundings.
    B. a system that can exchange energy, but not matter, with its surroundings.
    C. a system that cannot exchange matter or energy with its surroundings.
    D. a system that can exchange both matter and energy with its surroundings.

5. A device is built to mimic the force of the human heartbeat. One part of the device is a cylindrical container inside of which a gas presses on a piston.

The gas does 45 J of work on the piston while the gas is simultaneously given 70 J of heat energy. What is the energy change of this gas-piston system?
    A. −25 J
    B. 0 J
    C. +25 J
    D. 115 J

6. Which of the following pairs a chemical equation with a logical value for its change in entropy?
    A. A (g) + B (g) + C (l) → ABC (l); ΔS = +15 J/K
    B. A (g) + B (g) + C (l) → ABC (l); ΔS = −15 K/J
    C. AB (s) → A (g) + B (g); ΔS = +30 K/J
    D. AB (s) → A (g) + B (g); ΔS = +30 J/K

7. Some birds, such as raptors and vultures, can soar in the sky while exerting relatively little effort simply by allowing currents of warm air to carry them upward. These warm air currents represent which mechanism of heat transfer?
    A. Conduction
    B. Convection
    C. Radiation
    D. Transformation

8. In the PV-diagram shown below, process A can best be described as:

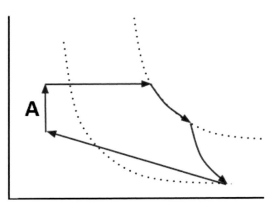

    A. isochoric.
    B. isobaric.
    C. isothermal.
    D. adiabatic.

Independent Question Explanations

1. C is correct. For an ideal gas, $v_{rms} = \sqrt{\frac{3RT}{M_m}}$. From this relationship, we can see that as molar mass (M_m) increases, we would expect v_{rms} to decrease. The other choices are false. Two gases held at the same temperature will have the same average kinetic energy (eliminate choice A). Kinetic energy is directly proportional to temperature (eliminate option B), and choice D is reversed; root mean square velocity is proportional to the square *root* of kinetic energy.

2. A is correct. The zeroth law of thermodynamics states that if one system ("System A") is in thermal equilibrium with two other systems ("System B" and "System C"), then System B and System C must also be in thermal equilibrium with each other. This is precisely what the question stem describes.

3. D is correct. To convert from Celsius to Kelvin, simply add 273 (or, to be precise, 273.15) to the Celsius temperature. Adding 273 to –293°C yields a Kelvin temperature of –20 K. However, negative Kelvin temperatures are impossible for a block of ice, as the lowest value on the Kelvin scale is absolute zero, or 0 K. (Note that, if we get into the realm of *much* more advanced physics, negative Kelvin temperatures are possible, but they could not exist for a solid such as a block of ice. For the sake of the MCAT, you can consider the lowest Kelvin temperature to be 0 K.)

4. B is correct. A closed system is one that can exchange energy (for example, heat energy) with its surroundings but cannot exchange matter. A good example of such a system is a closed vessel in which heat can still enter or exit. Note that choice C describes an isolated system, while option D represents an open system.

5. C is correct. For this problem, we can use the following equation (ΔU) as $\Delta U = Q - W$ to calculate the change in the internal energy of the gas. Since the gas is doing work, it must be losing some energy. Thus, W is positive and equal to 45 J. Next, since heat is added to the system, it must be gaining some energy. Thus, Q is positive and equal to 70 J. Our final answer is 70 J – 45 J = +25 J.

6. D is correct. We cannot possibly know the numerical value for the ΔS of any of these made-up reactions, so we must rely on the signs and the units. Entropy is measured in J/K, not K/J; for that reason alone, choices B and C can be eliminated. The equation in choice A shows three reactants (two gas and one liquid) combining to form a single liquid molecule; since this represents a transition from more "disorder" or more degrees of freedom to fewer, entropy should decrease. The given value of +15 J/K for choice A thus has the opposite of the correct sign, and it can be eliminated. Only choice D gives a logical value for the entropy, along with the correct units. Two solid molecules becoming two gas molecules would certainly be expected to coincide with a positive change in entropy.

7. B is correct. Convection is the transfer of heat by circulating fluids, including gases and liquids. Air currents represent convection. In contrast, conduction is heat transfer that occurs through physical contact between substances; conduction is often associated with solids, although it can take place between any states of matter. Finally, radiation is heat transfer through electromagnetic radiation.

8. A is correct. In a PV-diagram the x-axis represents volume. Therefore, transition labeled "A" involves no change in volume (since the line is drawn vertically upward, its x-coordinate does not change). A process in which volume remains constant is termed isochoric (aka isovolumetric). Isobaric refers to constant pressure, isothermal to constant temperature, and adiabatic to a process in which no heat exchange takes place.

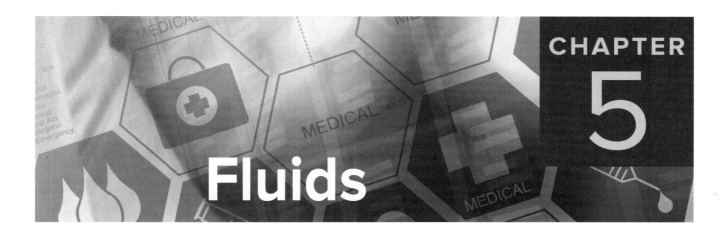

Fluids

CHAPTER 5

0. Introduction

In this chapter, we'll discuss fluids. It's fairly common for fluids to be a subject that MCAT students find challenging. As always, the MCAT rewards a very solid understanding of the fundamental principles of the subject, so our goal will be to review fluids with an emphasis on interconnections with other areas of physics and chemistry and on how the physics of fluids can be applied to understand biological systems.

The very first question we should address is the definition of a fluid. A fluid is defined as a substance that can change its shape to correspond to that of the container that it is put into. This means that both liquids and gases are fluids, whereas solids are not. Fluids are especially important for the MCAT because an understanding of the physics of fluids is helpful for analyzing several important physiological systems, especially the circulatory and respiratory systems. Be sure to review this chapter together with Chapter 9 of the Biology textbook, which discusses these systems and contains a detailed analysis of how the basic principles of fluid dynamics can be applied physiologically.

> **MCAT STRATEGY > > >**
>
> A slow, systematic approach to fluids is especially important (although it's a good idea for MCAT physics in general). Many problems with fluids arise because it's easy to skim through these sections and wind up with an 80% level of familiarity with the concepts, such that when a surprising question comes up under a stressful situation (like on Test Day), it's easy to get flustered. Strive to really *understand*, and be able to explain, every basic concept in this chapter before moving on.

1. Density and Pressure

Density is a quantity that we will refer to over and over again when discussing fluids. It is also a property of solids (and of all matter in general), but we tend to focus on it more when discussing fluids than when discussing solids, at least in the context of the MCAT. Density, which is denoted using the Greek lower case letter rho (ρ), is defined as mass divided by volume:

Equation 1.
$$\rho = \frac{m}{v}$$

There's a corny old joke that may help you solidify this definition: which is heavier, a pound of feathers or a pound of rocks? The answer, of course, is that they weigh the same. However, some people may be tricked into answering this because they give an immediate response based on intuitions they have about density. Of course, this joke is also a little scientifically unsound because it asks about weight rather than mass. This actually brings us to an important point: given the density of a material and its volume, you can easily calculate how much mass it contains by multiplying density times volume.

Equation 2.
$$\rho v = \left(\tfrac{m}{v}\right)v = m$$

Similar reasoning can be used when you have any quantity involving some absolute measurement divided by volume. For instance, although molarity is technically a general chemistry concept, it's worth pointing out the similarity between density and molarity. Molarity is defined as moles divided by liters, so if you need to find out how many moles you have of something given concentration and volume, you can just multiply molarity times volume. Since this kind of reasoning stretches across multiple content areas, you should be sure to develop it into a reflex.

It's important to take care with units when it comes to density. Two common sets of units that you may encounter are g/mL and g/cm^3, which are equivalent to each other. However, although these units of density are commonly encountered, neither of these are actually the SI unit for density, which is kg/m^3 (recall that kilograms are technically the standard base unit for mass in the SI system, although for many biological and chemical purposes it is much more practical to use grams). You also may encounter density expressed in terms of liters, although you should be careful to remember that a liter is not equivalent to a meter cubed. (Think about this one for a minute. A one-liter bottle is not approximately three feet tall and wide). Although you don't need to know many constants for the MCAT, one exception is the density of water at 4°C and 1 atm, which is given below in the various units that you may encounter:

Equation 3.
$$\rho_{water} = 1000\ \frac{kg}{m^3} = 1\frac{kg}{L} = 1\frac{g}{mL} = 1\frac{g}{cm^3}$$

Specific gravity is an exotic-sounding term that means something very simple: how dense something is compared to water. Theoretically speaking, specific gravity can be defined with regard to some other reference material, but water is almost always used, and you can assume that specific gravity refers to a comparison with water unless a question tells you otherwise. It is defined very simply:

Equation 4.
$$\text{specific gravity} = \frac{\rho}{\rho_{water}}$$

As long as you understand what specific gravity means, even this simple formula can be overkill. As noted above, the reference density of water is simply expressible as 1 if you are using units of kg/L, g/mL, or g/cm^3. Therefore, if you're given the density of a substance in units of kg/L, g/mL, or g/cm^3, its density is the same as its specific gravity, except that specific gravity is a dimensionless number. Thus, a substance with a density of 1.03 g/mL with have a specific gravity of 1.03.

There are two main reasons why the MCAT wants you to understand specific gravity. First, and most directly, it is very useful when analyzing buoyancy. Second, it is used in clinical contexts. For example, measuring the specific gravity of urine is a relatively quick and easy way of getting a sense of how many solutes are present, which can provide important clues about a patient's hydration and renal function.

Another parameter that we pay a lot of attention to when studying fluids is pressure. Similarly to density, pressure is not *only* a property of fluids—after all, a needle exerts pressure on the skin when an injection is given to a patient, and our solid (from the outside, anyway) bodies exert pressure on things all the time—but many of the applications of pressure that are interesting from the point of view of the MCAT do happen to involve fluids.

Pressure is defined as force divided by area. This is fairly intuitive if we envision exerting pressure on a surface by pushing it with our hands, for example.

Equation 5.
$$P = \frac{F}{A}$$

As this equation implies, the basic SI units for pressure are N/m², and 1 N/m² has been defined as a pascal (Pa), named after the 17th-century French mathematician, scientist, and philosopher Blaise Pascal. Since pressure has attracted the attention of researchers for centuries—that is, for much longer than SI units have been standardized—it is not surprising that a diverse range of customary non-SI units for pressure exist. It's not essential for you to memorize the conversions between the various units of pressure that are used in different contexts, but you should certainly recognize them as units of pressure and be able to convert them if necessary. In fact, asking a question about pressure using units that are different from those provided in a passage is an easy way for the MCAT to simultaneously test how attentively you read questions/figures and your ability to do the math necessary for conversions.

If you've ever taken a patient's vitals (or had your own vitals taken), you're at least somewhat familiar with one alternate set of units: millimeters of mercury (mmHg). The basic idea with mmHg is that you can measure the pressure difference between two fluids by the difference in the height of mercury in a container (usually U-shaped) that connects the two fluids. The same principle can be used with other fluids; for example, centimeters of water (cmH₂O) is a unit that is often used to measure pressures during the mechanical ventilation of patients. Another set of units of pressure is pounds per square inch (psi), which is often used in industrial/mechanical applications. For instance, most pressure gauges for bike tires are in units of psi.

Another set of units revolve around the concept of atmospheric pressure. This refers to the baseline pressure exerted on us by all of the air present between our location and the point where the Earth's atmosphere transitions to space. Atmospheric pressure varies with elevation, becoming lower as you go higher, and also varies over the course of weather events (you may occasionally hear reference to "high-pressure" and "low-pressure" weather systems with that in mind). However, based on the average value of the pressure at sea level, the unit of 1 standard atmosphere (1 atm) was defined. This is equal to approximately 101,000 Pa (sometimes expressed as 101 kPa), 760 mmHg, and 14.7 psi. The unit of a torr was defined to be exactly 1/760 of 1 atm, making 1 Torr almost equal to 1 mmHg (these units do differ on the scale of 0.000015%, meaning that they are equivalent for most practical purposes). As if this wasn't enough, the meteorologist Vilhelm Bjerknes (1862-1951) invented the bar, which is defined as 100,000 Pa, or slightly less than 1 atm. Millibars in particular are frequently used to talk about weather.

You certainly don't need to know the conversions between all of these units, although it can be helpful to recall that 1 Pa (the SI unit) is a very small unit of pressure in terms of our everyday experience, and that standard atmospheric pressure at sea level is 760 mmHg. Beyond that, you'll mostly want to just be able to recognize the other units of pressure, and be ready to perform conversions if necessary to answer the question.

The pressure exerted on an object submerged in a fluid is equal to the density of the object multiplied by g, multiplied by the depth of submersion:

Equation 6.
$$P_{sub} = \rho g h$$

In Equation 6, h indicates the depth of submersion (or the "height" of the fluid above the object). This is commonly applied to assessing the pressure experienced by an object submerged in water or another liquid, but is actually theoretically applicable to atmospheric pressure and pressure due to gases as well. The challenge in applying it to gases is that we have to may have to account for compressibility. In particular, the density of air at sea level is higher than the density of air at higher levels of the atmosphere. In contrast, for most applications, we can consider fluids to be incompressible. Water is compressible to some extent, but only under rather extreme conditions. Even at the bottom of the ocean, under tremendous pressures, water will only compress by a few percentage points.

We sometimes need to be more specific in our terminology about the pressure exerted on an object. If we're specifically interested in the pressure exerted by a liquid on an object submerged in it, we use the term hydrostatic pressure, which is defined according to Equation 6 ($P_{sub} = \rho gh$). In some other contexts, we may be interested in the total pressure exerted on such an object by *both* the hydrostatic pressure of the water and the atmosphere. This is called the absolute pressure, and it is simple to calculate: just add up the hydrostatic pressure and the pressure of the surrounding atmosphere:

Equation 7.
$$P_{abs} = P_{atm} + \rho gh$$

MCAT STRATEGY > > >

This section contains a lot of different terminology, and terminological confusion is one common source of difficulties on the MCAT. On one hand, there's no way around the fact that you need to memorize these terms and understand their definitions, but on the other hand, how you approach it can help. For every term you run into, don't just copy down the definition—ask yourself: when is this concept useful? Why did scientists develop it? This will help you memorize the content more efficiently *and* will help you develop good mental habits for problem-solving.

In a concrete problem-solving scenario, you do need to be careful to use the correct value for the surrounding atmosphere—don't just sub in 1 atm or 760 mmHg without checking to see if that is appropriate. You may be given a problem setup explaining that the system is at a higher elevation or immersed in a pressure cooker or some other apparatus to increase the ambient pressure.

Alternately, some additional terminology was developed for situations where we want to be absolutely clear that a given pressure reading does *not* reflect atmospheric pressure. The term gauge pressure is used for such measurements, usually made using gauges (hence the name) or other ways of measuring pressure in systems. A classic example of this is the gauge that you may use to measure the air level in your bike tires, although for that matter, gauge pressure is used when measuring blood pressure and in a tremendous range of other contexts. The equation for gauge pressure is:

Equation 8.
$$P_{gauge} = P_{system} - P_{atm}$$

Don't get bogged down in the equations for this, although you should be able to apply them if needed. The essential idea is simple, and you can remember it by focusing on the idea that a normal blood pressure reading is 120/80 mmHg, not 900/860 mmHg or whatever the corresponding result would be given the elevation and atmospheric conditions where the measurement is being taken, simply because we don't care about the atmospheric pressure when measuring someone's blood pressure.

2. Hydrostatics

Now that we've covered the basic principles of density and pressure that form the foundations of analyzing fluids, we'll move on to hydrostatics, which refers to the study of systems involving fluids that are not in motion.

One of the most basic applications of hydrostatics is buoyancy. For the purposes of the MCAT, we'll analyze buoyancy in the context of non-compressible fluids such as water (although you could conceivably encounter something more exotic, such as liquid mercury).

Buoyancy is an intuitively relatable concept. Some objects float on the surface of water and others sink. Whether an object floats or sinks is a property of its density. A very low-density object, such as a feather or a piece of driftwood, will float on the top of water, while higher-density objects, such as rocks, will sink. In fact, the degree to which an object is submerged in water is proportional to its specific gravity. If the specific gravity of an object is greater than 1, it is denser than water, so it will sink. If the specific gravity is exactly equal to 1, it will be completely submerged but at equilibrium. If the specific gravity of an object is less than 1, it will float, but it will be partially submerged in the water. In fact, the percentage it will be submerged is equal to its specific gravity, expressed as a percentage. What if we're not immersing the subject in water, or what if we're using water with a non-standard density (for example, salt water in the ocean is somewhat more dense than fresh water due to the solutes present in it)? In that case, we can just use the following equation:

Equation 9.
$$\% \ submerged = \frac{\rho_{object}}{\rho_{liquid}} \times 100$$

Understanding the principles behind this equation is a little bit more involved. The basic idea is that when an object is floating, the fluid it is floating in exerts an upward force on it. If the magnitude of this upward force, which is known as the buoyant force, exceeds that of the force of gravity that is pulling the object downward, then the object floats. If it does not, it sinks. This basic principle is illustrated in Figure 1.

MCAT STRATEGY > > >

Make yourself very familiar with Equation 9. It is a really useful shortcut to calculate how much an object is submerged. In physics classes, you may have been asked to solve questions about how much an object is submerged by starting with first principles, drawing out all the forces, and so on—but for the MCAT, you want to use shortcuts whenever possible, and this is a great one.

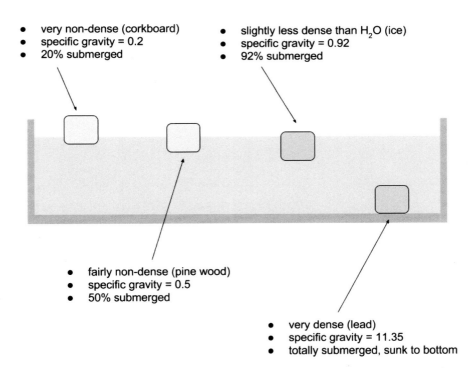

- very non-dense (corkboard)
- specific gravity = 0.2
- 20% submerged

- slightly less dense than H_2O (ice)
- specific gravity = 0.92
- 92% submerged

- fairly non-dense (pine wood)
- specific gravity = 0.5
- 50% submerged

- very dense (lead)
- specific gravity = 11.35
- totally submerged, sunk to bottom

Figure 1. Buoyancy and specific gravity.

However, we can be more specific than just saying that the fluid exerts a buoyant force on the object. The buoyant force is equal to the weight of the water that is displaced by the object. At this point, it may be useful to recall that weight = mg. We also know that $\rho = m/v$, meaning that $\rho v = m$. Therefore, we can substitute these variables and recognize that weight = ρvg. This is known as Archimedes' principle.

Equation 10. $\qquad\qquad\qquad\qquad$ weight = ρvg

The takeaway point here is that the buoyant force is therefore directly proportional to the *volume* of displaced fluid, as modified by the density of the water.

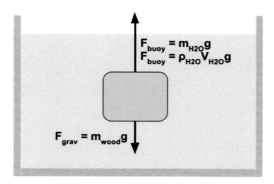

Figure 2. Buoyancy with forces indicated.

At this point we might ask ourselves why this is the case; after all, this is a pretty remarkable finding. One useful way of thinking about this is schematically shown in Figure 3. Imagine beginning to submerse a relatively large object in a relatively small container. Doing so visibly pushes the water upwards, meaning that a certain volume of water is located higher than it would be in its equilibrium state—which in turn means that can be thought of as "trying" to get back down to its original position. This energy can be thought of as the buoyant force.

Figure 3. Buoyant force.

Another important principle for hydrostatics is Pascal's law, which states that a change in pressure made at any location within an enclosed fluid will be transmitted equally to all points throughout that fluid. This is the basic principle underlying hydraulic lift, which uses this principle to generate mechanical advantage. In chapter 2, we discussed mechanical advantage as applied to levers and ramps. Recall that the basic principle of mechanical advantage is to leverage a clever physical setup to be able to perform the same amount of work with the input of less force. Figure 4 shows a schematic of how a hydraulic lift works.

Figure 4. Schematic diagram of a hydraulic lift.

In a hydraulic lift, the operator pushes down on the side with a smaller piston, creating a change in pressure that is transmitted to the side with a larger piston. Recall that pressure is defined as force divided by area. We know that the pressure must be constant, so we can set up the following equations, with F_1 and A_1 referring to the force and area on the side with a smaller piston that the operator depresses, and F_2 and A_2 referring to the force and area on the side with a larger area:

Equation 11.
$$\Delta P = \frac{F_1}{A_1} = \frac{F_2}{A_2}$$

Equation 12.
$$F_2 = \frac{A_2}{A_1} F_1$$

Recalling that $A_2 > A_1$, we can see that $F_2 > F_1$ by a factor equal to how much larger A_2 is than A_1. Since $A = \pi r^2$, the degree to which we can multiply force with a hydraulic lift increases with the square of the radius. This is why hydraulic lifts are often used to lift very heavy things, such as cars. Note, however, that as always with mechanical advantage, we still have to respect conservation of energy. The key idea here is understanding that the application of Pascal's principle to hydraulic lifts involves moving a fixed volume of fluid. In a cylinder, volume is equal to area times distance ($V = Ad$). This means that the smaller piston, to which a smaller force is applied, must be moved for a much greater distance in order to generate the greater force. Work is therefore conserved: $W = F_1d_1 = F_2d_2$.

A final important topic in hydrostatics for the MCAT is surface tension, which bridges physics and general chemistry, and even has implications for higher-level issues in biochemistry to a certain extent. To most efficiently approach surface tension, let's step back and ask a really basic question: why does a liquid hold together? This question overlaps with the analysis of phases of matter in general, which are discussed in more detail in Chapter 5 of the Chemistry and Organic Chemistry textbook. However, the short answer to this question is that a liquid is held together by the presence of intermolecular forces among molecules of the liquid. Hydrogen bonding, which is particularly characteristic of water, is an especially strong type of intermolecular force.

> > CONNECTIONS < <

Chapter 5 of Chemistry

With that in mind, let's consider what happens at the interface between air and water. Nothing particularly interesting happens to the molecules deep within the water: each such molecule experiences attractive forces from all of the other water molecules around it, and we can assume that they more or less balance out. However, the intermolecular forces from other water molecules act unevenly on water molecules that are on the surface of the water. These molecules experience attractive forces from the water molecules deeper in the liquid, but virtually no compensating interactions with the air (recall that air is virtually inert from the point of view of water; it's mostly composed of diatomic gases that offer little opportunity for intermolecular forces). This imbalance of forces acting on water molecules on the surface creates tension.

surface tension layer due to unbalanced intermolecular forces

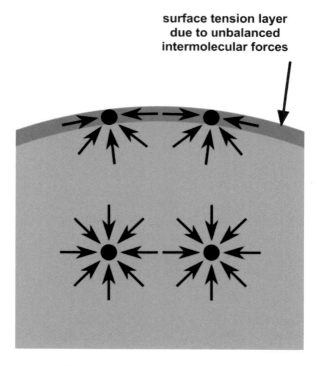

Figure 5. Surface tension.

Surface tension has units of force divided by length. This way of thinking about surface tension is especially useful to understand how it can be utilized by insects known as water striders, which have elaborate physical adaptations that allow them to leverage the surface tension of water to be able to walk on top of it.

However, it is also possible to express surface tension in terms of energy divided by area. This is important because it is a basic pattern in physics that all things being equal, systems will tend to adopt the lowest-energy conformation possible. More surface tension means more energy, so systems will want to minimize surface tension. The best way of doing this is to minimize surface area. This explains why liquids often condense into compact shapes—for instance, why water falls from the sky as raindrops. This principle is also an important lens through which you can understand the principle of "like dissolves like," or the tendency for hydrophobic and hydrophilic substances to isolate themselves from each other.

The effect of intermolecular forces within a given substance is known as cohesion. In the example of a water-air interface that we explored above, there were minimal interactions between the water and the air. However, it is also possible for a liquid to interact with a substance that it is in contact with. Such forces are known as adhesion forces. In general, as the name suggests, adhesion forces can be used to analyze how objects do or do not stick to each other.

When a liquid is placed in a container—especially a narrow tube of the type that is often used for making measurements—there's an interesting interaction that can take place between the cohesive forces within a liquid, which generate surface tension, and the adhesive forces between the liquid and the wall of the container. If the adhesive forces are stronger that the forces of surface tension, the liquid will crawl up the walls of the container to a slight extent. This results in the surface of the liquid becoming curved, which is known as a meniscus. Often, one of the first lessons students learn in a science lab is how to take the meniscus into account when measuring fluids; the correct way is to measure the amount of the fluid at the center of the meniscus, holding it at eye level. The meniscus formed by water is a concave meniscus. However, the opposite pattern holds if the fluid interacts more strongly with itself than with the walls of the container—that is, if the cohesive forces involved in surface tension outweigh the adhesive forces with the container. In this case, the fluid concentrates at the center, as if it is trying to avoid the walls of the container. This is known as a convex meniscus, and the classic example is mercury.

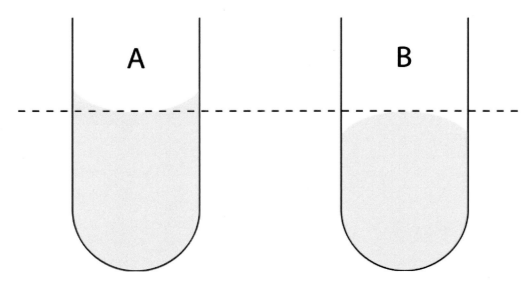

Figure 6. Meniscus shapes.

A very important phenomenon, capillary action, can be thought of as the more general statement of the mechanism through which a meniscus forms. Essentially, if you're using a narrow enough tube—and especially if the tube has been designed to optimize the adhesion forces between it and water—the interplay of adhesion forces and surface tension can allow liquids to rise up the tube in opposition to gravity. Capillary action is relevant in a surprising number of places in nature and science. For example, capillary action is the basic principle through which plants utilize water that is present in the soil. In science, a very familiar example is the use of capillary action in thin-layer chromatography, where it is responsible for the mobile layer moving up the plate.

> > CONNECTIONS < <

Chapter 5 of Biochemistry

> > CONNECTIONS < <

Chapter 9 of Biology

3. Fluid Dynamics

In this section, we discuss how fluids flow, a topic known as fluid dynamics. Fluid dynamics is a perhaps surprisingly complex field of physics, and accurately modeling the flow of fluids can take remarkable mathematical ingenuity and/or computational resources. Luckily, for the MCAT, you don't have to worry about those aspects of fluid dynamics. Instead, the MCAT is largely interested in fluid dynamics insofar as it is important for understanding physiological systems, such as the circulatory system. For that reason, Chapter 9 of the Biology textbook, which covers the circulatory system, provides a thorough overview of how concepts relating to fluid dynamics can be applied to analyze the circulation of blood in the body.

A large part of effectively studying fluid dynamics for the MCAT consists of understanding which analytical simplifications/assumptions are applied to which situations. This is sometimes challenging for students because it can seem arbitrary. Therefore, we'll start out this section by talking about how fluids flow in general. For the most part, in this section, you can assume that we're going to be talking about liquids (which are incompressible) rather than gases (which can be compressed), because the compressibility of gases adds an entire extra level of complexity that goes beyond the MCAT.

Let's start by talking about flow. By definition, liquids can flow, but some do so more easily than others. The property of being resistant to flow—or more technically, resistance to deformation by shear stress—is known as viscosity. Water is an example of a relatively non-viscous fluid, and honey is a classic example of a viscous fluid. All real fluids are viscous, but viscosity is often neglected, especially for problems involving water or aqueous solutions. Viscosity is represented by the Greek symbol η, and has units of Pa·s, or pressure multiplied by time. This is not necessarily a very intuitive set of units, so it may be useful to break it down into its components: $\frac{N \cdot s}{m^2}$. Interestingly, a newton-second (N·s) is equivalent to the SI units for momentum, so it may make sense to think of viscosity as something like momentum divided by surface area. However, momentum is not specifically tested on the MCAT, so you should only rely on this analogy if you happen to remember momentum from previous physics coursework and find it helpful.

On a molecular level, viscosity is caused by friction between layers of the fluid that are in motion relative to each other. Just like kinetic friction, therefore, it causes energy to be lost from the system over time. Therefore, just like how we neglect friction in many situations in which we use conservation of energy to analyze a problem, we neglect viscosity in many of the same scenarios. A final interesting property of viscosity is that it decreases as temperature increases.

In the above paragraph, we mentioned the presence of layers of fluid that are in motion relative to each other. This is an important aspect of flow. The term laminar flow is used to describe scenarios in which a flowing fluid is composed of parallel layers that may be moving at different velocities. In a nutshell, laminar flow corresponds to smooth, well-behaved flow that is easy to model.

In contrast, in turbulent flow, the smoothly regulated layers of laminar flow break down. Pressure and flow can vary dramatically and unpredictably in turbulent flow, as will be familiar to anyone who has experienced turbulence when flying in an airplane. Turbulent flow is, technically speaking, a mess, and is extremely common in real-world applications. At present, there exists no general model within physics of the internal states of turbulent flow, and it is not even clear whether such a model is possible.

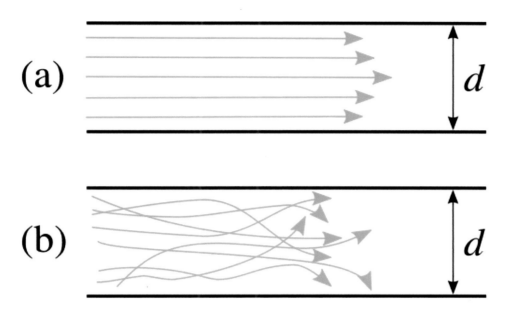

Figure 7. Laminar versus turbulent flow.

However, the onset of turbulence can be predicted to some extent using a value known as the Reynolds number: The Reynolds number (R_e) is a dimensionless constant; you are not expected to be able to calculate it for the MCAT, but it incorporates information about the velocity of a fluid, its density, its viscosity, and the linear dimensions of the area within which it is traveling. High values of R_e, which are directly related to the velocity and density of the fluid and inversely related to its viscosity, are associated with the onset of turbulence, but there is no single universal cut-off value of R_e for the onset of turbulent flow. The most important takeaway point you should understand about the Reynolds number is that the higher the velocity, the more likely flow is to become turbulent.

Returning to laminar flow, an important equation known as Poiseuille's law is used to describe laminar flow of incompressible fluids through a long cylindrical tube. An important fact about Poiseuille's law is that it accounts for viscosity. Poiseuille's law contains five variables, the most important of which are the flow rate, the pressure drop between both ends of the tube, and the radius of the tube. It can be written in two equivalent forms, depending on whether we are primarily interested in flow rate or the pressure drop. Both are given below:

Equation 13A.
$$Q = \frac{\pi r^4 \Delta P}{8\eta L}$$

Equation 13B.
$$\Delta P = \frac{8\eta L Q}{\pi r^4}$$

In these equations, Q is the flow rate, ΔP is the change in pressure from one end of the tube to the other, η is the viscosity, L is the length of the tube, and r is its radius. Equations 13A and 13B are completely equivalent, just rearranged. You may find it useful to memorize both, or you may prefer to memorize one form and derive the other on Test Day if necessary. It is very unlikely that you will be expected to perform a calculation using Poiseuille's law; instead, you should focus on the relationships that it encodes, which are summarized below:

> The flow rate (Q) and the pressure drop (ΔP) are proportional to each other. The best way to think about this is that a large pressure drop will cause flow rate to increase.

> Length (L) is proportional to the pressure drop (ΔP) and inversely proportional to the flow rate.
> Flow rate is proportional to the radius *to the fourth power*. This means that increasing the radius of the tube will dramatically increase the flow rate.
> The pressure drop (ΔP) is inversely proportional to the radius *to the fourth power*. This means that it we hold all other quantities equal, decreasing the radius will dramatically increase the amount of pressure necessary to push fluid through the pipe.
> This is covered in previous bullet points, but it's worth repeating: the radius term here is to the fourth power. This is quite rare in the content included on the MCAT, so it provides an excellent opportunity for the MCAT to test an exponential relationship beyond the commonly encountered direct square ($y = kx^2$), direct linear ($y = kx$), inverse linear ($y = k/x$), and inverse square ($y = k/x^2$) patterns.

Although Poiseuille's law accounts for viscosity, we can obtain some interesting results if we neglect viscosity. As discussed above, viscosity involves resistance to flow over time, and therefore is a way of transferring energy out of the fluid, similarly to how friction operates. This is a hint that we may be able to apply the principle of conservation to energy to fluids. It turns out that we can indeed do so, and the result is what's known as Bernoulli's law. To be absolutely clear, Bernoulli's law holds only for highly idealized fluids, for which we assume laminar flow, neglect viscosity, and neglect any interactions that may take place between the fluid and its container. Bernoulli's law is given below:

Equation 14.
$$P_1 + \frac{1}{2}\rho v_1^2 + \rho g h_1 = P_2 + \frac{1}{2}\rho v_2^2 + \rho g h_2$$

The terms $\frac{1}{2}\rho v^2$ and $\rho g h$ should just be thought of as corresponding to kinetic energy and potential energy, respectively. Note that they can be derived by dividing our standard terms for kinetic and potential energy, $\frac{1}{2}mv^2$ and mgh, by volume, because density equals mass divided by volume. This means that we're essentially talking about energy density here, and the reason for this is because it allows us to build a conceptual bridge to pressure (corresponding to the P_1 and P_2 terms).

At this point we need to step back and realize something interesting and non-obvious about pressure. In the first section of this chapter, we defined pressure as being equal to force divided by area, but what if we consider the entire volume of fluid that exerts pressure on its container? In this exposition, we'll use the equation $V = Ad$ (volume equals area times distance) for volume; although it is technically only true for cylinders, on the level of dimensional analysis it allows us to efficiently move from distance squared to distance cubed. We're working at a level of generality such that we don't really care about the specific shapes we're working with, so this simplification is helpful. First, let's take our standard expression for pressure, multiply through by distance, and rearrange:

Equation 15A.
$$P = \frac{F}{A}$$

Equation 15B.
$$P \cdot d = \frac{F \cdot d}{A}$$

Equation 15C.
$$P = \frac{F \cdot d}{A \cdot d}$$

Next, we can apply our formulas $V = Ad$ and $W = Fd$ (work equals force times distance) to transform this equation into:

Equation 16.
$$P = \frac{W}{V}$$

We saw this equation before in Chapters 3 and 4 where we analyzed PV curves. Since work has units of energy, this means that pressure is a measure of energy density, just like the terms $\frac{1}{2}\rho v^2$ and $\rho g h$ in the Bernoulli equation. This helps us see that Bernoulli's law is just conservation of energy applied in the context of the energy density of fluids. It tells us that a fluid contains energy in three forms: (1) the pressure it exerts against the walls of its container, (2) the kinetic energy that is proportional to its velocity squared, and (3) gravitational potential energy, and that these three forms of energy can be interconverted.

In physics class, you may have used Bernoulli's law to predict how pressure and velocity would change in the plumbing structures of large apartment buildings and the like. Problems like that are theoretically within the scope of the MCAT, but the major conceptual takeaway you should get from Bernoulli's equation is that, at a constant height, increasing the velocity of a liquid decreases the pressure that it exerts on its container.

A final important relationship is given by the continuity equation. This equation states that within a closed system, the flow rate of a liquid is constant. In particular, this implies a relationship between the velocity of the fluid and the cross-sectional area that it is flowing through:

Equation 17. $$V_1 A_1 = V_2 A_2$$

This equation means that as we increase the cross-sectional area through which a liquid is flowing, we decrease its velocity, and vice versa. As discussed in Chapter 9 of the Biology textbook, this can be applied to analyze blood flow in vessels of differing sizes throughout the body, but we have to be careful to compare the *entire* system at two points, not to compare various aspects of the subsystem. Therefore, we could use this to compare blood flow in the aorta, immediately after blood leaves the heart and enters the systematic circulation, to blood flow in the capillaries as a whole. Each capillary is relatively tiny, but there are so many of them that the total cross-sectional area is much larger than that of the aorta, meaning that blood will slow down as it moves towards the capillaries. Note, though, that if we compared the aorta with *a single* capillary, we could incorrectly make the opposite prediction.

> **> > CONNECTIONS < <**
>
> Chapter 9 of Biology

Conceptually, the continuity equation is best thought of as a consequence of the fact that liquids are essentially incompressible. This means that in a closed system through which a liquid is flowing, you can't have flow rates that differ from place to place.

Linking together the Bernoulli equation and the continuity equation, there are some important relationships that we can observe for ideal liquids (that is, if we neglect viscosity, turbulence, and interactions with the wall of the container):

> **>** Narrower tube → higher velocity
> **>** Narrower tube → lower pressure
> **>** Higher velocity → lower pressure

In particular, the fact that a narrower tube is associated with lower pressure is known as the Venturi effect. The fact that the Venturi effect is linked to velocity means that measuring the pressure drop across two areas of a pipe can be used to measure the velocity of fluid flow. Such an apparatus is shown in Figure 8. The Venturi effect is utilized in a wide range of industrial applications.

> **MCAT STRATEGY > > >**
>
> Study these relationships and make them instinctual. It is quite possible that you will only be asked to apply these concepts on the MCAT on a conceptual level, without needing to carry out specific calculations. Thoroughly internalizing these concepts will help you answer such questions quickly and efficiently.

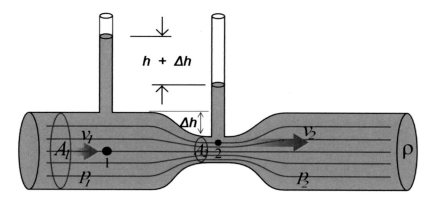

Figure 8. Venturi effect.

A final application of the principles that we have discussed in this section is known as the Pitot tube. This device is named after the 18th-century French engineer Henri Pitot, and is used to measure fluid velocity in several important contexts. For example, Pitot tubes are used to measure the speed of airplanes in flight, of ships traveling through the water, and to measure the speed of the wind for meteorological purposes. Pitot tubes rely on the same principle of conservation of energy that is expressed in Bernoulli's equation.

In its simplest form, a Pitot tube is just a one-ended tube that is pointed into the flow of the fluid that one wants to measure. Because it is a one-ended tube, the fluid that enters the tube can't exit. As this fluid gets "stuck," it exerts a pressure on the back of the tube, which is referred to as the stagnation pressure. In addition to this, a Pitot tube contains some way to measure what is referred to as the static pressure, which is essentially just the pressure along the sides of the tube. The difference between the static pressure and the stagnation pressure reflects the contribution of the flowing fluid, and is known as the dynamic pressure. The dynamic pressure is expressed as $\frac{1}{2}\rho v^2$, and can be used to calculate the velocity of the fluid. To summarize:

Equation 18.
$$P_{stag} - P_{static} = \frac{1}{2}\rho v^2$$

A Pitot tube is illustrated in Figure 9.

Figure 9. A Pitot tube.

4. Must-Knows

> - Density: $\rho = \frac{m}{v}$; solve for mass as $\rho v = \left(\frac{m}{v}\right)v = m$.
> - Density of water: $\rho_{water} = \frac{1000kg}{m^3} = 1\frac{kg}{L} = 1\frac{g}{mL} = 1\frac{g}{cm^3}$; specific gravity $= \frac{\rho}{\rho_{water}}$
> - Pressure = force divided by area
>   - When submerged in a fluid, $P_{sub} = \rho g h$
>   - Absolute pressure: $P_{abs} = P_{atm} + \rho g h$
>   - For measuring pressure in subsystems, gauge pressure: $P_{gauge} = P_{system} - P_{atm}$
> - Buoyancy:
>   - When an object is submerged: $\% \; submerged = \frac{\rho_{object}}{\rho_{liquid}} \times 100$
>   - Archimedes' principle: weight $= \rho v g$
> - Mechanical advantage in a hydraulic lift: $F_2 = \frac{A_2}{A_1}F1$; idea is that same *volume* of fluid is being moved, but the force necessary depends on *area*.
> - Surface tension: caused by uneven intermolecular interactions at an interface between two surfaces.
>   - If cohesive forces within a molecule are stronger than adhesive forces to walls of a container, a convex meniscus results (mercury)
>   - If adhesive forces to walls of a container are stronger than cohesive forces within a molecule, a concave meniscus results (water)
> - Viscosity: on an intuitive level = resistance to flow (technically resistance to deformation by shear stress). Water = relatively non-viscous.
> - Laminar flow → flow of smoothly regulated layers; turbulent flow is chaotic
> - Poiseuille's law (applies to laminar flow, accounting for viscosity): $Q = \frac{\pi r^4 \Delta P}{8\eta L}$ or $\Delta P = \frac{8\eta L Q}{\pi r^4}$.
> - Bernoulli's law (applies to ideal fluids with laminar flow and no viscosity):
>   - $P_1 + \frac{1}{2}\rho v_1^2 + \rho g h_1 = P_2 + \frac{1}{2}\rho v_2^2 + \rho g h_2$
>   - Like conservation of energy for fluids (more technically, conservation of energy *density*).
> - Continuity equation: $V_1 A_1 = V_2 A_2$ within a closed system
>   - Due to incompressibility of liquids
> - Key relationships (from Bernoulli's law & continuity equation):
>   - Narrower tube → lower pressure (Venturi effect), higher velocity
>   - Higher velocity → lower pressure
> - Pitot tube can be used to calculate velocity of a fluid: $P_{stag} - P_{static} = \frac{1}{2}\rho v^2$

Practice Passage

A Galileo's thermometer consists of a large cylinder of liquid filled with small glass bulbs, each partially filled with liquid. These bulbs function as weights and the internal liquids are brightly colored for decorative purposes. Once the bulbs have been sealed and dropped into the large cylinder, their densities are adjusted by attaching metal tags with temperature labels. Each bulb and metal tag has a predetermined density.

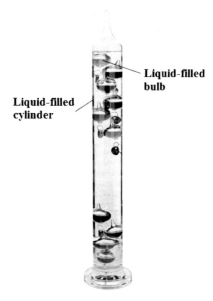

Figure 1. Galileo's thermometer

The clear liquid inside the cylinder is often water, but is more often an organic liquid, such as ethanol. Organic liquids such as ethanol (melting point -114 °C; boiling point 78 °C) are commonly chosen for their sensitive temperature-dependent density variations (Figure 2). The relative densities of the bulbs and the liquid medium allow for some bulbs to sink while others float.

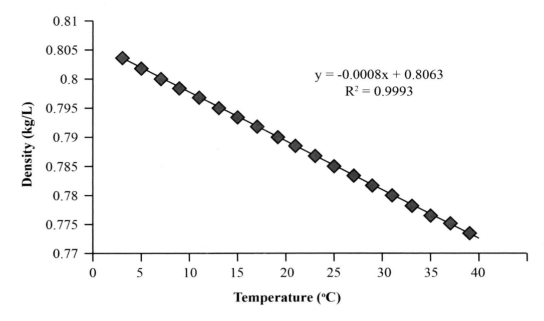

Figure 2. A plot of density versus temperature for pure ethanol, including the equation for the best-fit line.

The temperature of the liquid inside the bulbs is such that there will be some bulbs floating near the top of the cylinder, some bulbs that sink to the bottom, and one bulb will be suspended in the middle of the liquid. This is possible because of slight pressure differences (ΔP) acting on the bottom and top of the bulbs. This difference is dependent upon the density (ρ) of the liquid, the acceleration due to gravity (g) and the depth (h) below the surface of the bulb within the liquid, according to $\Delta P = \rho gh$.

1. What is the approximate weight of a glass bulb suspended in the middle of a Galileo's thermometer whose temperature is 298 K, assuming that the bulb can be approximated as a sphere and the diameter of the bulb is 2.0 cm?
   A. 32 mN
   B. 41 mN
   C. 130 mN
   D. 160 mN

2. What is the net force acting on a glass bulb suspended in the middle of a Galileo's thermometer whose temperature is 298 K?
   A. 0 N
   B. +0.032 N
   C. -0.032 N
   D. -0.041 N

3. Based on information in the passage, which of the following must be true concerning the buoyant force and the weight of a bulb that is suspended in the middle of the surrounding fluid of a Galileo's thermometer?
   A. The force of gravity acting on the bulb is less than the buoyant force acting on the bulb.
   B. The force of gravity acting on the bulb is greater than the buoyant force acting on the bulb.
   C. The force of gravity acting on the bulb is equal to the buoyant force acting on the bulb.
   D. There is no way to predict the relative magnitudes of gravity and the buoyant force.

4. An alternative design for a Galileo's thermometer involves using hollow metal cubes with the length of a side being 1.0 cm. What is the pressure difference at 25°C that the ethanol exerts on the top-side, as compared with the bottom-side of the cube, when the center of mass of the cube is located 10.0 cm below the surface. The diameter of the thermometer is 3.0 cm and the total height is 25.0 cm. Note that 1 Pascal (Pa) of pressure is equivalent to a Newton per square meter.
   A. 77 Pa
   B. 308 Pa
   C. 616 Pa
   D. 756 Pa

5. What fraction of a bulb will be above the surface of ethanol at 7 °C, if the density of the bulb is 1 kg/L?
   A. 0
   B. 0.1
   C. 0.2
   D. 0.8

6. All of the following directly contribute to the surface tension of the ethanol at the top of the cylinder EXCEPT:
   A. liquid temperature.
   B. hydrogen bonds.
   C. liquid density.
   D. intramolecular forces.

7. Which of the following bulbs is most likely to be found at the greatest depth inside the cylinder?
   A. Bulb 1, ρ = 1.6 g/ml, V = 1 mm^3
   B. Bulb 2, ρ = 3.2 g/ml, V = 6 mm^3
   C. Bulb 3, ρ = 6.4 g/ml, V = 15 mm^3
   D. Each of the bulbs listed would sink to approximately the same depth.

Practice Passage Explanations

A Galileo's thermometer consists of a large cylinder of liquid filled with small glass bulbs, each partially filled with liquid. These bulbs function as weights and the internal liquids are brightly colored for decorative purposes. Once the bulbs have been sealed and dropped into the large cylinder, their densities are adjusted by attaching metal tags with temperature labels. Each bulb and metal tag has a predetermined density.

Key terms: Galileo's thermometer, density

Cause and effect: floating vs. sinking is determined the adjusted density of the fluid-filled bulb

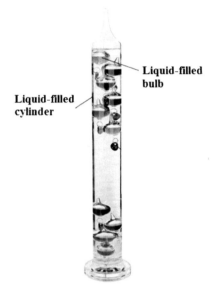

Figure 1. Galileo's thermometer

Figure 1 shows the bulbs with densities that match the T-dependent range of fluid density; T can be determined by observing bulb movement

The clear liquid inside the cylinder is often water, but is more often an organic liquid, such as ethanol. Organic liquids such as ethanol (melting point -114 °C; boiling point 78 °C) are commonly chosen for their sensitive temperature-dependent density variations (Figure 2). The relative densities of the bulbs and the liquid medium allow for some bulbs to sink while others float.

Key terms: organic liquids, T-dependent density, ethanol, melting/boiling point

Cause and effect: organic solvents are used inside cylinder due to their t-dependent density

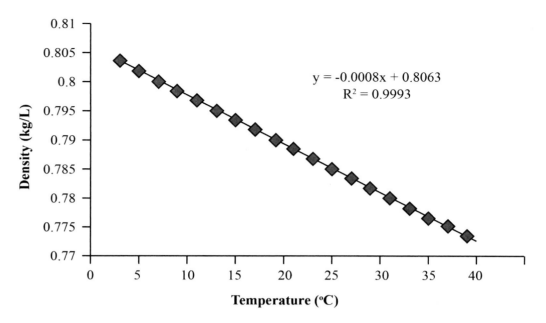

Figure 2. A plot of density versus temperature for pure ethanol, including the equation for the best-fit line.

Figure 2 shows that the density of ethanol is inversely proportional to temperature; the correlation is very strong

The temperature of the liquid inside the bulbs is such that there will be some bulbs floating near the top of the cylinder, some bulbs that sink to the bottom, and one bulb will be suspended in the middle of the liquid. This is possible because of slight pressure differences (ΔP) acting on the bottom and top of the bulbs. This difference is dependent upon the density (ρ) of the liquid, the acceleration due to gravity (g) and the depth (h) below the surface of the bulb within the liquid, according to $\Delta P = \rho gh$.

Key terms: pressure differences, gravity, depth

Cause and effect: if overall ρ_{bulb} is just less than ρ_{liquid}, the bulb will appear to be suspended motionless within the liquid, because the pressure of the fluid on the bulb bottom will be just greater than the pressure of the fluid on the bulb top, resulting in equilibrium between buoyancy, upward pressure, weight and downward pressure

1. A is correct. The volume of a sphere is $4/3\ \pi r^3$ and the radius of the bulb is 1.0 cm, giving a volume of $4/3(3.14)$ $(1)3 \sim 4\ cm^3$. Using Figure 1, the estimated density of ethanol at 25°C (273 + 25 = 298 K) is 0.785 kg/L or 0.785 g/cm³, which is about 0.8 g/cm³. If the bulb is suspended in the ethanol, the density of the bulb must be essentially the same as the liquid. The mass of the bulb can be determined from using the density, 0.8(4) = 3.2 g. To determine the weight you must convert the mass to kilograms and multiply by the acceleration of gravity, 0.0032(10) ~ 0.032 N or 32 mN.
    B, C, D: These answers are a result of miscalculation. If you simply use the volume, and don't use the density, you would get choice B. If you use the diameter of 2.0 cm in the volume equation, you get choices C or D.

2. A is correct. If the bulb is "suspended in the middle" of the thermometer, the bulb is not accelerating and the sum of all the forces acting on the bulb must equal zero. Choice A is the correct answer.
    B, C, D: Choices B and C would be approximately the buoyant force and the force of gravity acting on the bulb, but not the net force. D is a result of miscalculation.

3. B is correct. For a bulb suspended in the middle of the fluid (ethanol), the net force in the vertical direction must equal zero. The passage indicates that there will be a pressure difference that the fluid exerts on the top and bottom surfaces of the bulb, with the latter being slightly greater than the former. Therefore, the upward pressure is slightly greater than the downward pressure, and the upward buoyant force must be slightly less than the downward weight of the bulb.

   A, C, D: These answers are a result of miscalculation. If choices A and C were true, taking into account the differences in pressure acting upward and downward, the bulb should float to the surface of the surrounding fluid. Choice D can be eliminated, since an analysis of the forces of pressure, buoyancy and weight can make satisfactory predictions.

4. A is correct. The difference in height from the top to the bottom of the cube is 1 cm or 0.01 m. From Figure 2, the density of the ethanol at 25°C is 0.785 kg/L, which is 785 kg/m³ (10^3 L = 1 m³). Inserting the variables into Equation 1 gives, $\Delta P = (785)(9.8)(0.01) = 77$ N/m².

5. A is correct. From Figure 2, the density of the bulb (1 kg/L) is greater than the density of the ethanol (0.8 kg/L) at 7°C. The bulb will sink and be completely submerged in the ethanol. Choice A is the correct answer. If the density of the bulb and the density of the fluid are confused, then you might think that the bulb will float, which would give some fraction of the bulb above the surface which is related to the ratio of the densities. The bulb would only have a portion of its volume below the surface, such that the weight of liquid displaced equals the weight of the bulb.

   A, B, C: If the density of the bulb and the density of the fluid are confused, then you might think that the bulb will float, which would give some fraction of the blub above the surface which is related to the ratio of the densities. The bulb would only have a portion of its volume below the surface, such that the weight of liquid displaced equals the weight of the bulb.

6. D is correct. Surface tension is represents the net force or "tension" at the interface between the liquid and surrounding air. Surface tension represents the energy required to increase the surface area of a liquid by a unit of area. The surface tension of a liquid results from an imbalance of intermolecular attractive forces (such as hydrogen bonds, choice B) at the liquid-air boundary. While a molecule within the liquid experiences attractive forces with other molecules in all directions, a liquid molecule at the surface of a liquid experiences only net inward attractive forces since there is no layer of liquid above the surface. The individual bonds within the ethanol molecules (intramolecular bonds) would not directly contribute to the surface area or attraction between ethanol molecules.

   A, C: Temperature of the ethanol directly effects its density, and both will affect the weight and surface area of the liquid/air boundary. Thus, both would impact the surface tension of the system.

7. D is correct. When it comes to floating vs. sinking, the factor that will determine this is overall object density. Do not be distracted by the size/volume of the bulb. All of the bulbs are much more dense than ethanol so they would all sink to the bottom and be at the same depth.

Independent Questions

1. An open tank at STP contains water to a depth of 10 meters. What is the approximate ratio of the absolute pressure at a point 4 meters below the surface of the water to the absolute pressure at a point 2 meters below the surface of the water?
   A. 2:1
   B. 4:1
   C. 16:1
   D. 7:6

2. If a pipe containing an ideal fluid widens such that its cross-sectional area increases from 20 cm^2 to 40 cm^2, which of the following accurately describes the change in fluid velocity?
   A. The velocity doubles.
   B. The velocity is halved.
   C. The velocity remains constant.
   D. The velocity quadruples.

3. Which of the following is NOT required for a fluid to be considered ideal?
   A. The fluid is incompressible.
   B. The fluid is not viscous.
   C. The fluid particles flow at a constant velocity.
   D. The fluid exhibits laminar flow.

4. The Hay's test is a simple procedure to test for the presence of amphipathic bile salts in urine. Fine sulfur powder is sprinkled over the surface of a urine sample. Which of the following accurately describes a result indicative of bile salts in the urine sample?
   A. The sulfur powder coats the surface of the urine sample due to increased surface tension.
   B. The sulfur powder coats the surface of the urine sample due to reduced surface tension.
   C. The sulfur powder sinks to the bottom of the urine sample due to increased surface tension.
   D. The sulfur powder sinks to the bottom of the urine sample due to reduced surface tension.

5. A large bucket is filled to the brim with water and a small hole is drilled in the wall of the bucket. If the bucket is 50 centimeters deep and water escapes from the hole at a speed of 2 m/s, where is the hole located?
   A. 30 centimeters above the bottom of the bucket
   B. 20 centimeters above the bottom of the bucket
   C. 10 centimeters above the bottom of the bucket
   D. 4 centimeters above the bottom of the bucket

6. An object has a specific gravity of 0.60. What percent of the object's volume will be found above water when it is placed in a liquid with a specific gravity of 2.0?
   A. 30%
   B. 40%
   C. 60%
   D. 70%

7. Large ships traveling close together on parallel paths are in danger of colliding. One valid explanation for this is:
   A. As water is forced between the two ships, its velocity increases and its pressure increases.
   B. As water is forced between the two ships, its velocity increases and its pressure decreases.
   C. As water is forced between the two ships, its velocity decreases and its pressure increases.
   D. As water is forced between the two ships, its velocity decreases and its pressure decreases.

8. Which of the following is not a scalar quantity?
   A. Flow speed
   B. Gauge pressure
   C. Total pressure
   D. Buoyant force

Independent Question Explanations

1. D is correct. Do not fall for answer choice A here; we are dealing with absolute pressure, not gauge pressure! Absolute pressure is the sum of gauge pressure and atmospheric pressure, given by:

$$P_{abs} = P_{atm} + \rho gh$$

The ratio of the absolute pressure values at each depth is obtained by:

$$\frac{P_2}{P_1} = \frac{P_{atm} + \rho gh_2}{P_{atm} + \rho gh_1} = \frac{(1.015 \times 10^5 \text{ Pa}) + (1000 \frac{\text{kg}}{\text{m}^3})(10 \frac{\text{N}}{\text{kg}})(4 \text{ m})}{(1.015 \times 10^5 \text{ Pa}) + (1000 \frac{\text{kg}}{\text{m}^3})(10 \frac{\text{N}}{\text{kg}})(2 \text{ m})}$$
$$\approx \frac{1.4 \times 10^5 \text{ Pa}}{1.2 \times 10^5 \text{ Pa}} = 76$$

2. B is correct. This question relates to the continuity equation, which is given as follows:

$$v_1 A_1 = v_2 A_2$$

Thus, fluid velocity and cross-sectional area are inversely proportional. An increase in cross-sectional area by a factor of two necessitates that velocity be reduced by half.

3. C is correct. The volume flow rate of an ideal fluid is constant at all points in a pipe system at a given time. However, the velocity at which individual particles flow is distinct from the volume flow rate. This velocity is not necessarily constant; simply imagine fluid particles speeding up as they enter a narrower region of the pipe. All of the other choices describe properties of ideal fluids.

4. D is correct. Reduced surface tension would allow the powder to sink, while high surface tension would support the powder on the surface of the fluid, eliminating choices B and C. Since bile salts are amphipathic, they will disrupt the network of hydrogen bonds between water molecules at the surface of the urine. This results in a reduction of surface tension and allows the powder to sink. This effect is similar to that of a surfactant, as you may have read in your review of biology content.

5. A is correct. The velocity of fluid leaving a small hole on the side of an open container can be solved using Bernoulli's equation, shown below:

$$P_1 + \tfrac{1}{2} \rho v_1^2 + \rho gh_1 = P_2 + \tfrac{1}{2} \rho v_2^2 + \rho gh_2$$

P_1 and P_2 are both equal to atmospheric pressure, so those terms drop out. The velocity of the fluid at the surface (v_1) can be estimated as 0, as can the height when the fluid leaves the hole (h_2). (Of course, the fluid does still have some height above the ground, but it has converted its potential energy at the surface to kinetic energy exiting the hole.) As such, we can simplify Bernoulli's equation to the form shown below:

$$\rho gh_1 = \tfrac{1}{2} \rho v_2^2$$
$$gh_1 = \tfrac{1}{2} v_2^2$$
$$2gh_1 = v_2^2$$
$$v_2 = \sqrt{2gh_1} \rightarrow h_1 = \frac{v_2^2}{2g} = \frac{(2 \frac{\text{m}}{\text{s}})^2}{20 \frac{\text{m}}{\text{s}^2}} = 0.2 \text{ m}$$

This value (20 centimeters) reflects the distance between the hole and the surface of the fluid. Since the bucket is filled to the brim, this implies the hole is located 30 centimeters above the bottom of the bucket.

6. D is correct. The equation for the percent of an object's volume that is submerged in a liquid is given below:

$$\% \text{ submerged} = \frac{\rho_{object}}{\rho_{liquid}} \times 100$$

Here, $\rho_{object} = 0.60$, while $\rho_{liquid} = 2.0$. Plugging in values to the equation above shows us that 30% of the object is submerged. However, this problem is asking for the percent found *above* water—in other words, the percent *not* submerged. This amount can be found by subtracting 30% from 100%, yielding an answer of 70%.

7. B is correct. According to the continuity equation, flow velocity increases when a fluid is forced through a confined space such as that created between the two large ships. According to the Bernoulli principle, this increased flow speed will result in a zone of low pressure, which puts the ships in danger of being pushed together by the higher pressure of the surrounding seawater.

8. D is correct. Scalar quantities do not have direction. Pressure and speed are scalar quantities, but forces are vector quantities.

This page left intentionally blank.

Electricity

CHAPTER 6

0. Introduction

In this chapter, we'll be covering the basics of electricity, focusing on charges, their behavior, and electric fields and electric potential. Sometimes these topics are known as electrostatics, in contrast to the study of how charge moves in circuits, which we will explore in Chapter 7.

As mentioned in Chapter 2 on forces, the electromagnetic force is one of the four distinct forces in nature, along with the strong and weak nuclear forces and the gravitational force. Gravitation acts between substances that have the fundamental property of mass, and electromagnetism acts on substances that have the fundamental property of charge. Sometimes students are curious about what charge really "is," which is a difficult question to answer, because it is just as basic of a property as mass is. The difference is that our everyday experiences have led us to have an intuitive sense of what mass, or at least what the mass-derived quantity of weight means, but charge may be less accessible. For this reason, we often use analogies when talking about charge. In this chapter, we will build analogies between electricity and gravitation, and in Chapter 7, where we discuss how charges flow, we will use analogies with the flow of water.

As is often the case with MCAT physics, your number one goal should be to develop a strong intuitive understanding of the basic principles of electricity, linked to a knowledge of the key equations and of common applications. For many students, electrostatics, circuits, and magnetism (our main topics for this chapter and the next chapter) are notorious for involving complicated problem setups and the need to derive deep theoretical conclusions about non-obvious properties of reality. This aspect of studying physics is minimized on the MCAT, where instead the crucial skill that you need to develop is quickly recognizing what a question is asking and being able to decisively determine how to answer it.

1. Charges and Coulomb's Law

As we've already mentioned, charge is a basic property of matter. The unit of charge is the coulomb (C), which is defined as the amount of charge carried by a current of 1 ampere (A) in 1 second. More specifically, it is a property of the subatomic particles known as protons and electrons. Protons have positive charges, while electrons have negative charges. Neutrons are neutrally charged, as the name implies. In this context, it may be useful to review the basic properties of subatomic particles, as shown in Table 1.

	PROTON	NEUTRON	ELECTRON
Mass	1.672×10^{-27} kg (1 Da, 1 amu)	1.674×10^{-27} kg (1 Da, 1 amu)	9.019×10^{-31} kg (5.486×10^{-4} Da/amu)
Charge	1.602×10^{-19} C (+1 e)	0 C (0 e)	-1.602×10^{-19} C (−1 e)

Table 1. Mass and charge of subatomic particles.

You don't need to know the precise masses or charge (in coulombs) of the various particles, but there are a few points worth noting here. First, the quantities involved in terms of standard SI units are so tiny that alternate units have been developed. Protons and neutrons are defined as having a mass of 1 dalton (Da) or 1 atomic mass unit (amu) (these terms are not technically equivalent, but for MCAT purposes they can be treated as such). Similarly, the elementary unit of charge (e) is used to refer to the magnitude of charge possessed by a single proton or a single electron. You may also want to note that while all subatomic particles are tiny, electrons have a particularly small mass, and are notably less massive than protons or neutrons. For more details about subatomic structures, see Chapter 10.

> > **CONNECTIONS** < <

Chapter 10 of Physics

MCAT STRATEGY > > >

If you ever find yourself in doubt about which particle carries which charge, you can always remember that **p**rotons are **p**ositive.

The fact that charge is carried by subatomic particles implies that the flow of charge is due to the flow of subatomic particles. This is essentially correct. Materials through which charge can move easily are known as conductors. Many conductors are metals, which are characterized by the presence of abundant electrons that are not especially tightly localized near the nucleus, allowing them to move around and conduct charge. For the same reason, solutions with ions can also be good conductors. In contrast, materials that do not allow charges to flow readily are known as insulators. Some common examples include glass, paper, and many types of plastic.

The degree to which a substance readily allows current (that is, moving charge) to be propagated can be quantified in terms of resistivity and conductivity. Resistivity and conductivity are essentially inverse concepts: high resistivity means that charge does not readily flow through a substance, while high conductivity means that it does. Resistivity (R) and conductivity (G) are defined below:

Equations 1 and 2.
$$R = \rho\frac{\ell}{A} \text{ and } G = \sigma\frac{A}{\ell}$$

In these equations, ℓ is the length of the conductor and A is its cross-sectional area. Essentially, what this tells us—in both equations—is that a large cross-sectional area and a short length favor the conduction of charge. The constants ρ and σ are material-specific constants that are reciprocals of each other (that is, $\rho = 1/\sigma$ and vice-versa). For MCAT-level physics, you will most often encounter ρ, which is known as resistivity and is defined in terms of ohm-meters. We will explore more about resistance in the next chapter on circuits. From the point of view of this chapter, you just have to understand that conductors are defined by low resistance and high conductivity, while insulators are defined by high resistance and low conductivity. As this implies, the distinction between insulators and conductors is a spectrum; there are no perfect insulators or perfect conductors under standard conditions, although certain materials can exhibit superconductivity in extremely low temperatures.

As mentioned above, protons are positively charged, while electrons are negatively charged. The fact that charge can be negative or positive is one of the basic facts about charge as a physical property. Moreover, like charges (such as two positive charges or two negative charges) repel each other, while opposite charges (one negative and one positive) attract each other. This is the origin of the relationship cliché that "opposites attract." To be more precise, we can characterize the force that exists between two charged objects using Coulomb's law:

Equation 3.
$$F = \frac{kq_1q_2}{r^2}$$

In this equation, F is the electric force present between two charges, q_1 and q_2 are two point charges, and r is the distance between q_1 and q_2. The constant k is known as Coulomb's constant. It is equal to 8.99×10^9 N•m²/C², and is also sometimes expressed as $\frac{1}{4\pi\varepsilon_0}$. The constant ε_0 is equal to 8.85×10^{-12} F/m, where F stands for farads, a unit used to measure capacitance. It is known as the permittivity of free space and is a basic physical constant; it tends to be used in contexts where it's important to analyze electromagnetic phenomena on a theoretically deeper level than is required for the MCAT.

In general, Coulomb's constant is one of those constants that you should be aware of but not spend a ton of energy worrying about. However, it is worth taking a quick look at the units. If we rewrite the units of k as $N\frac{m^2}{C^2}$ and note that the rest of the equation, $\frac{q_1q_2}{r^2}$, has units of $\frac{C^2}{m^2}$, then it is easy to see that the units of k are designed to cancel out the rest of the equation and ensure that the final value winds up being in newtons, as is appropriate for force.

> > **CONNECTIONS** < <

Chapter 7 of Physics

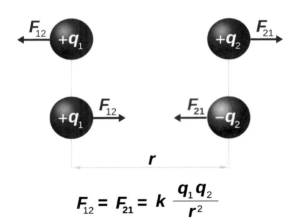

Figure 1. Coulomb's law.

Since the MCAT does not give you any direct rewards for showing your work, we don't have to be *too* careful about sign conventions with this equation, because within the limits of what the MCAT will ask you to solve, you will be able to identify the direction of the force just by qualitatively applying the rule that opposite charges attract and like charges repel. However, note that according to Coulomb's law, two positive charges and two negative charges would both result in a positive force, while unlike charges would result in a negative force, meaning that positive values for this equation indicate repulsion while negative values indicate attraction.

A notable fact about Coulomb's law is that it is structurally identical to the corresponding law of gravitation. This fact received much attention when foundational research was being conducted into electricity in the 18th and 19th centuries, but for our purposes, it's mostly useful to help consolidate your knowledge of both equations. Both are inversely proportional to distance squared and directly proportional to the mass or charge of each component, respectively.

Coulomb's law has an interesting consequence for conductors. Let's imagine a spherical conductor with an overall negative charge. On a subatomic level, this would correspond to an excess of electrons. Coulomb's law indicates that each of those negative point charges will experience repulsive forces from all of the other negative point charges. This means that in the absence of some external stimuli affecting the distribution of charges, charges will become evenly distributed across the surface of a conductor in order to minimize the energy of the system.

2. Electric Fields

Recall from Chapter 2 that any object with mass causes a gravitational field to be present. This is just a somewhat more abstract and general way of talking about gravity. The idea is that it would get tiresome to talk about the gravitational force as existing just between two objects: we'd have to refer to the relationship between the Earth and the moon differently from the relationship between the Earth and a satellite, which would be different from the relationship between the Earth and us as individual humans, and so on. This way of talking about things would clearly miss the basic point that the earth will exert a meaningful gravitational force on *any* object with mass that we place within a reasonable distance. This tendency is what we describe when we refer to a gravitational field.

A similar idea applies to electricity. The fact that a force exists between any two point charges, according to Coulomb's law, logically means that a single point charge must be capable of exerting a force on any other charge. We describe this in terms of an electric field, and we can formalize the magnitude of an electric field by dividing the force experienced by a charge in that electric field (a so-called 'test charge') by the magnitude of the test charge. Dividing by the magnitude of the test charge allows us to simplify our life by controlling for the possibility of having different test charges. (Otherwise, we'd have to account for the details of every single test charge, and this would be just as irritating and counterproductive as accounting for the specific mass of every single object that experiences gravity). This useful simplification is presented in the equation below:

Equation 4.
$$E = \frac{F}{q}$$

In this equation, E is the magnitude of the electric field, F is the force experienced by the test charge, and q is the magnitude of the test charge. However, by applying Coulomb's law, which provides a definition of the force between two point charges, we can modify this equation as follows:

Equation 5.
$$E = \frac{F}{q} = \frac{\frac{kqQ}{r^2}}{q} = \frac{kQ}{r^2}$$

In this equation, q is the magnitude of the test charge and Q is the magnitude of the charge that is originating the electric field. This formulation has two major advantages: first, it captures the fact that the magnitude of an electric field diminishes with the square of distance (just like electrical forces) and second, it allows us to calculate the magnitude of the electric field only in terms of Q, the source charge, for any distance r. However, the expression $E = \frac{F}{q}$ is also useful, in that it allows the force experienced by a charge q to be determined straightforwardly if you know the strength of the electric field:

Equation 6.
$$F = qE$$

Field lines are used to graphically indicate the direction and magnitude of electric fields. The arrows in field lines point in the direction that a positive test charge would travel in the electric field—that is, away from a positive charge and towards a negative charge. Figure 2 shows a simple source charge.

Figure 2. Simple source charge.

Fleshing out our comparison with gravity, field lines are like what you would get if you drew a map of the landscape indicating in what direction a ball would travel if you put it on the ground at rest. In fact, something similar is actually done by scientists who study water resources: watershed maps provide an indication of what river/drainage basin a drop of rain that falls somewhere will eventually wind up in. However, things are a little bit more complicated for electrical fields because we need to account for attractive and repulsive forces, whereas gravity is only an attractive force.

Drawing field lines for simple source charges is easy, as shown in Figure 2. You just draw them radiating out evenly from the source charge. Things get a little bit more complicated when you have more than one source charge,

MCAT STRATEGY > > >

When dealing with electricity and waves, we will often have to both address what is *true* and what is *useful*. Alternate forms of equations may exist, with certain forms being more useful in some contexts than others. Cultivating the habit of thinking about physics equations as tools that are useful for solving certain problems is helpful, because doing so helps you master the materials more actively and create some of the mental habits that will pay off on Test Day.

though, because the path a test charge takes will be affected by multiple source charges. There are a few especially common patterns that you should be aware of for the MCAT, which we will review below.

The first common setup for an electric field is if you have two equal but opposite source charges. A positive test charge will move away from the positive source charge and towards the negative charge. This results in the electric field shown below in Figure 3:

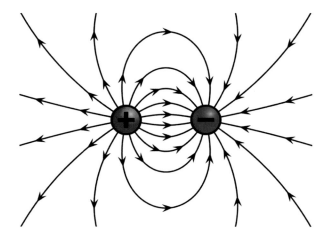

Figure 3. Electric field with two equal but opposite test charges.

Your next question might be what would happen if we had two identical charges (that is, both positive or negative). Our approach to drawing the field lines will be similar, but in this case the field lines will never connect the two point charges—instead, the field lines emanating from each of the charges will bend away from each other. This is shown below in Figure 4, for a scenario involving two negative charges.

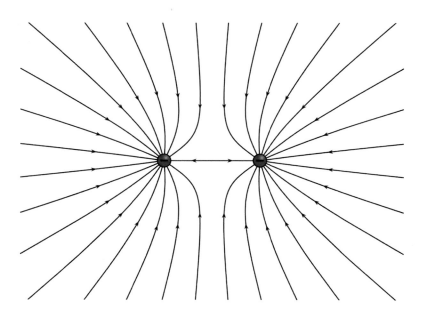

Figure 4. Electric field with two equal negative charges.

MCAT STRATEGY > > >

Technically speaking, charges aren't animate and can't "try" to do anything, but it can be helpful to think of things in terms of what a positive or negative charge would "want" to do as a way of solidifying your intuitions about charge.

In Figure 4, note the line drawn in the middle. This might initially seem surprising, but just reflects the fact that a positive test charge dropped in the middle of two negative charges will immediately be drawn towards one or the other of the source charges. If we drew a figure with two positive charges, we would not have such a line. Remember that by convention, field lines represent the movement of a *positive* test charge. A positive test charge placed between two positive source charges would "try" to get out of that situation as quickly as possible, so you would not have that line connecting the two charges.

Another scenario to be aware of is what happens if you were to take the electric field between two equal but opposite point charges shown in Figure 3 and stretch out the source charges such that they are distributed over a long linear surface. This results in an electric field that is uniform between those surfaces, as shown in Figure 5.

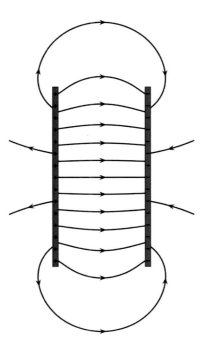

Figure 5. Electric field in a capacitor.

This setup is characteristic of devices known as capacitors, which are discussed more in the next chapter. However, it can be applied to any situation in which source charges are arranged linearly. One physiological example would be if you took a longitudinal cross-section of an axon, the long linear part of the body of a neuron. The extracellular environment is more positive than the intracellular environment, so an electric field much like the one illustrated in Figure 5 is established.

In Figure 3, we saw an electrical field between two equal but opposite charges. You might look at this and ask: shouldn't those source charges themselves be attracted to each other and therefore crash into each other, changing the shape of the electric field? All things being equal, that would be a real possibility. However, it is possible to construct devices that stably maintain areas of opposite charge on different ends of an object. Such objects are known as dipoles. You may recognize this term from chemistry, and the resemblance isn't a coincidence, because some dipoles do exist in molecules. In the context of physics, we usually abstract away from the specific shapes of molecules and consider a dipole to be a linear object with opposite charges on each end.

> **MCAT STRATEGY > > >**
>
> The uniform electrical field along an axon is an important example to remember, because it provides the MCAT with a way of testing both electricity and physiology at the same time.

While dipoles can generate electric fields of their own, it also turns out that they show interesting properties when placed into a uniform electric field like that shown in Figure 5. For the purposes of this discussion, we'll assume that the electric field generated by the dipole itself is negligible compared to the field that it is placed in. When we place the dipole into a uniform electric field, the negatively-charged end of the dipole will be pulled towards the positive source charge of the electric field, and the positively-charged end of the dipole will be pulled towards the negative source charge of the electric field (following the field lines). This will cause rotation that will align the dipole with the field.

Since there is rotation, there must be torque. An important point to appreciate here is that the forces involved are equal but opposite, but the corresponding *torques* don't cancel out, because the relevant directionality of torque is clockwise/counterclockwise. Also remember that because the forces balance out, the center of the dipole does not move. Therefore, in the setup shown in Figure 6, the positive charge will move down—in a counterclockwise direction—to align with the field, and the negative charge will move up, which is *also* in a counterclockwise direction.

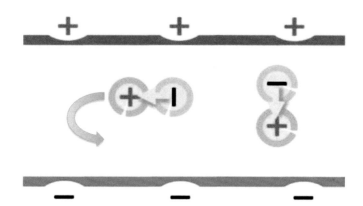

Figure 6. Dipole aligning in a uniform electric field.

The MCAT is much more likely to test the behavior of dipoles in electric fields in qualitative terms than in quantitative terms, but if you are asked to carry out a calculation related to this idea, you have the necessary tools: recall that $\tau = Fd\sin(\theta)$, $F = qE$, and that the point about which each charge is pivoting corresponds to the *midpoint* of the dipole—that is, $d = \frac{\ell}{2}$, where ℓ is the length separating the charges in the dipole.

3. Electric Potential

The next major topic to cover regarding electricity is another area with some conceptual overlap with gravity. Just as gravitational potential energy is an extremely important facet of problem-solving in setups focused on moving masses around, electric potential is a ubiquitous topic in electrostatics and circuits. As we explore electric potential, we'll focus on developing the analogy with gravity; although they're not perfect equivalents, the similarities will help you get an intuitive grasp of electric potential that you can apply on the MCAT.

Consider a simple electric field emanating from a single positive source charge, as shown below in Figure 7. The field lines indicate that a positive test charge would be repelled from the source charge, and would travel off into the distance—theoretically into infinity, although the fact that electric force is proportional to $\frac{1}{r^2}$ means that realistically, there will come a point where the force becomes negligible. Next, let's imagine that we had some kind of magical tweezers that we could use to pick up that positive point charge and drag it back to be in proximity to the original source charge. In order to do so, we'd have to exert some force to overcome the repulsive electric force emanating from the source charge, and we'd have to exert force continuously over a distance to get the test charge back to where we want it to be.

Figure 7. Simple electric field.

At this point, we've said a set of magic words: force exerted over a distance. This means that work is being done! Note also that work is being done when the electric field repels the test charge. That work is spontaneous, so we denote it with a negative sign by convention. Our next task is to take our familiar equation $W = \vec{F}d$ and translate it into terms that are more useful for talking about electricity. To do so, we can once again take advantage of Coulomb's law. Recognizing that the d term $W = \vec{F}d$ is the same as the r term in $F = \frac{kq_1q_2}{r^2}$, and using the common convention in electric fields of denoting the source charge as Q and the test charge as q, we can define the work performed in this setup as follows:

Equation 7.
$$W = Fd = \frac{kQq}{r^2}(r) = \frac{kQq}{r}$$

Note that we're talking about work that is done in a very specific context here—namely, work that is exerted on a charged particle by or against an electric field—and recall that work is the same thing as change in energy. The energy that we're dealing with here is known as electric potential energy, and can be thought of as analogous to gravitational potential energy. You can think of a positive test charge being repulsed by a positive source charge as analogous to a ball rolling down a hill, and a negative test charge being attracted by a positive source charge as analogous to a ball rolling into a funnel. From a theoretical point of view, this analogy isn't perfect, because in the gravitation example the landscape is changing, not the magnitude of the gravitational force, but this example suffices to develop your intuition around electric potential energy.

We can formalize this connection between work and potential energy in the following equation, where U is electric potential energy:

Equation 8.
$$U = \frac{kQq}{r}$$

With both electric and gravitational potential energy, we're faced with the problem of defining a reference point. For gravitational potential energy, we just define $y = 0$ based on whatever is convenient for a given problem. However, for electric potential energy, we use infinity as the reference point. This may seem weird at first, but it's just a mathematically more precise way to articulate what we did in the thought experiment above where we let a positive source charge repel a positive test charge as far as it would go, until some point (i.e., infinity) where the electric force becomes negligible. Practically speaking, this point doesn't have many consequences for you on the MCAT. The takeaway point is essentially just that when we analyze the electric potential energy of an object, we care about *changes* in its location relative to the source of the electric field.

Recall from section 2 that when we defined the strength of an electric field at a given point, we needed to divide force by charge in order to get a reliable measurement of the field itself that didn't depend on the magnitude of the test charge. Doing so gives us a quantity known as electric potential (which is not exactly the same as electric potential energy). It is denoted by V and measured in volts, and can be defined as follows:

Equation 9.

$$V = \frac{U}{q} = \frac{\frac{kQq}{r}}{q} = \frac{kQ}{r}$$

MCAT STRATEGY > > >

Take care not to confuse electric potential energy with electric potential, which is normalized for charge. The more precise gravitational analogy for electric potential might be *gh* instead of *mgh*. The idea is that for electric potential, we care about differences in the potential energy due to location in the field, not due to characteristics of individual charges. The equivalent for gravity would be to just focus on height and gravitational acceleration, not the mass of the object.

As implied by the equation $V = \frac{U}{q}$, a volt is defined as 1 V = 1 J/C. In other words, it is a measure of how much energy you need to move a certain amount of charge to get to whatever point in the electric field you're measuring electric potential at (or the amount of work done by the charge to get there, if that movement is spontaneous).

Based on this reasoning, we can see that different distances from a single source charge will be associated with different electric potentials. We can draw lines connecting all points that have the same electric potential; such lines are known as equipotential lines. For a simple electric field consisting of a single source charge, these lines will be shown as two-dimensional circles radiating out from the source charge, as shown below in Figure 8.

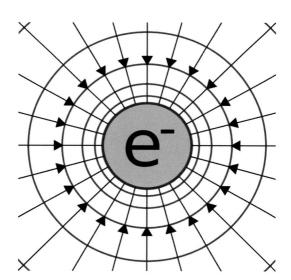

Figure 8. Simple equipotential lines.

In Figure 8, the black lines are field lines pointing into the negative charge, and the red circles are equipotential lines. In real-world situations, maps of equipotential lines can be considerably more complex. A useful comparison can be made with topographical maps that contain contour lines corresponding to specific elevations. The key point to realize is that equipotential lines and field lines are just two different ways of representing an electric field.

Next, let's consider two points with different electric potentials—that is, two points that lie on different equipotential lines. In such a case, the potential difference (ΔV) between these points—also known as voltage—can be defined as follows:

Equation 10.
$$\Delta V = V_2 - V_1$$

At this point, it is useful to revisit our previous discussion of electric potential and work. We can rewrite this equation as follows, with the goal of assessing the electric potential difference for a single charge q at these two points:

Equation 11.
$$\Delta V = \frac{U_2}{q} - \frac{U_1}{q} = \frac{U_2 - U_1}{q} = \frac{\Delta U_{2-1}}{q} = \frac{W_{2-1}}{q}$$

In other words, we note in this expression that q is a common denominator. Therefore, the numerator winds up being the change in electric potential energy between points 1 and 2, which is equivalent to the work done to move the charge between the two points.

There are few important points to note about the connection between potential difference (voltage) and work. First, recall that work in general is a conservative quantity. It doesn't matter what path you take to get between points 1 and 2 in the above example; the net work done by or against the electric field will be the same. Second, and perhaps somewhat counterintuitively, no work by or against the electric field is done if a charged particle moves around on an equipotential line. By definition, $\Delta V = 0$ in such a case, meaning that $\frac{W_{2-1}}{q} = 0$, indicating that the net work is zero. The corresponding concept in the domain of gravity is that no work is done by or against gravity if you move something along a flat surface.

The concepts of charge, electric field, and voltage that we've discussed will help set you up to understand how they are applied in the context of circuits, as described in the next chapter. The material discussed in this chapter is also useful for the MCAT because it addresses the physical underpinnings of several important biological phenomena, such as membrane potential and the transmission of action potentials.

4. Must-Knows

> Charge: a property of subatomic particles; electrons are negatively charged and protons are positively charged.
> – Like charges repel, opposite charges attract.
> Resistivity (R) and conductivity (G): $R = \rho\frac{\ell}{A}$ and $G = \sigma\frac{A}{\ell}$
> Electric fields: created by any source charge:
> – $E = \frac{F}{q} = \frac{\frac{kqQ}{r^2}}{q} = \frac{kQ}{r^2}$
> Field lines in an electric field point in the direction that a positive charge would move.
> Dipole: substance with two stable charges at each end.
> – Dipole in a uniform electric field → will align with electric field lines.
> – To analyze a dipole in a uniform field: $\tau = Fd\sin(\theta)$, $F = qE$, and $d = \frac{\ell}{2}$, where ℓ is the length separating the charges in the dipole.
> Electric potential energy: measure of how much work is needed or is performed to drag a charge from infinity to a given location within an electric field:
> – $U = \frac{kQq}{r}$
> Electric potential (V): a measure of electric potential energy normalized for charge:
> – $V = \frac{U}{q} = \frac{\frac{kQq}{r}}{q} = \frac{kQ}{r}$
> Equipotential lines: lines connecting points with equal electric potential; no work is done moving charges along equipotential lines.
> ΔV is equal to the work needed to move a charge between two points with different electric potential.

Practice Passage

The human cerebral cortex is a convoluted sheet with an area of ~2000 cm², a thickness of 2.5 mm and ~10^5 neurons/mm³. It has a resting magnetic field of approximately 10^{-12} T. Astrocytes in the brain surround both synapses and capillaries, and they are responsible for neurotransmitter recycling, which requires large amounts of energy. To satisfy this need, cerebral blood flow (CBF) increases the local blood flow in reaction to the demand for glucose and oxygen.

The blood oxygen level dependent (BOLD) signal from functional magnetic resonance imaging (fMRI) comes from hydrogen atoms in the brain. When placed in a magnetic field, hydrogen atoms align with the field and are excited by energy that is applied via radio frequency. After absorption of this energy, the hydrogen atoms emit energy until they gradually return to their equilibrium state (time = T1). Figure 1 shows the measured cortical response in a subject who was asked to open and close their left hand. A 2 T fMRI and 64 MHz radio-frequency excitation signal was used in the experiment.

Figure 1. (a) BOLD and (b) CBF response in the primary motor cortex to experimental stimulus

The scanner measures the sum total of the emitted radio-frequency energy. The radio-frequency signal decays over time due to variance in the magnetic field. Greater magnetic variance causes decreased image intensity, because each hydrogen atom experiences a slightly different magnetic field strength, and after a short time has passed (called T2), their radio-frequency emissions cancel out one another. Deoxyhemoglobin introduces an inhomogeneity into the nearby magnetic field, while oxyhemoglobin does not. Physiological noise and motion effects present challenges for fMRI studies of the brainstem and spinal cord, and these effects may interfere with detection of BOLD responses.

(Note: $\mu_0 = 4\pi \times 10^{-7}$ T•m/A; 1 T = 10^4 G)

Adapted from Stroman, P. W., Bosma, et al. (2016). Continuous Descending Modulation of the Spinal Cord Revealed by Functional MRI. PLoS ONE, 11(12), under CCBY 4.0

1. If the fMRI coil used in the experiment is doubled in diameter, while all other parameters remain the same, what will be the strength of the magnetic field inside the coil?
   A. 0.5 T
   B. 1.0 T
   C. 2.0 T
   D. 4.0 T

2. The BOLD effect arises because of which electromagnetic phenomena?
   A. Deoxyhemoglobin is diamagnetic, while oxyhemoglobin is paramagnetic
   B. Water is paramagnetic, while oxyhemoglobin is diamagnetic
   C. Deoxyhemoglobin is paramagnetic, while oxyhemoglobin is diamagnetic
   D. Water is diamagnetic, while oxyhemoglobin is paramagnetic

3. In order to monitor hand movements made inside the fMRI chamber during the experiment, researchers need to shield the specialized glove from the magnetic field. Which material should the researchers use to build this shield?
   A. Wood
   B. Rubber
   C. Copper
   D. Lead

4. Which of the following is a fundamental assumption that underlies the use of the BOLD signal as it is used in the experiment?
   A. Blood flow is inversely proportional to synaptic activity
   B. Blood flow is independent of synaptic activity
   C. Increased synaptic activity follows directly from increased blood flow
   D. Blood flow follows directly from increased synaptic activity

5. According to the data presented in Figure 1, how long were the subjects engaged in the motor task?
   A. 2 s
   B. 3 s
   C. 5 s
   D. 6 s

6. If the total magnetic field of the brain can be idealized as the sum of all contributions from individual neurons, what is the approximate magnetic field strength emitted by a single neuron in the cerebral cortex?
   A. 2×10^{-19} G
   B. 5×10^{-2} G
   C. 2×10^{-2} G
   D. 5 G

7. If subjects are put on supplemental oxygen to assist their motor activity, what is the most likely effect of this change on the intensity of their fMRI images?
   A. Image intensity will increase
   B. Image intensity will decrease
   C. Image intensity will remain the same
   D. Image intensity will decrease, then increase

Practice Passage Explanations

The human cerebral cortex is a convoluted sheet with an area of ~2000 cm², a thickness of 2.5 mm and ~10^5 neurons/mm³. It has a resting magnetic field of approximately 10^{-12} T. Astrocytes in the brain surround both synapses and capillaries, and they are responsible for neurotransmitter recycling, which requires large amounts of energy. To satisfy this need, cerebral blood flow (CBF) increases the local blood flow in reaction to the demand for glucose and oxygen.

Key terms: cerebral cortex, resting magnetic field, CBF

Cause and effect: increased neural activity → increased need for NT recycling → increased blood supply

The blood oxygen level dependent (BOLD) signal from functional magnetic resonance imaging (fMRI) comes from hydrogen atoms in the brain. When placed in a magnetic field, hydrogen atoms align with the field and are excited by energy that is applied via radio frequency. After absorption of this energy, the hydrogen atoms emit energy until they gradually return to their equilibrium state (time = T1). Figure 1 shows the measured cortical response in a subject who was asked to open and close their left hand. A 2 T fMRI and 64 MHz radio-frequency excitation signal was used in the experiment.

Key terms: BOLD, radio frequency excitation, absorption

Cause and effect: use B field to orient H atoms → RF excitation of H → E emission by H; experiment on hand movement

Figure 1 (a) BOLD and (b) CBF response in the primary motor cortex to experimental stimulus

Figure 1 shows a + change in blood blow and blood oxygenation as a result of voluntary hand movement; note the CBF response peaks before the BOLD response

The scanner measures the sum total of the emitted radio-frequency energy. The radio-frequency signal decays over time due to variance in the magnetic field. Greater magnetic variance causes decreased image intensity, because each hydrogen atom experiences a slightly different magnetic field strength, and after a short time has passed (called T2*), their radio-frequency emissions cancel out one another. Deoxyhemoglobin introduces an inhomogeneity into the nearby magnetic field, while oxyhemoglobin does not. Physiological noise and motion effects present challenges for fMRI studies of the brainstem and spinal cord, and these effects may interfere with detection of BOLD responses.

(Note: $\mu_0 = 4\pi \times 10^{-7}$ T•m/A; 1 T = 10^4 G)

Key terms: scanner, image intensity

Cause and effect: deoxygenation of Hb → variance in B field → lower image intensity; movement and body "noise" affect BOLD signal

Adapted from Stroman, P. W., Bosma, et al. (2016). Continuous Descending Modulation of the Spinal Cord Revealed by Functional MRI. PLoS ONE, 11(12), under CCBY 4.0

1. B is correct. The strength of a magnetic field in the center of a current loop is given by the following equation:

$$B = \mu_0 I/2r$$

where I is current, r is the radius of the loop, and μ_0 is the permeability of vacuum. Do not rush to do calculations. We are told what the original field strength was in paragraph 1 (2 T), so we can deduce that doubling the diameter (equivalent to doubling the radius) will halve the magnetic field strength to 1 T.

2. C is correct. Paragraph 3 tells us that deoxyhemoglobin introduces variance into the magnetic field, suggesting it has magnetic properties while oxyhemoglobin does not. When two electrons are paired in an orbital, or their total spin is 0, they are diamagnetic electrons. Paramagnetic refers to the magnetic state of an atom with one or more unpaired electrons. The unpaired electrons will be attracted by a magnetic field due to the electrons' magnetic dipole moments. The BOLD effect related to neural activity arises because when hemoglobin loses its oxygen to become deoxyhemoglobin, the magnetic properties of the protein change (deoxyhemoglobin is paramagnetic) and this alters the magnetic susceptibility of blood.

3. C is correct. Magnetic fields cannot be blocked, meaning there is no material that can be used as a magnetic insulator. This is because there are no magnetic monopoles. With electric fields, we can separate electric monopoles (i.e. + and - charges) such that an electric field does not have to terminate on the opposite charge. However, we cannot do this with magnetic poles since there is no such thing as "magnetic charge." All magnetic field lines must terminate on the opposite pole, we cannot block the magnetic field lines from going to an opposite pole. However, magnetic fields can be re-routed. By surrounding an object with a material which can conduct magnetic flux better than the materials around it, the magnetic field will tend to flow along this material and avoid the objects inside. This is a form of magnetic shielding employed by microwaves and Faraday cages, and is a big part of any MRI-concurrent measurements.
A, B, D: These are all either electrical insulators (A, B) or poor conductors of electrical or magnetic flux (D) and would be ineffective at rerouting the magnetic field.

4. D is correct. In order for the BOLD signal to be indicative of neuronal activity, there must be a direct, positive correlation between increased brain activity and the outcome measure of fMRI, which is blood oxygenation changes. Choice C is tempting, but would imply that blood flow will change before the metabolic needs of the tissue change, which is incorrect and contradicts the information given in paragraph 1.

5. B is correct. Examining the figure, we see that the x-axis is time measured in seconds. The block representing the motor stimulus appears to extend from 1s to 4s, for a total span of 3 seconds.

6. A is correct. The answers are numbers, so we must look for numbers related to the cerebral cortex. According to paragraph 1, the human cerebral cortex has an area of 2000 cm^2, a thickness of 2.5 mm and has 10^5 neurons/mm^3. The entire region has a resting magnetic field of approximately 10^{-8} gauss. We can first calculate the cortical volume.

2000 cm^2 × 2.5 mm × (1 mm^2/0.1^2 cm^2) = 5 × 10^5 mm^3

Next we calculate the total number of cortical neurons.

5 × 10^5 mm^3 × 10^5 neurons/1 mm^3 = 5 × 10^{10} neurons

Finally we calculate the approximate magnetic field strength of each neuron.

10^{-12} T × (10^4 gauss/1 T) × (1/(5 × 10^{10} neurons)) = (10^{-12})(10^4) / (5 × 10^{10}) = 0.2 × 10^{-18} = 2 × 10^{-19} G/neuron

7. A is correct. Placing a patient on supplemental oxygen means we are increasing the total amount of oxygen they are breathing in, thus increasing the total oxygenation of their blood. Paragraph 3 tells us that deoxyhemoglobin introduces an inhomogeneity into the nearby magnetic field, while oxyhemoglobin does not. This means that increased deoxyhemoglobin will increase magnetic variance to the field, causing a decrease in image intensity, while a decrease in deoxyhemoglobin causes an increase in image intensity.

Independent Questions

1. The electric field lines between two parallel plates of infinite area and opposite charge are most accurately described as:
   A. parallel to the plates and to each other.
   B. parallel to each other, directed from the positive plate to the negative plate.
   C. parallel to each other, directed from the negative plate to the positive plate.
   D. random in their individual directions, but with an average direction pointing toward the negative plate.

2. Two positive point charges, each bearing a charge of magnitude Q, are separated by a distance d. A third positive point charge of magnitude q is placed in line with the other charges as depicted below.

Which of the following expressions describes the net electric force on the charge q?
   A. $\dfrac{5kqQ}{4d^2}$
   B. $\dfrac{4kqQ}{5d^2}$
   C. $\dfrac{5kqQ^2}{4d^2}$
   D. $\dfrac{3kqQ}{2d^2}$

3. If a solid insulating sphere is brought very close to a source of negative charge without touching it, which of the following accurately describes the resulting system?
   A. The electrons in the interior of the insulating sphere will move to the surface.
   B. The insulating sphere will be attracted to the source of negative charge.
   C. The insulating sphere will be repelled by the source of negative charge.
   D. The insulating sphere will develop an excess of electrons.

4. A point charge $q = +6$ C moves through an electric field from a potential of 900 V to a potential of 1800 V. What change in potential energy is experienced by the charge q?
   A. +5400 J
   B. +3200 J
   C. −5400 J
   D. −3200 J

5. Two oppositely-charged, infinite parallel plates are separated by a distance of 1 mm. A 12-μC point charge is traveling along a path parallel to the plates at a distance 0.5 mm away from each plate. Approximately how much work is done by the electric field after the charge has traveled a distance of 0.5 meters?
   A. 1200 J
   B. 3500 J
   C. 16,000 J
   D. 0 J

6. Which of the following sections of copper wire will exhibit the lowest resistance?
   A. A 5-meter section with a diameter of 8 mm
   B. A 5-meter section with a diameter of 3 mm
   C. A 2-meter section with a diameter of 4 mm
   D. A 2-meter section with a diameter of 1 mm

7. Joules per coulomb are units that can be used to denote:
   A. electric field strength.
   B. charge.
   C. electric potential.
   D. electrostatic force.

8. Two opposite point charges are separated by a distance of 4 meters. Each charge has a magnitude of 25 μC. What is the electric potential at a point exactly halfway between these charges?
   A. 0 V
   B. 24,000 V
   C. 50,000 V
   D. 240,000 V

Independent Question Explanations

1. B is correct. By convention, electric field lines are directed from positive charges to negative charges. The electric field between two infinite parallel plates is represented by parallel lines directed from the positive plate to the negative plate.

2. A is correct. The sum of the electric forces from each of the two equivalent charges on the third charge is given by:

$$F_{net} = k\frac{qQ}{d^2} + k\frac{qQ}{(2d)^2} = k\frac{qQ}{d^2} + k\frac{qQ}{4d^2} = \frac{kq}{d^2}\left[Q + \frac{Q}{4}\right] = \frac{5kqQ}{4d^2}$$

3. B is correct. Electrons do not move freely within insulating materials (choice A is wrong), but polarization does occur on an atomic level. As a result, the insulator develops a slightly asymmetric distribution of charge as electrons move away from the source of negative charge. The result is an excess of positive charge on the side of the insulator closest to the external charge, and a net attraction between them.

4. A is correct. We are given the change in electric *potential*, and we need to find the change in electric potential *energy*. Remember, electric potential is equal to electric potential energy divided by charge; electric potential energy, then, must equal the product of electric potential and charge.

$$\Delta PE = (q)(\Delta V) = (q)(1800\ V - 900\ V) = (6\ C)(900\ V) = 5400\ J$$

5. D is correct. The charge is traveling along a path that is perpendicular to the electric field lines, so the electric field does no work on the charge. Alternatively, one might consider that the electrical potential energy of the charge must not change if its distance between the two plates is constant.

6. A is correct. Resistance decreases with decreasing length and increasing radius. Choices B and D can be eliminated immediately, since an equivalent length of wire with a smaller radius will always have a higher resistance. We are left with choices A and C. Resistance as a function of wire dimensions is given by:

$$R = \rho\frac{L}{A}$$

Since all of the wires are made of copper and resistivity is an intrinsic property, the resistivity values will be identical across all sections. Using the above equation, the ratio of the resistance values of choices A and C is:

$$\frac{R_{5\text{-meter section}}}{R_{2\text{-meter section}}} = \frac{\frac{5\ m}{(\pi)(4 \times 10^{-3}\ m)^2}}{\frac{2\ m}{(\pi)(2 \times 10^{-3}\ m)^2}} = \frac{\frac{5}{16}}{\frac{1}{2}} = \frac{5}{8}$$

Thus, the 5-meter section of wire has a lower resistance than the 2-meter section.

7. C is correct. Joules per coulomb (J/C) are the units for electric potential; these units are equivalent to volts. The units for electric field strength are newtons per coulomb (N/C) or volts per meter (V/m) (eliminate choice A). Charge has units of coulombs alone, not joules per coulomb (eliminate option B). Electrostatic force, like force in general, is measured in newtons (eliminate choice D).

8. A is correct. Electric potential is given by the equation below.

$$\text{Electric potential} = k\frac{Q_1}{r}$$

The total electrical potential at the midpoint between the two charges is given by the scalar addition of the electrical potential due to each individual point charge, such that:

$$\text{Tot. electric pot.} = k\frac{Q_1}{r} + k\frac{Q_2}{r} = k\left[\frac{25\ \mu C}{2\ m} + \frac{-25\ \mu C}{2\ m}\right] = 0$$

Note that one of these point charges is negative, so we must make one of them -25.

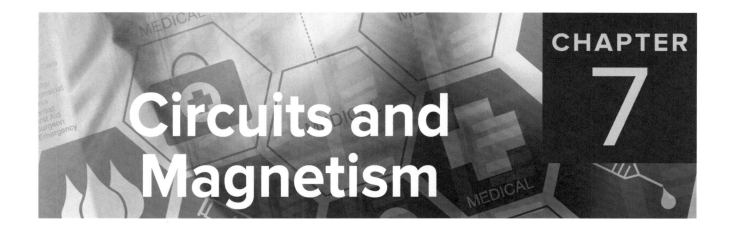

Circuits and Magnetism

0. Introduction

Just like for fluids, where we made a major distinction between fluids in static equilibrium (hydrostatics) and fluids in motion (fluid dynamics), in this chapter we will move on from discussing electric fields and charges at equilibrium to talking about what happens when we put charges in motion in a systematic and deliberate way. In other words, it is time to talk about circuits. We will also discuss magnetism, which is a conceptually important phenomenon (after all, this topic as a whole is referred to as "electromagnetism," which underscores how electricity and magnetism are two sides of the same coin) with some important real-world applications, although magnetism tends to be emphasized a bit less on the MCAT.

1. Current, Resistance, and Voltage

When charge flows through a conductor in a specific direction, that movement of charge is known as current. Although current in a conductor is mediated by the flow of electrons (which have a negative charge), by convention we talk about current in conductors running in the direction taken by positive charge. This may seem confusing at first—and it's hard to deny that this is not the most intuitive convention in the world—but it may help to remember that an overall positive charge just means a deficiency of electrons, so that when we follow the flow of a current, we're tracing the movement of electron-deficient areas. It may also be helpful to just remember that the direction in which current flows is opposite that of the actual flow of electrons.

Current (I) is defined as the amount of charge that flows through a location over an interval of time: that is, current equals charge divided by time. The SI unit of current is the ampere (A), and is defined as follows: $1 \text{ A} = \frac{1 \text{ C}}{1 \text{ s}}$. That is, 1 ampere equals 1 coulomb over 1 second.

On the MCAT, you will always be asked to analyze current that moves in a single direction through a circuit. This is known as direct current (DC), and is commonly found in batteries (as well as in some other applications). If the direction of current flow changes, that is known as alternating current (AC). Most real-world applications of electricity are AC; the details go beyond the scope of the MCAT, but the idea is that AC enables certain improvements in the safety and feasibility of long-distance transmission, like what is seen along power lines. You should know that AC circuits exist, but you will not be asked to analyze them on the MCAT.

The next question we need to address is *why* current moves through a conductor. Essentially, in circuits, the motion of current is driven by voltage differentials. Recall from Chapter 6 that voltage is a measure of difference in electrical potential, and for that reason charges spontaneously flow across voltage differentials. In a standard DC setup, current flows from a positive point of voltage to a relatively negative point of voltage (recall that we follow the movement of positive charge). The voltage differential that powers a circuit is sometimes referred to as the electromotive force (emf). This terminology is misleading: voltage is *not* a force. Instead, a better analogy for voltage—as we also explored in Chapter 6—is gravitational potential energy. You can think of circuits as operating as if current is flowing "downhill" from an area of high voltage to an area of low voltage.

MCAT STRATEGY > > >

The term "emf" is used because voltage is felt to be the factor that sets the whole circuit in motion, kind of like how a force puts an object into motion. Messing with technically incorrect but appealing terminology is dangerous for the MCAT, but it can still be useful to think about voltage differentials as making a circuit "go."

MCAT STRATEGY > > >

Without resistors (or capacitors, as we'll see later in this chapter), there would be no point to a circuit. In fact, there wouldn't even be a circuit in any meaningful sense. You should strive to see voltage, current, and resistance as three fundamentally linked properties.

In Chapter 6, we discussed how different materials conduct electricity to different degrees, defining the inverse concepts of conductivity and resistivity. To reiterate the basic equation from that chapter, $R = \rho \frac{\ell}{A}$; that is, resistance depends directly on length and the inherent resistivity of an object, and inversely on cross-sectional area. Circuits are defined as including elements, such as resistors, capacitors, and other electronic components that are beyond the scope of the MCAT, that are connected by conductive wire. Generally, when analyzing a circuit, we consider the resistance of the conductive wire to be negligible, and focus on the resistance present in the resistors.

You might wonder why we would include resistors in a circuit. The way we've described circuits so far, it sounds like resistance is a bad thing, as it gets in the way of conductivity. However, resistance is actually very useful, because it allows the kinetic energy present in the electrons moving through the wire to be transformed into other kinds of energy, like heat or light. An everyday example is a traditional incandescent lightbulb: current is conducted smoothly through the wire that links the wall plug to the lightbulb, but then passes through a coil of tungsten, which is a strong resistor. The energy of the current is then converted to light (and heat). A useful analogy for approaching resistance is to consider it as something similar to how energy is dissipated by kinetic friction.

The three quantities of current, voltage, and resistance are linked together in an equation that is absolutely fundamental to analyzing circuits. This is known as Ohm's law:

Equation 1A.
$$V = IR$$

In other words, voltage equals current times resistance. This is the most common way this equation is presented, but it can of course be rewritten. In particular, it may be helpful from the point of view of gaining an intuitive understanding of what this means to rewrite the equation to focus on current:

Equation 1B.
$$I = \frac{V}{R}$$

Here, we can see that current is proportional to voltage (i.e., the electric potential difference that can be thought of as what "pushes" the current to flow "downhill") divided by resistance (the degree to which the flow of current is blocked by the resistance of a circuit).

This equation can also be rewritten to focus on resistance, as follows:

Equation 1C.
$$R = \frac{V}{I}$$

Writing the equation this way is mostly useful because it allows us to define the units of resistance. Resistance has units of ohms (Ω). Ohms can be defined in several ways, but the most straightforward follows from $R = \frac{V}{I}$: $1 \, \Omega = \frac{1 \, V}{1 \, A}$, or 1 ohm equals 1 volt divided by 1 ampere (the unit of current).

As stated above, resistors function to convert the energy of electron flow into other forms of energy. When we hear 'energy', we should also think of power, because work has units of energy, and the fact that power equals work divided by time is a basic definition in physics.

It turns out that by the clever application of some of the laws we have already derived, we can get an equation for the power dissipated in a resistor in terms of the basic circuit properties of current and voltage. Recall from Chapter 6 that voltage is defined as the electric potential energy of a charge at a given point in an electric field divided by the magnitude of that charge ($V = \frac{U}{q}$). The key insight here is that U (electric potential energy) has the same units as work, such that we can even consider W to be equal to ΔU if we're limiting ourselves to work done by electric potential energy (which is a reasonable assumption). Therefore, we can take the definition of voltage, slightly modify it to fit our circumstances, and derive a neat expression for work in terms of voltage and charge:

Equation 2.
$$V = \frac{U}{q} \rightarrow V = \frac{\Delta U}{q} \rightarrow V = \frac{W}{q} \rightarrow W = Vq$$

Now that we have an expression for work, we can use this to derive an expression for power, as follows:

Equation 3.
$$P = \frac{W}{t} \rightarrow P = \frac{Vq}{t} \rightarrow P = V\left(\frac{q}{t}\right) \rightarrow P = VI$$

In this derivation, we utilize the fact that the change in charge over time is current to derive the equation $P = VI$, more commonly given as $P = IV$.

Utilizing Ohm's law to identify ways of rewriting the quantities of voltage and current in terms of resistance, we can derive the following set of equivalent equations for the power dissipated by a resistor:

Equation 4.
$$P = IV = I^2R = \frac{V^2}{R}$$

Whether you choose to memorize all three forms of this equation or to derive them on the fly from Ohm's law ($V = IR$) is up to you, but you should be aware that the MCAT will expect you to be able to calculate power if you're given any two of the three potential variables of current, voltage, and resistance.

With all of this in mind, let's assess the diagram of a simple circuit given in Figure 1. This figure contains a simple circuit containing one resistor, with all of its components labeled. Since the MCAT requires you to move quickly, though, it is worth making sure that you understand what all the labeled components refer to before moving on.

MCAT STRATEGY > > >

You don't have to memorize the derivation of $P = IV$, although you certainly do need to know the equation itself, but working through the derivation will help you connect circuits with the topics discussed in the previous chapter on electricity, develop better intuitions for how electricity- and circuit-related concepts fit together, and demystify these often challenging topics.

Figure 1. Labeled simple circuit.

On the basis of the simple circuit presented in Figure 1, let's take a closer look at how exactly the drop in voltage across the circuit happens. At first you might think that the voltage drop is distributed evenly throughout the circuit, but that's not quite correct. The equation $V = IR$ can be applied to the circuit as a whole, but it can also be applied to its subcomponents. The current-carrying part of the circuit can be broken down into two main components: the conductive wire and the resistor. Let's analyze these two components separately using Ohm's law. While doing so, it's important to remember that there's always an implicit "Δ" when we use V—much like work is defined as *change* in energy, voltage is defined as a *difference* in electric potential. To clarify this point, when analyzing voltage in specific components of a circuit, we often use the term "voltage drop" to refer to the change in electric potential that occurs across a circuit element.

First, let's look at the voltage drop in the conductive wire. By definition, the conductive wire will have very low resistance. The voltage drop is directly proportional to resistance, by $V = IR$, so therefore the conductive wire will have a very low voltage drop. For most circuit problems, we would go so far as to assume that $R = 0\ \Omega$ for the conductive wire and that the voltage drop would therefore be 0 V. (This is an oversimplification; in reality, non-superconductive wires do display *some* resistance, but it should always be relatively quite small).

MCAT STRATEGY > > >

Understanding that resistors are where the action happens in terms of resistance may seem like an obvious statement, but it's actually an important prerequisite that sets up our discussion of how to combine resistors in the next section. Be sure you understand this point before continuing.

In contrast, consider the voltage drop across the resistor. R will be much bigger for the resistor, so the voltage drop will be much larger. In fact, in a simple idealized circuit with a single resistor, that resistor will account for the entire voltage drop of the circuit. The reason for this is articulated in a set of principles known as Kirchhoff's laws, which are essentially adaptations of conservation of mass/energy in the context of electrical circuits.

Kirchhoff's first law applies to currents and states that for any junction in a circuit, the sum of current entering the junction must equal the sum of current exiting the junction. Kirchhoff's second law applies to voltage and states that for a closed circuit, the sum of the voltage drops throughout the circuit is equal to the source voltage (or emf) of the circuit as a whole. They can be summarized as follows:

Equations 5 and 6.

1: At a junction: $I_{in} = I_{out}$

2: Over a closed circuit: $V_{source} = \Sigma V_{circuit}$

Kirchhoff's first law is definitely worth paying specific attention to because it can be applied in concrete problem-solving situations, in which you may be asked to analyze a junction in a circuit and determine the current flowing through various wires. Kirchhoff's second law, for the purposes of the MCAT, is more like interesting background information, in that it provides a theoretical justification for some of the assumptions we make about how voltage plays out in circuits (which we will explore in more detail in the next section), but is rarely something that you will specifically leverage to solve a problem.

2. Circuits: Series and Parallel

In section 1 of this chapter, we carefully walked through how to analyze a very simple circuit containing a single resistor. Our next task is to figure out what happens when you add more than one resistor to a circuit. Resistors can be added either in series or in parallel. As the name implies, resistors added in series are added one after another such that an uninterrupted flow of current goes first through one resistor, then another, and so on. In contrast, resistors added in parallel involve the current being split, such that one branch of the current goes through one resistor and one branch of the current goes through another. This is shown in Figure 2.

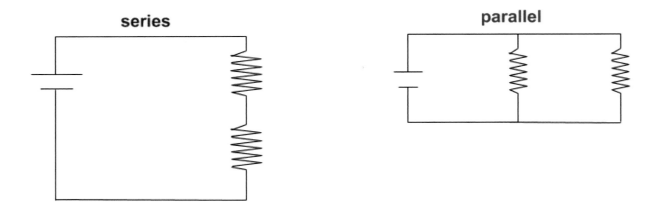

Figure 2. Simple series and parallel resistors.

First, let's consider a set of resistors in series. The circuit as a whole will still have its properties of overall voltage, current, and resistance; however, unlike when we were analyzing a single-resistor circuit, now that we have multiple resistors, we need to be able to analyze how they each contribute to the overall properties of the circuit.

The first conclusion we can draw is that the total current of the circuit will be the same as the current that flows through each of the resistors. This is a simple consequence of Kirchhoff's first law, given that we have a scenario in which no junctions are present in the circuit. Based on Kirchhoff's second law, we can conclude that the voltage drops in each of the resistors must add up to equal the overall source voltage (or emf) of the circuit, and it is also intuitively reasonable that the resistances of each resistor add up to form the total resistance of the circuit.

To summarize, for a circuit with resistors R_1, R_2, ... R_n wired in series:

Equation 7. $$I_{total} = I_1 = I_2 = \ldots = I_n$$

Equation 8. $$V_{source} = V_1 + V_2 + \ldots + V_n$$

Equation 9. $$R_{total} = R_1 + R_2 + \ldots + R_n$$

At this point, it's worth briefly touching on a point of mathematical hygiene. Voltage differentials can be positive or negative, and the voltage drops within the circuit have the opposite sign as that of the source voltage or emf. Another way of saying this would be to say that the voltage drops contributed by the resistors in the circuit act to gradually dissipate the difference in electric potential contributed by the source voltage. An analogy with gravitational potential energy might state that the source voltage/emf is similar to lifting a heavy load up above the ground by a certain distance, and then the voltage drops in the resistors correspond to gradually lowering it, bit by bit, until it reaches the ground again. For this reason, a more mathematically precise version of how voltages add together for resistors in series (and of Kirchhoff's law in general) would be $V_{source} = -(V_1 + V_2 + \ldots + V_n)$. However, this is one of the many points where the practicalities of MCAT physics fail to correspond exactly to what you may remember having worried about in physics problem sets—as long as you understand that the two sets of voltages 'cancel each other out,' so to speak, you should be fine.

MCAT STRATEGY > > >

Your first and foremost goal for studying MCAT science is conceptual clarity. Notation comes second. The reason for this is that on Test Day, you will have to apply fundamental physics concepts quickly, accurately, and in new contexts—but no physics professor will be checking your notes and deducting points.

Resistors added in parallel behave quite differently. The basic reason for this is that the current is split up and travels separately through each resistor, before rejoining at the end of the circuit. Therefore, to analyze current, we'll have to apply Kirchhoff's first law and conclude that the currents running through the various resistors must be added up to obtain the total current of the circuit. The voltage drops across the resistors, however, must be identical to each other and to the voltage of the circuit as a whole, because all the resistors start at the same voltage (equal to the source voltage) and end at the same final voltage. Resistance, however, behaves unusually; you might think that resistance would add in the same way that current does, but instead, for parallel circuits, resistance adds reciprocally.

Therefore, for a circuit with resistors $R_1, R_2, \ldots R_n$ wired in parallel:

Equation 10.
$$I_{total} = I_1 + I_2 + \ldots + I_n$$

Equation 11.
$$V_{total} = V_1 = V_2 = \ldots = V_3$$

Equation 12.
$$\frac{1}{R_{total}} = \frac{1}{R_1} + \frac{1}{R_2} + \ldots + \frac{1}{R_n}$$

On Test Day, it will be extremely important for you to know which equations to apply to which circuits (or which components of a circuit, as a large circuit can contain *both* series and parallel components), and for you to be able to make that decision quickly and accurately. The best way to approach this is to carefully work through the logic of how current and voltage work in both types of circuits. These are reasonably intuitive equations, and you may find it helpful to use analogies such as waterfalls or water slides, with water corresponding to current and vertical displacement corresponding to the voltage drop.

The final main thing that you have to remember is the fact that resistance adds directly in series circuits, but reciprocally in parallel circuits. The challenge here is that it may be difficult to develop an intuitive sense for what reciprocal addition means and how that connects to the underlying physics. To understand why this is the case, recall that resistance is the opposite (mathematically, the inverse) of conductance. Adding branches to the circuit makes it easier, overall, for the current to make it through the multi-branched circuit, and this can be thought of both as an increase in overall conductance and a decrease in overall resistance. This decrease in overall resistance is expressed through reciprocal addition.

Having covered the basics of series and parallel circuits, we're now in the position to cover how current, voltage, and resistance can be measured at various points in a circuit.

Current is measured using ammeters (think amperes, the unit of current). An ammeter is inserted in series into a circuit, which makes sense because it has to be able to 'capture' the entire flow of current in order to be able to measure it. Ammeters measure a current based on the magnetic field induced by current moving through a wire (as we'll talk about more in section 4). In order to have a minimal effect on the circuit as a whole, an ideal ammeter would have zero resistance.

> ## MCAT STRATEGY > > >
>
> A simple but less conceptually insightful trick is to remember that in a series-connected circuit, you have resistors that are lined up one after the other, so you add them up one after the other. In contrast, the alignment in parallel circuits is less straightforward, which corresponds to the less straightforward mathematical operation of reciprocal addition. Essentially, you just have to remember that you apply the weird math to the weird situation.

A voltmeter, in contrast, is connected to a resistor in parallel. The idea of a voltmeter is that it has a known resistance and siphons off some current, which is measured to calculate voltage based on Ohm's law ($V = IR$). Ideally, a voltmeter should use the least current possible in order to disturb the rest of the circuit to the least extent possible. Therefore, to do so, it should have an extremely high resistance. Since resistance adds reciprocally, this also means that it will have a minimal effect on the overall resistance of the circuit.

Ohmmeters, in turn, are used to measure resistance. There are two basic ohmmeter designs you should be aware of: in one, a known voltage is supplied across a resistor and the resulting current is measured, and in the other, a constant and known current is supplied across a resistor and the voltage drop is measured. The basic principle of both designs is the same, in that Ohm's law is used to calculate resistance based on current and voltage. The only difference has to do with which parameter is controlled and which is measured.

3. Capacitors

A capacitor is a device containing two physically separated components in which opposite charges are accumulated. The MCAT will ask you to analyze idealized capacitors that consist of two parallel, conductive plates separated by a non-conductive, insulating material that is known as a dielectric material. In this section, we will review the basic properties of capacitors, how they can be integrated into circuits, and some common ways in which they are tested on the MCAT.

The model of a capacitor tested on the MCAT involves parallel, flat, thin plates that can accumulate charge, as schematically shown in Figure 3.

Figure 3. Schematic diagram of a capacitor.

The accumulation of charge in a capacitor is caused by the application of a voltage, and the degree to which a capacitor can store charge is defined as its capacitance. The most important equation relating to capacitance (C) is the following equation, which can be written in two equivalent ways, shown in Equations 13A and 13B:

Equation 13A. $$C = \frac{Q}{V}$$

Equation 13B. $$Q = VC$$

MCAT STRATEGY > > >

There is a well-known TV shopping channel named QVC, which—among other things—sells electronics. This association might help you remember the equation $Q = VC$.

As such, capacitance is defined as the amount of charge stored in a capacitor for a given voltage. This relationship is also often presented as $Q = VC$, which helps make this concept more intuitive by clarifying that there are two ways to increase the charge in a capacitor: (1) to increase the voltage, because a greater electric potential difference will drive the accumulation of more charge; and (2) to increase the capacitance, which is a measure of how well the capacitor itself, as a device, can store charge.

As implied by the above equation, capacitance is defined in units of charge divided by voltage. The unit of capacitance is the farad (F), and $1 \text{ F} = \frac{1 \text{ C}}{1 \text{ V}}$. Capacitance itself is affected by two main parameters: (1) the geometry of the capacitor itself and (2) the insulating (dielectric) material separating the two plates.

In terms of the geometry of the capacitor, as already mentioned, the MCAT will limit you to the relatively simple case of two parallel plates. For such a capacitor in a vacuum, assuming that the plates have the same area and are oriented such that they overlap with each other, the capacitance is given by the following equation:

Equation 14. $$C = \varepsilon_0 \frac{A}{d}$$

In this equation, ε_0 is a constant known as the permittivity of free space. It is defined as 8.85×10^{-12} F/m. There is no need for you to memorize this constant, but it is worth dwelling on conceptually briefly. As the name "permittivity of free space" implies, permittivity is a more general concept. The name "permittivity" is actually somewhat misleading, because it is best thought of as a measure of how much resistance occurs to the formation of an electric field. ε_0 is the lowest possible value of permittivity, and corresponds to the permittivity of pure vacuum. The details go far beyond the MCAT; for our purposes, it is more than enough to know that ε_0 is a fundamental physical constant that reappears in a surprising number of contexts and equations if one studies electromagnetism in depth. A in this equation is the overlapping cross-sectional area of the plates (if the plates completely overlap, as is usually the case, you can just use the area of a single plate), and d is the distance between them. The takeaway point is that increasing the area of the plates and bringing them closer together will increase the capacitance.

MCAT STRATEGY > > >

Note that capacitance is a property that has a *linear* inverse relationship with distance, unlike the inverse square relationship we have seen with the gravitational and electric forces.

The equation $C = \varepsilon_0 \frac{A}{d}$ is truly remarkable, because it links capacitance to a basic physical constant of the universe and the geometric properties of the capacitor itself.

However, an assumption that we made for the equation $C = \varepsilon_0 \frac{A}{d}$ was that the capacitor was located in a vacuum. This is obviously unrealistic. Our next task is to figure out what happens if a material other than vacuum separates the plates of a capacitor. Recall that the plates of a capacitor contain accumulations of opposite charges, which are attracted to each other. The insulating property of the material separating the plates of the capacitor is what prevents the charges from equalizing. The greater the insulation provided, the greater the charge that can be built up at a given voltage before a discharge occurs that equalizes the charges. (An interesting example of such a discharge is lightning). Non-conductive (dielectric) materials all have individual values of ε, permittivity, and it turns out that all values of ε are greater than ε_0, the permittivity of free space. Therefore, in order to streamline comparisons of the dielectric properties of various substances to that of vacuum, we define the dielectric constant (κ) of a substance as the ratio of its permittivity (ε) to ε_0:

Equation 15.
$$\kappa = \frac{\varepsilon}{\varepsilon_0}$$

The greater the dielectric constant, the more charge a capacitor can store at a given voltage. By definition, since $C = \frac{Q}{V}$, this means that materials with greater dielectric constants increase the capacitance of a capacitor. Moreover, since C is linearly proportional to ε, the new capacitance increases proportionally to κ, as expressed in the following equation, in which C' indicates the modified capacitance and C indicates the capacitance under vacuum conditions:

Equation 16.
$$C' = \kappa C$$

There is no need to memorize values of κ for various materials, but an important fact to be aware of is that the dielectric constant of air is very close to that of pure vacuum, to the point that the difference is generally considered to be negligible for MCAT problem-solving setups.

Now that we've covered some of the basic properties of capacitors and capacitance, you may find yourself wondering why they're important. In addition to some practical applications, which we will cover below, it turns out that capacitors have several noteworthy electric properties.

MCAT STRATEGY > > >

The practical point of the equation $C' = \kappa C$ is that using an insulating material increases capacitance.

First, capacitors create uniform electric fields, as discussed in Chapter 6. Figure 4 shows an example of such a field.

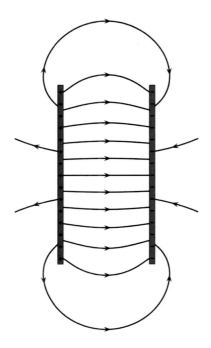

Figure 4. Uniform electric field in a capacitor.

In a uniform electric field, there is another useful equation we can derive, which states that the strength of an electric field is equal to the voltage difference divided by the distance between the plates:

Equation 17.
$$E = \frac{V}{d}$$

Be careful with this equation, though: it applies *only* to uniform electric fields, whereas the equation $E = \frac{F}{q}$ applies to electric fields in general.

Another interesting property of capacitors has to do with their function of storing energy in the form of the electrical field that they generate. This is a form of potential energy, and can be expressed using the following equation:

Equation 18.
$$PE = \tfrac{1}{2}CV^2$$

An interesting fact about this equation is that although it expresses a form of potential energy, it looks more reminiscent of kinetic energy equations that we have encountered before. The underlying theoretical mechanics aren't particularly important for the MCAT, but you may want to be aware of this point just to avoid any confusion that might occur due to the form of the equation.

So far, we've been talking about capacitors in isolation, but they can also be incorporated into a circuit. When included in a battery-powered DC circuit of the type that we've analyzed in this chapter, the emf of the battery will cause charge to accumulate in the capacitor. Capacitors can be added in series or in parallel, just like resistors, but their mathematical properties are flipped: capacitors in series add reciprocally, while capacitors in parallel add directly:

Equation 19.
$$(\text{series}): \frac{1}{C_{total}} = \frac{1}{C_1} + \frac{1}{C_2} + \ldots + \frac{1}{C_n}$$

Equation 20.
$$(\text{parallel}): C_{total} = C_1 + C_2 + \ldots + C_n$$

As always, simple memorization is one way of approaching this distinction, but it may be helpful to at least have a sense of the underlying logic. Figure 5 shows capacitors connected in series and in parallel. Recalling that by definition, no charge flows across capacitors, it is fairly easy to appreciate on an intuitive level that adding capacitors in series is not very effective. In fact, what winds up happening is that the circuit acts like it has a single equivalent capacitor with a greater distance between the plates. The greater distance diminishes the capacitance. The mathematical relationship of reciprocal addition that we see for capacitors in series is a way of expressing this idea. In contrast, if capacitors are connected in parallel, they each have the same voltage drop associated with them, and can each function independently. The net effect is to increase the total surface area of the capacitor, which increases the overall capacitance, and this straightforward relationship is reflected in the fact that capacitors in parallel add directly.

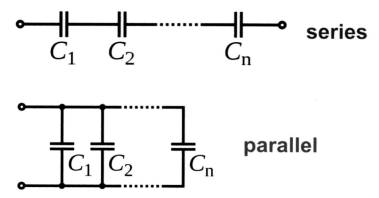

Figure 5. Series and parallel capacitors.

As a final note, we might reflect on why the MCAT is so interested in capacitors. In addition to the fact that they display a range of important electric properties and are widely incorporated into real-world electronics, they have some specific biomedical parallels. One example of a capacitor in real-world use is a defibrillator, which stores electric energy that is discharged when needed as an electric current that helps shock the heart back into rhythm. Another example is the charge differential across the plasma membranes in cells. This may seem counterintuitive, but recall that the potential difference is normally on the order of –70 mV, and in the right circumstances (such as cross-sections of neurons) the two-dimensional geometry is similar to the parallel-plate model that we have used. As a result, a uniform electric field is generated across a plasma membrane at rest, and this could be used as the basis for questions linking the physics of electricity with some crucial aspects of cellular physiology.

4. Magnetism

The final topic we will analyze in this section is magnetism. Magnetism is not tested in depth on the MCAT, but it is tested regularly; while you may not have to know as much about magnetism as you do for many physics courses, you do have to have a very solid grasp of the basic information that is covered.

Magnetic fields are like electric fields in that they act on charges, but different in that magnetic fields only affect *moving* charges. The unit of the strength of magnetic fields is the tesla (T), named after Nikola Tesla. Like many units we encounter in electromagnetism, the tesla can be expressed in many ways, but it is best to focus on the conceptual core of the unit: a tesla is defined as the magnitude of a magnetic field through which a particle with a charge of 1 C moving perpendicularly to the field at 1 m/s experiences a force of 1 N, or $1 \text{ T} = 1 \frac{\text{N·s}}{\text{C·m}}$. One point to be aware of with teslas is that they are a very large unit; a refrigerator magnet might have a field on the order of approximately 5 mT, while fields on the order of 3 T are about as strong as you will encounter in magnetic resonance imaging (MRI) systems.

Magnetic fields are generated in two main ways: by magnetic materials and by moving charges.

Multiple terms exist to describe the magnetic behavior of various materials. To best understand these terms, it's useful to first review the subatomic basis of magnetism. Electrons are very tiny magnetic dipoles, and their behavior as dipoles is described by the quantum property of spin. A filled orbital contains two paired electrons, the dipoles of which cancel each other out. As such, materials

> **MCAT STRATEGY > > >**
>
> No matter what, *never* let an MCAT question trick you into thinking that a magnetic field will exert a force on an uncharged particle or on a charged particle at rest. Remember that an object affected by magnetism *must* be charged *and* moving.

with paired electrons do not generate a magnetic field and cannot become magnetized. Such materials are known as diamagnetic, and they include a wide range of materials in everyday life, such as fabric, glass, water, and so on.

The behavior of materials that do have unpaired electrons also varies depending on what happens to those unpaired electrons. In many materials, the unpaired electrons have random spins, meaning that the material as a whole has no net magnetic dipole on its own. Such materials are known as paramagnetic. Interestingly, though, while paramagnetic materials do not generate magnetic fields on their own, they are weakly attracted by external magnetic fields. They can also be magnetically polarized by an external field. Ferromagnetic materials, in contrast, are materials with unpaired electrons in which the spin of the electrons can be permanently affected by the application of an external magnetic field. This is the process through which everyday magnets are generated.

Note that we have been discussing magnetic fields in terms of dipoles. This reflects a basic difference between magnetism and electricity; while we can have positive or negative electric charges in isolation, magnets always have both a north and a south pole (these terms are used instead of positive and negative, but the idea is the same: north and south are attracted, while north/north and south/south pairs exhibit repulsion). This tendency, along with the resultant magnetic field lines, is shown in Figure 6 below for a bar magnet similar to what you might have on your refrigerator at home.

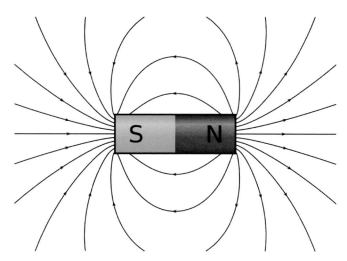

Figure 6. Magnetic dipole in a bar magnet.

Next, let's turn to magnetic fields induced by moving charges. Although "moving charges" is a very general term, it also is a description of what happens in a wire or a circuit, and for the MCAT, the example of the magnetic field generated by current moving through a wire is the major example that illustrates this phenomenon. The strength of this field is given by the following equation:

Equation 21.
$$B = \frac{\mu_0 I}{2\pi r}$$

In this equation, μ_0 is the permeability of free space. This is a fundamental quantity of the universe that describes how magnetic fields spread through the vacuum, akin to ε_0, which we saw for electricity. It is defined as $4\pi \times 10^{-7}$ N/A^2, but its numerical value should not be memorized for the magnet. I is the current running through the wire, and r is the distance from the wire. Note that the strength of B is directly proportional to current, which makes sense since the field is caused by the movement of charges, and inversely but *linearly* proportional to r, unlike the equations for the strength of electric and gravitational fields, which are inverse *square* laws with respect to r.

The magnetic field around a current-carrying wire has field lines that run in concentric circles, and the directionality of such magnetic fields is determined by one of the two right-hand rules we will encounter in this chapter. As shown below in Figure 7, to determine the direction of the magnetic field at a point around a current-carrying wire, simply align your right thumb with the direction of the current flow, and your fingers will curve around in the direction of the field.

Figure 7. Right-hand rule for current-carrying wires.

Now that we've covered the main MCAT-relevant ways that magnetic fields are generated, let's turn to how they affect particles. As mentioned in the beginning of this section, magnetic fields act on moving charges. In particular, the force exerted by a magnetic field on a moving particle with velocity v and charge q is given by the following equation:

Equation 22.

$$\vec{F}_B = q\vec{v}\,\vec{B}\sin(\theta)$$

This form of the equation emphasizes that the force is a vector quantity, as are velocity and the magnetic field itself. Technically speaking, cross multiplication is necessary to do the math correctly, but for the purposes of the MCAT, we can use the $\sin(\theta)$ term to account for the angle of the velocity of the particle to the magnetic field (note that the force will be maximized when the motion is perpendicular) and use a second right-hand rule to account for the direction of the various forces.

The right-hand rule used to determine the effects of a magnetic field on a moving particle is shown in Figure 8. Your thumb is used to indicate the direction in which the charge is moving, and your fingers are used to indicate the direction of the magnetic field. The resulting force either points up or down from your palm. It points up if the charge is positive, while it points down from the back of your hand if the charge is negative. The other way of accounting for the effect of positive versus negative charge in this system is to learn this system as it applies to *positive charges only*, such that if you're given a moving negative charge in a problem set-up, you simply reverse the direction of the particle to indicate how a negative charge *would* move in such a context.

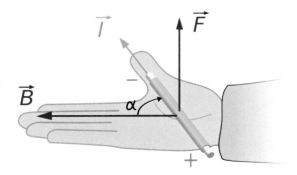

Figure 8. Right-hand rule for force exerted by magnetic fields.

A few interesting consequences are associated with the effects of magnetic fields on moving charges. First, as a point of test-taking skills, be sure not to fall for any trickily-worded questions about magnetic fields. In particular, make sure that you understand how to apply the two right-hand rules that we've covered and be sure to check that a particle is actually moving before you try to calculate the force exerted on it by a magnetic field. Second, the fact that the force exerted by the magnetic field is always perpendicular to a particle's motion means that within a uniform magnetic field, a particle will experience circular motion (the idea here is similar to how Earth's gravitation is always acting perpendicularly to the motion of a satellite). Recalling that rotational acceleration is defined as $\frac{v^2}{r}$, and that $F = ma$, we can set ma equal to the equation for magnetic force given above, as follows:

Equation 23.
$$m\left(\frac{v^2}{r}\right) = qvB$$

Rearranging and solving for r, we obtain the following expression for the radius of circular motion of a charged particle in a uniform magnetic field:

Equation 24.
$$r = \frac{mv}{qB}$$

This equation is useful in many high-energy physics applications, because the momentum (mv, although this technically goes beyond the scope of the MCAT) of a particle can be calculated based on measurements of its motion and knowledge of its charge and the strength of the magnetic field.

As we've discussed before, the fact that current is simply an aggregation of moving charges means that we often discuss magnetism-related topics related both to individual charges and to current-carrying wires. Indeed, the equation we saw above for the force exerted by a magnetic field on a moving charge can be modified to obtain the force exerted on a current-carrying wire, as follows:

Equation 25.
$$\vec{F}_B = \vec{I}\,\ell\,\vec{B}\sin(\theta)$$

The terms for B (the strength of the magnetic force) and $\sin(\theta)$ are the same as what we saw before. The idea here is that instead of talking about a single charge moving at a given velocity, we're dealing with a current I, in which a certain quantity of charge moves through a length ℓ in a certain time interval. In other words, the velocity term is essentially buried in the current (I) term, but the concept is the same.

Finally, you should be aware of the term 'Lorentz force.' This term is used to refer to the cumulative force exerted on a charged particle by an electric field and a magnetic field, because in reality, these fields generally co-occur. The equation describing the total Lorentz force is simply a summation of the forces due to electric and magnetic fields, as shown below:

Equation 26A.
$$\vec{F}_{total} = \vec{F}_{electric} + \vec{F}_{magnetic}$$

Equation 26B.
$$\vec{F}_{total} = q\vec{E} + q\vec{v}\,\vec{B}\sin(\theta)$$

5. Must-Knows

> Current: charge over time; $1 \text{ A} = \frac{1 \text{ C}}{1 \text{ s}}$
> In a circuit, ΔV = electromotive force (emf)—not actually a force!
> Resistance: units of ohms ($1 \text{ } \Omega = \frac{1 \text{ V}}{1 \text{ A}}$); resistors convert current to other forms of useful energy in a circuit.
> Ohm's law: $V = IR$
> Power dissipated by a resistor: $P = IV = I^2R = \frac{V^2}{R}$
> Kirchhoff's laws:
>   – At a junction: $I_{in} = I_{out}$
>   – Over a closed circuit: $V_{source} = \Sigma V_{circuit}$
> For a circuit with resistors $R_1, R_2, \ldots R_n$ wired in series:
>   – $I_{total} = I_1 = I_2 = \ldots = I_n$
>   – $V_{source} = V_1 + V_2 + \ldots + V_n$
>   – $R_{total} = R_1 + R_2 + \ldots + R_n$
> For a circuit with resistors $R_1, R_2, \ldots R_n$ wired in parallel:
>   – $I_{total} = I_1 + I_2 + \ldots + I_n$
>   – $V_{total} = V_1 = V_2 = \ldots = V_3$
>   – $\frac{1}{R_{total}} = \frac{1}{R_1} + \frac{1}{R_2} + \ldots + \frac{1}{R_n}$
> Capacitors: store charge in parallel plates, $Q = VC$, $C = \varepsilon_0 \frac{A}{d}$.
> Dielectric insulators: increase capacitance; $C' = \kappa C$, where $\kappa = \frac{\varepsilon}{\varepsilon_0}$.
> Capacitors create a uniform electric field, where $E = \frac{V}{d}$.
> Capacitors in circuits:
>   – series: $\frac{1}{C_{total}} = \frac{1}{C_1} + \frac{1}{C_2} + \ldots + \frac{1}{C_n}$
>   – parallel: $C_{total} = C_1 + C_2 + \ldots + C_n$
> Magnetic fields: generated by magnetic materials and moving charges, affect moving charges.
> Strength of a magnetic field generated by a current: $B = \frac{\mu_0 I}{2\pi r}$
> Direction of magnetic fields: given by right-hand rule when generated by a current.
> Force of a magnetic field on a moving charge: $\vec{F}_B = q\vec{v}\vec{B}\sin(\theta)$
>   – Direction: right-hand rule with thumb for motion of charge, fingers for magnetic field lines, and up/down from palm for direction of force
> Magnetic force on a current-carrying wire: $\vec{F}_B = \vec{I}\ell\vec{B}\sin(\theta)$

Practice Passage

A physician with Doctors Without Borders discovered that an electrical monitor had malfunctioned due to a problem with the electrical generator that was used by the clinic. Opening up the casing revealed that a power surge may have burned out several resistors and capacitors.

The clinic had a battery-operated meter with which it could measure voltages and currents in the circuit. The meter used to monitor current and voltages can influence the circuit it is connected to if it is not properly designed and calibrated. There is also a box of various resistors and capacitors. Resistance and capacitance of an individual component is determined using a color code shown in Table 1.

Table 1. Color Code for 4-band and 5-band Resistors

Color	Digit	Multiplier	Tolerance (%)
Black	0	10^0	
Brown	1	10^1	1
Red	2	10^2	2
Orange	3	10^3	
Yellow	4	10^4	
Green	5	10^5	0.5
Blue	6	10^6	0.25
Violet	7	10^7	0.1
Grey	8	10^8	
White	9	10^9	
Gold		10^{-1}	5
Silver		10^{-2}	10
(none)			20

Figure 1 shows examples for a 4-band and a 5-band resistor. A 5-band resistor colored Brown-Green-Grey-Silver-Red would be 1.58 Ω with a tolerance of ± 2%. When looking to replace the burned-out components, there was not always the exact equivalent resistor or capacitor so technicians were forced to determine appropriate series or parallel component combinations.

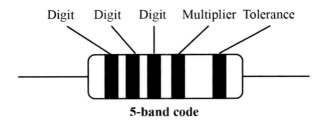

4-band code

5-band code

Figure 1. Resistor band codes

1. The multimeter was used to measure the current in the circuit below between points B and C.

If the multimeter has an internal resistance of 2.5 Ω, what will be the ratio of the measured current to the true current between those two points?

    A. < 1
    B. = 1
    C. > 1
    D. > 2

2. If a resistor is taken from the broken monitor and the bands are read out as Brown-Gold-Black-Red. What was the correct resistance and tolerance of component?
    A. 2 Ω ± 1 %
    B. 0.2 Ω ± 2 %
    C. 1 Ω ± 2 %
    D. 10 Ω ± 2 %

3. If a single 100 mF capacitor failed inside the monitor, what combinations of capacitors could NOT be used to replace it?
   A. Two 200 mF capacitors in series
   B. Two 50 mF capacitors in parallel
   C. Three 100 mF capacitors in series
   D. One 200 mF and two 400 mF capacitors in series

4. Which of the following could be measured to most accurately monitor the total current running through the device once it is repaired?
   A. Electric field
   B. Magnetic field
   C. Temperature
   D. Electromotive force

5. The electrodes used to connect the monitor to patients are covered in a Ag-Cl gel in order to facilitate optimal conductance of electrical signals. What would be the units used to quantify this conductance?
   A. $(kg \cdot m^2)/(s^2 \cdot A^3)$
   B. $(C \cdot m)/s^2 \cdot A^2$
   C. $(C^2 \cdot s)/(kg \cdot m^2)$
   D. $(s^3 \cdot A^3)/(kg \cdot m^2)$

6. The technicians are testing the charging capacity of a Yellow-Orange-Black-Red capacitor prior to placing it into the damaged monitor. Which of the following graphs would indicate the capacitor is charging correctly?

A.

B.

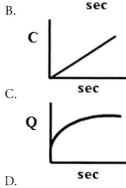

C.

D.

7. An Orange-Yellow-Black-Green-Violet capacitor is taken out of the box and charged. If the dielectric material is removed from and the capacitor is charged again, what will be observed?
   A. The electric potential across the capacitor is lower without the dielectric.
   B. The electric field strength of the capacitor is higher without the dielectric.
   C. The capacitance of the capacitor is higher without the dielectric.
   D. The charge stored on the capacitor is lower with the dielectric.

Practice Passage Explanations

A physician with Doctors Without Borders discovered that an electrical monitor had malfunctioned due to a problem with the electrical generator that was used by the clinic. Opening up the casing revealed that a power surge may have burned out several resistors and capacitors.

Key terms: power surge, burned out resistors, capacitors

Cause and effect: a voltage surge overwhelmed and damaged electrical components due to excess energy

The clinic had a battery-operated meter with which it could measure voltages and currents in the circuit. The meter used to monitor current and voltages can influence the circuit it is connected to if it is not properly designed and calibrated. There is also a box of various resistors and capacitors. Resistance and capacitance of an individual component is determined using a color code shown in Table 1.

Key terms: resistor color code, 4-band, 5-band, combinations

Cause and effect: codes are sued to determine C_{eq} or R_{eq}; parallel/series combinations; meter will effect measured V, I due to its internal resistance

Table 1. Color Code for 4-band and 5-band Resistors

Color	Digit	Multiplier	Tolerance (%)
Black	0	10^0	
Brown	1	10^1	1
Red	2	10^2	2
Orange	3	10^3	
Yellow	4	10^4	
Green	5	10^5	0.5
Blue	6	10^6	0.25
Violet	7	10^7	0.1
Grey	8	10^8	
White	9	10^9	
Gold		10^{-1}	5
Silver		10^{-2}	10
(none)			20

Table 1 allows the determination the resistance or capacitance

Figure 1 shows examples for a 4-band and a 5-band resistor. A 5-band resistor colored Brown-Green-Grey-Silver-Red would be 1.58 Ω with a tolerance of ± 2%. When looking to replace the burned-out components, there was not always the exact equivalent resistor or capacitor so technicians were forced to determine appropriate series or parallel component combinations.

Key terms: resistor color code, 4-band, 5-band, combinations

Cause and effect: equivalent capacitance or resistance was used to replace missing components, anticipate equations on the rules of parallel/series combinations

4-band code

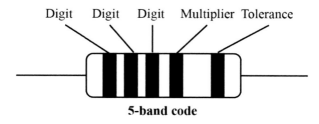

5-band code

Figure 1. Resistor band codes

Figure 1 shows how we must read the bands left to right with the band indicating the tolerance on the far right

1. A is correct. The ideal ammeter has zero internal resistance, so that the circuit loses as little voltage as possible as electrons flow through it. This ideal resistance value is exactly opposite as that of an ideal voltmeter, where we want near infinite resistance. We can do the calculations, but on Test Day we want to work smarter, not harder. It is impossible to change the total resistance of a circuit yet have the total current remain the same (eliminate choice B). Increasing the total resistance will lower the total current. This means that the current with the ammeter attached (the measured current) will be less than the true current.

   With the ammeter disconnected, total resistance of the circuit is calculated as:
   $$1/R_{eq} = 1/15 + 1/7.5 = 3/15$$
   $$R_{eq} = 15/3 = 5 \text{ Ω}$$

   Using Ohm's law (V = IR) we can calculate $I_{eq} = V_{eq}/R_{eq} = 10 \text{ V}/5 \text{ Ω} = 2$ A entering point A.

   With the ammeter connected, the total resistance becomes 15 Ω in series with the 2.5 Ω ammeter, and both of these components in parallel with the 7.5 Ω resistor.
   $$\text{A to C } R_{eq} = 15 + 2.5 = 17.5 \text{ Ω}$$
   $$\text{A to D } R_{eq} = 7.5 \text{ Ω}$$
   $$1/R_{eq} = 1/17.5 + 1/7.5 = 2/35 + 5/35 \approx 7/35 \text{ Ω (Note: We approximated 1/7.5 to 1/7)}$$
   $$R_{eq} \approx 35/7 \approx 5 \text{ Ω}$$

$I_{eq} = V_{eq}/R_{eq} = 10$ V/5 Ω = 2 A, but do not be so quick to choose choice B. We approximated 1/7.5 as 1/7, making the value artificially larger than it really is, thus making our R_{eq} smaller than it actually is. If our R_{eq} is too small, our I_{eq} will be too large, and thus the real value of I_{eq} will be just under 2 A.

2. A is correct. If the resistor is read in the order given as a 4-band resistor, the first digit (Brown) is 1, but Gold does not have a digit value. This must be because the resistor is turned around and the presented order is backwards. The order of bands should be read Red-Black-Gold-Brown. Read this way, the first digit is 2, the second digit is 0, the multiplier is 10^{-1} and the tolerance is 1%. This gives $20 \times 10^{-1} = 2 \pm 1\%$.
   B, C, D: These answers are a result of miscalculation or failure to realize that gold cannot be read as the 2nd band in an accurate reading.

3. C is correct. There are two ways to combine capacitors: in parallel or in series. The equivalent capacitance (C_{eq}) of capacitors in parallel is the sum of the individual ($C_{eq} = C_1 + C_2$ ...). For capacitors in series, the inverse of the equivalent capacitance is equal to the sum of the inverse individual capacitances ($1/C_{eq} = 1/C_1 + 1/C_2$...). In choice C, placing the capacitors in series gives:
$$1/C_{eq} = (1/100) + (1/100) + (1/100) = 3/100$$
$$C_{eq} = 100/3 = 33 \text{ mF}$$
   A: Connecting the two capacitors in series, gives:
$$1/C_{eq} = (1/200) + (1/200)$$
$$1/C_{eq} = 2/200 = 1/100$$
$$C_{eq} = 100 \text{ mF}$$
   B: Connecting the two capacitors in parallel, gives:
$$C_{eq} = 50 + 50 = 100 \text{ mF}$$
   D: Connecting the three resistors in series, gives:
$$1/C_{eq} = (1/400) + (1/400) + (1/200) = (2/400) + (1/200) = (2/400) + (2/400) = 4/400$$
$$C_{eq} = 400/4 = 100 \text{ mF}$$

4. B is correct. All current-carrying wires produce a magnetic field, the strength of which is in direct proportion to the strength of the current. By building an instrument that measures the strength of that magnetic field, a no-contact ammeter can be produced.
   A: Electric field would not allow us to monitor the current, as any charge, moving or not, will generate an electric field.
   C: Some of the components will give off heat as a waste product due to the voltage they dissipate, but this will not be as reliable nor as accurate as magnetic field.
   D: Electromotive force, aka voltage, will help determine the relative size of the current through the device, but will not allow us to directly measure the current though the components, as they may change with time while the battery voltage remains constant.

5. C is correct. Conductance, or conductivity, is a measure of the ease with which current flows through a conductor. Conductance is the inverse of resistance (Ohms). Since we should know that V = IR, we can deduce that R = V/I = Ohms (Ω).
$$1/R = 1/\Omega = I/V = A/V = (C/s) / (J/C) = C^2/(J{\bullet}s) = C^2/(N{\bullet}m{\bullet}s) = C^2/((kg{\bullet}m/s^2){\bullet}m{\bullet}s) = C^2{\bullet}s/kg{\bullet}m^2$$

6. D is correct. When a capacitor is charging, it continues to store charge until it reaches its total capacitance and the plates can no longer hold more or the battery charging the capacitor has insufficient energy to place more charge on the plates. This will result in a horizontal asymptotic plot, once which approaches a plateau value.
   B, C: While the capacitor is charging, it is total charge, not capacitance, which should change with time. The capacitance is constant, determined by the properties and dimensions of the capacitor itself.

7. B is correct. Capacitance is the ratio of charge to voltage ($C = Q/V$) while the electric field between the plates of a capacitor can be related via $V = Ed$, where d is the distance between the two plates. Introducing a dielectric into a capacitor decreases the total electric field strength between the plates, which decreases the voltage, which increases the capacitance. A capacitor with a dielectric will store the same charge as it does without a dielectric, but at a lower voltage. Thus, a capacitor with a dielectric in it is more effective and removing the dielectric will have the opposite effect. Removing the dielectric increases the total electric field strength between the plates, which increases the voltage, which decreases the capacitance.

Independent Questions

1. A complex electrical circuit operates in an industrial building at room temperature. A malfunction results in loss of power to the building, and the circuit shuts down. Following this shutdown, which of the following is expected to be true of the conduction electrons in the metal wires of this circuit?
   A. All of them stop moving entirely once the voltage across the circuit drops to zero, since no electric field is present.
   B. They move in only one direction, which is determined by the applied electric field.
   C. They move randomly, but their net movement is opposite the direction of the electric field.
   D. They move randomly, but there is no net movement of electrons.

2. A simple circuit consists of a battery connected in series to a parallel-plate capacitor. The capacitor is charged and the battery remains connected to the circuit. Which of the following subsequent actions would *decrease* the charge on the capacitor?
   A. Doubling the distance between the plates of the capacitor
   B. Halving the distance between the plates of the capacitor
   C. Placing a dielectric material between the plates of the capacitor
   D. Increasing the voltage supplied by the battery

3. A particle with charge $+q$ initially traveling at a constant velocity v enters a constant magnetic field directed perpendicular to its path. If the particle adopts a circular path with radius r and the strength of the magnetic field is B, which of the following expressions describes the mass of the particle?
   A. $\frac{rqB}{v^2}$
   B. $\frac{rqB}{v}$
   C. $\frac{2rqB}{v}$
   D. $\frac{2rqB}{v^2}$

4. A simple circuit is shown below.

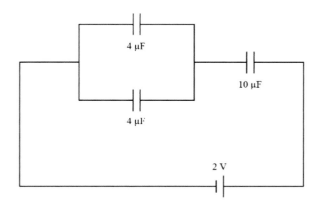

After the battery has been connected for a long time and all capacitors are fully charged, what will be the approximate charge on one of the 4-μF capacitors?
   A. 16 μC
   B. 10 μC
   C. 4 μC
   D. 2 μC

5. Which of the following is NOT a correct unit for current?
   A. C/s
   B. V/Ω
   C. J/s
   D. W/V

6. A material is said to obey Ohm's law if which of the following is true?
   A. Its resistance does not change with increasing current.
   B. Its resistance does not change with temperature.
   C. Its resistivity depends only on its extrinsic properties.
   D. Its resistance at 0°C is virtually zero.

7. Three 5-Ω resistors are connected in series to a 15-V battery and to each other. What is the power dissipated by each resistor?
   A. 5 W
   B. 2 W
   C. 0.2 W
   D. 0.1 W

Independent Question Explanations

1. D is correct. Conduction electrons move freely among the atoms that make up the metal wire. In the absence of an applied electric field, this movement is random. The *net* movement is zero, and there is said to be no current in the wire. In the presence of an external electric field, the electrons still move randomly, but their net movement is in the direction opposite the electric field lines.

2. A is correct. The amount of charge stored by a capacitor per unit voltage is described by the value of the capacitance. Capacitance increases as the distance between the parallel plates decreases (eliminate option B). It also increases when a dielectric is inserted between the plates (eliminate choice C). Option D can also be eliminated, since voltage and charge stored on the plates are directly proportional, meaning that increasing the voltage would increase the stored charge. However, capacitance decreases with increasing distance between the parallel plates, making choice A the correct answer.

3. B is correct. The force exerted by a magnetic field directed perpendicular to the path of a charged particle is given by $F_B = qvB$. This force causes the particle to curve as it enters the magnetic field. Since the magnetic force is always perpendicular to the path of the particle, it cannot alter the speed of the particle. Therefore, the particle assumes uniform circular motion and the centripetal force is given by:

$$\frac{mv^2}{r} = qvB \rightarrow m = \frac{rqB}{v}$$

4. C is correct. The two 4-μF capacitors are connected in parallel and are equivalent to a single 8-μF capacitor. This equivalent 8-μF capacitor is connected in series to the 10-μF capacitor. Capacitors in series share the same charge, but may not have the same voltage drop. The equivalent capacitance of the entire circuit is given by:
    C_1 = the equivalent capacitance of the two 4-μF capacitors
    C_2 = the 10-μF capacitor
    Step 1. Set up the equation to determine capacitance

$$\frac{1}{C_{eq}} = \frac{1}{C_1} + \frac{1}{C_2}$$

Step 2. Find a common denominator for the fractions so that they can be added

$$\frac{1}{C_{eq}} = \frac{C_2}{C_1C2} + \frac{C_1}{C_1C_2}$$

Step 3. Add the fractions

$$\frac{1}{C_{eq}} = \frac{C_1 + C_2}{C_1C_2}$$

Step 4. Flip the fractions to find the inverse, or equivalent capacitance

$$C_{eq} = \frac{C_1C_2}{C_1 + C_2} = \frac{8\ \mu F \times 10\ \mu F}{8\ \mu F + 10\ \mu F} = \frac{80}{18}\ \mu F = \frac{40}{9}\ \mu F \approx 4\ \mu F$$

The charge on each of the capacitors in series is given by $Q = CV = (4\ \mu F)(2\ V) = 8\ \mu C$. Since the equivalent 8-μF capacitor is actually two identical capacitors in parallel, the charge is distributed evenly between the two. Each 4-μF capacitor carries approximately 4 μC of charge.

5. C is correct. Current is the movement of charge, which is appropriately described by units of C/s. Since current is related to voltage and resistance by $V = IR$ and to power and voltage by $P = IV$, current can also be described in units of V/Ω or W/V. The watt, which is a unit of power, is equivalent to one J/s, making choice C the correct answer.

6. A is correct. Materials that obey Ohm's law support the relationship between voltage and current according to $V = IR$. That is, for a constant resistance, voltage and current are directly proportional. If current is increased, then, voltage should increase proportionally while resistance remains unchanged. On the other hand, if a resistor displayed a resistance value that changed in response to changing current, this material would not obey Ohm's law.

7. A is correct. The equivalent resistance of the circuit is given by the sum of the three individual resistance values and is thus equal to 15 Ω. The current flowing through the circuit is given by $I = V/R = \frac{15\ V}{15\ \Omega} = 1\ A$. Since resistors in series share the same current, this is also the current flowing through each individual resistor. The power dissipated by a single resistor is given by $P = I^2 \times R = (1\ A)^2(5\ \Omega) = 5\ W$.

0. Introduction

In this chapter, we cover two of the most fundamental physics concepts for the MCAT: waves in general, and sound waves in particular. The concept of waves is profoundly important because it also forms the basis for our study of light in the next chapter and, to some extent, the review of nuclear physics and atomic structure in Chapter 10. Sound, in turn, is relevant for the MCAT both because of the role it plays in our perception of the world, making it one of the relatively few bridges between physics and psychology content on the MCAT, and because technologies such as ultrasound are extremely important in medical imaging.

In this chapter, we first review the basics of waves in general by covering periodic motion and the general properties of waves. Then, we move on to discuss sound waves in detail, focusing first on the basic properties of sound and then covering specific applications such as resonance, the Doppler effect, and interference and beats.

1. Periodic Motion

Periodic motion is the basis from which we can develop a theory of waves. It refers to a form of motion defined relative to a midpoint, from which an object is first displaced by a certain distance (let's call it y), then moves back to the midpoint, is displaced by the same amount in the opposite direction ($-y$), and returns to the midpoint, at which point the cycle begins again.

Physically, periodic motion can take many forms, although some especially common examples include the motion of a pendulum and the motion of a mass oscillating back and forth on an ideal spring. For all of these types of motion, a graph of displacement over time will yield a sinusoidal curve, as shown below in Figure 1.

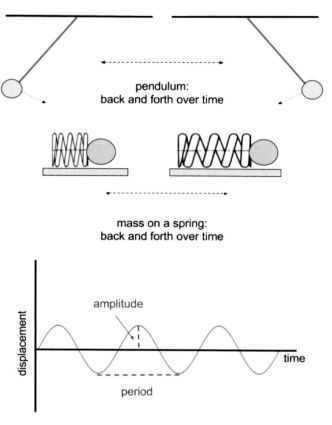

Figure 1. Types of periodic motion.

Based on this curve, we can define several important parameters. The extent of displacement ($|y|$) is referred to as the amplitude of the motion. The period of the motion (hence the term "periodic motion") is defined as the time T that separates adjacent peaks, and the frequency of the motion is defined as $1/T$. Frequency has units of hertz (Hz), with 1 Hz defined as being equal to 1 s⁻¹. To get a sense of how these quantities are related, consider the example of a pendulum that completes a cycle of motion every 5 seconds. We'd say that its period is 5 seconds, and its frequency is either once per 5 seconds or, more technically, 0.2 Hz. We could also describe the frequency of this pendulum verbally as 12 times per minute, although this doesn't correspond to the official units of hertz.

Two objects in periodic motion can have the same frequency but still be out of sync. The technical term for this property is that they are out of phase. The phase difference between two objects in motion can be visualized as the time difference (Δt) between x-intercepts on graphs of their motion over time.

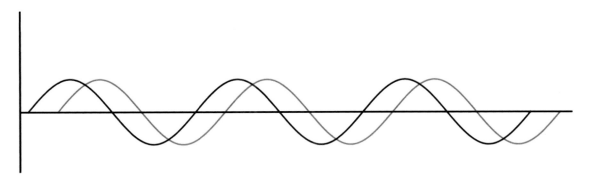

Figure 2. Phase differences.

In addition to the basic properties of amplitude, frequency, and phase, periodic motion is connected with conservation of energy. In particular, periodic motion involves a constant interchange between kinetic energy and potential energy. At the peak of an object's motion, its velocity is zero and all of its energy is in the form of potential energy (mgh for a pendulum and $\frac{1}{2}kx^2$ for a mass on an ideal spring). When it passes through the equilibrium point ($y = 0$), its energy is entirely in the form of kinetic energy ($\frac{1}{2}mv^2$), and then is again converted to potential energy at the opposite peak.

> ### MCAT STRATEGY > > >
>
> These examples of periodic motion are definitely underemphasized on the MCAT compared to what you may remember from physics class. You should definitely understand the interplay of KE and PE on a conceptual level, but beyond that, you should only focus on memorizing Equations 1 and 2 once you have already mastered everything else in this chapter.

In both of the classic examples of periodic motion (mass on a spring and pendulum motion), periodic motion is maintained by a restoring force that acts to pull the object back towards the equilibrium point. In the case of the mass on a spring, the restoring force is expressed by Hooke's law: $F = -kx$, and in the case of a pendulum, the restoring force is gravity (mg). The derivation goes far beyond the scope of the MCAT, but special expressions exist for the period of these two special cases. For a mass on a spring, $T = 2\pi\sqrt{\frac{m}{k}}$. Keeping in mind that a large value for T indicates a low frequency; this means that a spring with a mass attached to it will oscillate quickly if it has a small mass and a relatively large value of k (corresponding to greater stiffness), whereas it will oscillate slowly if it has a large mass or a small value of k. For a pendulum, $T = 2\pi\sqrt{\frac{L}{g}}$. Since gravity is considered constant on Earth, this means that for all MCAT-related purposes, the period of a pendulum is only related to its length, with longer pendulums having greater periods and lower frequencies.

Equation 1 (spring). $T = 2\pi\sqrt{\frac{m}{k}}$

Equation 2 (pendulum). $T = 2\pi\sqrt{\frac{L}{g}}$

These points are summarized in Table 1 below.

		PERIODIC MOTION IN GENERAL	MASS ON AN IDEAL SPRING	MASS ON A PENDULUM
Peak	Energy	100% PE, 0% KE	$\frac{1}{2}kx^2$	mgh
	Velocity	0		
Equilibrium point	Energy	0% PE, 100% KE	$\frac{1}{2}mv^2$	$\frac{1}{2}mv^2$
	Velocity	v_{max}		
Period		T = time for cycle of motion to repeat	$T = 2\pi\sqrt{\frac{m}{k}}$	$T = 2\pi\sqrt{\frac{L}{g}}$

Table 1. Main examples of periodic motion.

To address an important possible misconception, these examples of periodic motion are not themselves waves. However, a solid understanding of periodic motion helps set the stage for waves, which are discussed in the next section.

2. General Properties of Waves

Waves refer to what happens when a pattern of periodic motion (or oscillation) propagates through space. In this chapter, we will focus on the properties of mechanical waves, or waves that involve the actual physical motion of particles. In the next chapter, we will discuss light as an example of an electromagnetic wave that can move through vacuum.

Mechanical waves can be subdivided into transverse and longitudinal waves, depending on whether the direction of the displacement of the particles is perpendicular or parallel to the axis through which the wave propagates, respectively.

A classic example of a transverse wave is a wave moving through water, like the kind that you can surf. The wave itself moves along the surface of the water, which we would usually denote as the x-axis, and the molecules of water that are participating in the wave move up and down (along the y-axis). This means that the wave can potentially propagate across very long distances although all its constituent parts stay in the same place on the x-axis. An example that might help solidify this point is "the wave" that is often done at sports games, in which successive groups of spectators raise their arms; this "wave" propagates around the stadium although no one actually gets up out of their seats and moves anywhere.

Longitudinal waves are mechanical waves in which the particles move in the same direction in which the wave propagates. This essentially results in a pushing-and-pulling motion, which is why these waves are sometimes known as compression waves. However, the same basic principle holds in that the particles involved in the wave stay within the region bounded by the amplitude of the wave. To put this in somewhat more formal mathematical language, imagine that a longitudinal wave has an amplitude A. A particle that starts at the point $\{x_0\}$ on the x-axis will oscillate back and forth between the points $\{x_0 - A\}$ and $\{x_0 + A\}$.

The spatial interval over which a waveform repeats itself is known as its wavelength (λ). For a transverse wave, the wavelength is usually visualized as a line connecting two crests on the same side of the x-axis. For a longitudinal wave, you can visualize the wavelength as a line connecting two areas of compression.

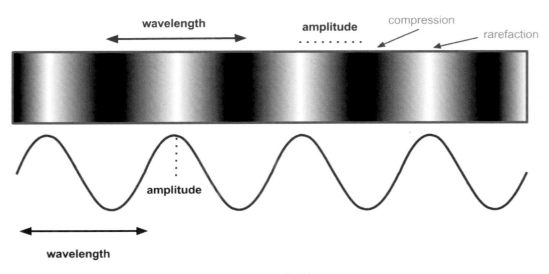

Figure 3. Wavelength and amplitude in transverse and longitudinal waves.

The speed with which a wave signal spreads through space is known as its propagation speed. An important fact is that the propagation speed depends on the medium. The term velocity (v) is sometimes used to refer to propagation speed, but you should be very careful not to confuse the velocity of the wave (i.e., its propagation speed) with the velocity of the particles in the wave. Frequency (f) and period (T) can be defined in the same way that we saw above for periodic motion. Remember that the unit of frequency is the hertz (Hz), defined as $1 \text{ Hz} = 1 \text{ s}^{-1}$.

Propagation speed, wavelength, and frequency are related in the following equation, which is absolutely fundamental for the study of waves on the MCAT. We will refer to it again and again in this chapter and the next.

Equation 3. $$v = \lambda f$$

In this equation, λ is the wavelength, f is the frequency, and v is the propagation speed. Because this equation is so essential, let's do a quick unit check. Velocity has units of meters per second, wavelength has units of meters, and frequency has units of inverse seconds, so we get meters per second on both sides of the equation. The most common way this equation is applied is to calculate wavelength or frequency if we know the propagation speed.

However, as mentioned above, the propagation speed of a wave depends on the medium through which it passes. With very few exceptions, such as the speed of light (discussed in the next chapter) and some general characteristics about the speed of sound in different phases of matter, you don't need to be aware of the detailed properties of various media, but you do need to be aware of this general fact. Thus, let's explore what happens when the v term changes in the equation $v = \lambda f$. At first, it might not seem like we have enough information to be able to predict the consequences of changing v, but it actually turns out that the frequency of a wave does not change when it enters a new medium. This may appear counterintuitive, but upon some thought, it's consistent with common sense: after all, a wave has a pre-existing frequency and for a wave to be transmitted into a new medium, that frequency must be transmitted too. Therefore, wavelength must change. In fact, a higher speed of propagation is associated with a greater wavelength.

While $v = \lambda f$ implies an inverse relationship between wavelength and frequency given a constant speed of propagation, you should take care to remember that all three of these quantities are independent and distinct properties. In particular, be sure that you understand the difference between speed of propagation and frequency, because both of these concepts sometimes get blurred together under the general category of "fast versus slow," which is in and of itself not an especially helpful way of looking at waves.

MCAT STRATEGY > > >

Don't skim through the basic properties of waves. On Test Day, you'll have to apply these principles quickly and under stress, so now is the time to invest energy into understanding them backwards and forwards. One useful strategy is to draw out examples of waves that exemplify contrasting qualities: can you imagine a wave with low frequency and high speed of propagation? Or vice versa? Doing so will help solidify the difference between these concepts.

So far, we've only been considering the properties of a single wave at a time. However, in real-world situations, it's very common for multiples waves to interact in a given space. When multiple waves are present in a given location, they exhibit interference: that is, the amplitudes associated with each wave at a given location add together to predict the behavior of a particle, which then itself can be modeled as part of a wave. Another way of thinking about this is to say that waves exhibit summation, resulting in a "new" wave, the amplitude of which is precisely equal to the sum of its parts.

When overlapping waves have amplitudes with the same directionality (i.e., $y>0$ or $y<0$), the amplitudes of each component wave add up, meaning that the product wave exhibits an amplitude greater than that of any of its component waves. This is known as constructive interference, and plays a major role in the phenomenon of "rogue waves" in the ocean, in which a single wave may unexpectedly be much larger than surrounding waves. For constructive interference to take place, it does not necessarily have to be the case that the two waves are perfectly in phase, although that would certainly optimize the effect. Amplitudes add linearly; if two waves with amplitude y are in perfect sync, the resulting amplitude would be $2y$.

In contrast, when overlapping waves have amplitudes with the opposite directionality, they tend to cancel each other out to some extent. This is known as destructive interference. Similarly to constructive interference, if two waves with amplitude y were perfectly out of sync, they could cancel each other out completely, resulting in a final amplitude of zero. This principle is used in some state-of-the-art approaches to noise cancellation.

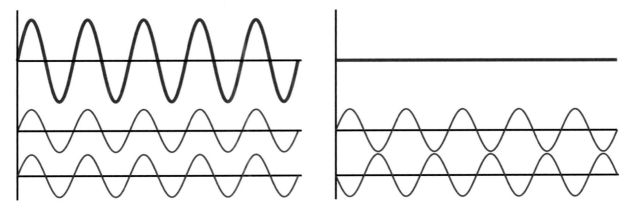

Figure 4. Constructive and destructive interference.

So far, we've been talking about what happens as waves propagate through a medium, but what happens if they encounter a barrier? For example, if we were to create transverse waves in water by dropping a rock into a pool surrounded by concrete, it's pretty clear that the waves will not propagate through the concrete in any meaningful manner. Instead, the waves will reflect back at an angle equal but opposite to the angle with which they hit the barrier. We will explore this at length in the next chapter on optics, but you should be aware that it is a property of waves in general.

A final note in this section: the crucial equation $v = \lambda f$ applies both to transverse waves and to longitudinal waves, as does everything else relating to the basic properties of waves. While it is important that you understand the difference between transverse and longitudinal waves, it is also important that you understand their fundamental similarities, in order to be able to confidently apply these principles on Test Day.

3. Sound Waves

For the rest of this chapter, we'll be dealing with sound. Sound is sometimes treated as an afterthought in physics classes that place more of an emphasis on waves in general and then focus especially closely on electromagnetic waves in particular, but sound is very important as a topic in its own right for the MCAT.

Sound is made up of longitudinal, compressive waves. We produce sound through our vocal tract, and sound is also produced by the displacement of air caused by the movements of and interactions between various objects in the environment. We sense sound via our ears and perceive it through a chain of transmission events that "translate" the pressure signals sensed by the ears into neurological stimuli processed by our brains, as discussed in greater detail in Chapter 2 in the Psychology and Sociology textbook.

> > **CONNECTIONS** < <

Chapter 2 of Psychology

The fact that we sense sound in terms of pressure is important to understand. This is connected with the fact that sound is a longitudinal wave. Imagine what happens when a longitudinal sound wave is transmitted through air and then bounces off a reflective surface (such as our ears)—this reflection is mediated through the impact of the air molecules involved in the wave, and that impact is felt as pressure, which has units of force divided by area.

As mentioned above, the propagation speed of waves depends on the medium they are propagating through. Since sound waves are compression waves, the compressibility of a substance affects the speed through which energy is transmitted via sound waves. In particular, sound waves move more quickly through relatively *non*-compressible, or stiffer media. The degree to which a material resists compression is measured via the bulk modulus (B), which measures how much pressure is needed to compress a substance by a certain amount. High values of the bulk modulus indicate non-compressibility. The equation for the speed of sound also depends on density (ρ) to some extent, as shown below:

Equation 4.

$$v_{sound} = \sqrt{\frac{B}{\rho}}$$

For the MCAT, you only need to know about general trends in the speed of sound across different phases of matter, not in great detail about specific examples of media. At this level of granularity, bulk modulus is much more important than density. Air is much more compressible than liquids, which are much more compressible than solids; therefore, solids tend to have the highest bulk modulus values, followed by liquids, followed by gases. As this suggests, sounds moves fastest through extremely incompressible solids, somewhat slower through liquids, and much more slowly through gases. To give you a sense of the scale of this variation, the speed of sound in air under standard conditions is 343 m/s, while its speed in water is 1,484 m/s and its speed in aluminum is 5,130 m/s. The speed of sound is also affected by environmental considerations such as temperature, but to a much lesser extent.

The intensity (I) of sound is defined as a measure of the power delivered by sound over a given area, or as watts divided by meters squared ($\frac{W}{m^2}$). Intensity is not exactly the same as "loudness," because loudness has to do with how the intensity of sound is perceived by the human sensory and perceptual apparatus; however, these quantities are related and for most MCAT-related purposes can be considered near-equivalents. Intensity and loudness are both related to various parameters of the sound wave, but the most important modifiable parameter that affects intensity and loudness is amplitude, as intensity is proportional to the amplitude squared. The derivation for this fact goes well beyond the scope of MCAT physics, but on an intuitive level, it is reasonable that a higher amplitude means higher energy because, all things being equal, the particles in a wave with a higher amplitude have to travel further in the same amount of time. This increases their kinetic energy upon contact with a surface, thereby increasing the power that is transmitted.

MCAT STRATEGY > > >

The association between intensity and amplitude should become automatic. Don't let any question trick you into thinking that intensity is a property of propagation speed, frequency, or wavelength!

Although the SI units for intensity are $\frac{W}{m^2}$, for most practical purposes, intensity is measured in terms of decibels (dB). The decibel scale is a logarithmic scale expressing the intensity of a sound as its ratio to that of the smallest detectable sound intensity, which corresponds to 1×10^{-12} W/m^2. The range of sound intensity values we encounter in real-life is tremendous; very loud rock concerts can reach intensities of up to 1 W/m^2, and even louder sounds have been documented in contexts like the takeoff of jets. To put this in perspective, 12 orders of magnitude separate macroscopic units of length such as tens of meters from the atomic and subatomic scale. This scale is much too broad to work with for practical purposes, so a logarithmic scale was created as way to compress these differences into an intuitively accessible scale.

The intensity ratio of sound in decibels is defined as follows:

Equation 5.

$$dB = 10\log\left(\frac{I}{I_0}\right)$$

In this equation, I is the intensity of a given sound in W/m^2, and I_0 is the reference value of 1×10^{-12} W/m^2. The purpose of the $\log\left(\frac{I}{I_0}\right)$ term is to identify by how many orders of magnitude (i.e., powers of 10) I is greater than I_0, and the purpose of multiplying by 10 is to make the results more intuitive by spreading out decibel values on a scale ranging from 1 to ~120-130 (although larger values are possible) instead of a scale of 1 to ~12-13. Let's explore how this works in practice by working through examples going both from intensity to decibels and from decibels to intensity.

Let's first see how we would calculate the dB value of a sound wave with an intensity of 1×10^{-6} W/m². First, we need to evaluate the ratio: $\dfrac{1 \times 10^{-6} \frac{W}{m^2}}{1 \times 10^{-12} \frac{W}{m^2}} = 10^6$. Note that the units cancel out and the decibels are a dimensionless ratio. This simply tells us that the sound wave we're interested in is 10^6 times as intense as our reference value. Now we need to apply the logarithmic transformation. $\text{Log}(10^6) = 6$, which tells us that our sound wave is 6 orders of magnitude more intense than the reference value. Finally, we multiply this value by 10 to get a final value of 60 dB. Next, let's reverse this reasoning and start with decibels. We might wonder how many more times more intense a sound of 75 dB is than a sound of 35 dB. Subtracting these values, we need to account for a difference of 40 dB. First, we divide this by 10; the resulting value of 4 tells us that the 75-dB sound is four orders of magnitude louder than the 35-dB sound. We reverse the logarithmic transform by raising 10 to the power in question, so we can determine that the 75-dB sound is 10^4 times as intense as the 35-dB sound.

A familiar fact from our own everyday experience is that the intensity of sound decreases over distance. To some extent, this reflects the fact that energy transmission through real media is not perfectly efficient, which is a general issue with mechanical waves. This is known as attenuation, or damping, and can generally be neglected for the purposes of the MCAT (similarly to how we generally neglect friction in kinematics problems).

However, the more fundamental reason for the decrease of sound intensity with distance has to do with how intensity is defined. In particular, intensity is defined as power (or energy divided by time) per units of area. Sound propagates in all directions from a source, and we can envision this as concentric spheres arranged around a simple source of sound. The surface areas of these spheres increase exponentially as we get further and further from the source, as the surface area of a sphere is equal to $4\pi r^2$. This means that the intensity of sound decreases exponentially as we move away from its source; interestingly, this is similar to what occurs with the strength of gravitational and electrical forces.

> ## MCAT STRATEGY > > >
>
> For the MCAT, you want to be sure that you can go back and forth using the decibel formula to identify ratios in the intensity of sounds quickly. This is a common way the MCAT can simultaneously test you on the physics of sound and your ability to do logarithmic calculations using scientific notation, so be prepared!

While amplitude is the property of sound waves that contributes most directly to our perception of loudness, frequency is correlated to our perception of the quality of a sound. The term "pitch" is used to refer to our perception of a sound as high or low, with high-frequency sounds corresponding to high pitch and low-frequency sounds corresponding to low pitch. The range of human hearing extends from 20 Hz to 20 kHz, although this varies to some extent with age, as hearing loss tends to first occur for high-pitch sounds. The range of hearing perception varies considerably across species; in particular, many species are able to perceive higher-pitch sounds than humans. Such sounds are classified as falling within the ultrasound range. This fact has led to applications familiar to many pet owners; for example, certain types of dog whistles emit sounds that are too high-frequency for humans to perceive but that are easily perceptible to dogs.

4. Doppler Effect and Applications

So far, we've only considered stationary sounds. What happens if the sound source, observer, or both are in motion? The well-known Doppler effect deals with precisely this scenario. In this section, we'll discuss simple examples of the Doppler effect as a way of developing the general Doppler equation, and then move on to cover MCAT-relevant applications of the Doppler effect, such as shock waves and ultrasound.

Let's start by analyzing what happens if a source of sound is moving while the observer remains still. A classic example of this is an ambulance with sirens blazing, because we're all familiar with how an approaching siren sounds different from a siren disappearing off into the distance. As the ambulance moves, its siren emits sound with a constant frequency, but as it gets closer and closer to the observer, the sound waves 'bunch up,' causing them to be perceived as having a higher frequency. The opposite effect happens as the ambulance moves away from the observer: the sound waves get 'stretched out' because the ambulance is further and further away as each successive sound wave is emitted. This is illustrated below in Figure 5.

Figure 5. Simple illustration of the Doppler effect.

A similar pattern would happen if you had a stationary source of sound and a moving observer. As the observer moves closer to the source, the waves 'bunch up', resulting in a higher perceived frequency, and as the observer moves away, it will take longer for him/her to perceive each wave, resulting in a lower perceived frequency. The same basic analysis can also be applied to a scenario in which *both* the observer and the source are moving. It turns out that the change in perceived frequency is proportional to the degree to which the velocity of the source and/or observer adds to the propagation speed of the wave. This insight is ultimately connected to our master equation in this chapter $v = \lambda f$; by putting the source and/or observer of the wave into motion, we're changing v while holding λ constant, which means that f has to change. (Technically speaking, we're talking about the frequency from the point of view of the observer here; the source of the wave still emits it at the same actual frequency).

The full version of the Doppler equation is given below:

Equation 6.
$$f' = f_0 \frac{(v_{sound} + v_{observer})}{(v_{sound} + v_{source})}$$

Using the Doppler equation on the MCAT requires some care. First and foremost, don't jump so quickly into memorizing the equation that you forget to obtain an intuitively accessible understanding of what it says. Essentially, it's just saying that the observed frequency is obtained by multiplying the frequency of the sound when no motion is involved (f_0) by a factor that expresses how much the effective velocity of the sound waves is changing due to the motion of the source and/or observer.

Second, extreme care must be taken with the sign conventions. The term $v_{observer}$ is considered positive if the observer is moving toward the source, while v_{source} is considered positive if the source is moving away from the observer. This can be quite tricky, so it's helpful to connect this with physical reality. If the observer and source are moving towards each other, the perceived frequency will increase, which means that the numerator (the top of the fraction) must be greater than the denominator (the bottom of the fraction). The only way to guarantee this is for $v_{observer}$ to be >0 and for v_{source} to be <0. Similarly, if the observer and source are moving away from each other, the perceived frequency will decrease, which means that the numerator (the top of the fraction) must be smaller than the denominator (the bottom of the fraction). The only way to guarantee this is for $v_{observer}$ to be <0 and for v_{source} to be >0.

Note that absolutely nothing that we said above was contingent on analyzing a longitudinal wave. In fact, the Doppler effect is a property of waves in general, even though it is by far most commonly tested on the MCAT as applied to sound waves. In fact, the application of the Doppler effect to light is fundamental in astronomy, because shifts in the spectra of distant objects such as galaxies allow us to determine whether they are moving towards us or away from us. You shouldn't necessarily prepare to analyze that problem specifically for the MCAT, but you should be aware that the principle of the Doppler effect can be generalized to waves and motion more broadly.

In the Doppler effect scenarios we presented above, the velocity of the object was relatively small compared to the speed of sound. When sound waves are emitted by an object traveling at or above the speed of sound, it is impossible for sound waves to move in front of the object emitting them. The result is that they build up. When superimposed on each other, constructive interference increases the overall amplitude, resulting in a sudden high-pressure gradient known as a shock wave, which is followed by an area of low pressure. A common example of this is the "sonic boom" that occurs when an airplane traveling faster than the speed of sound (about 767 miles per hour) passes by.

A final application of the Doppler effect that you should be aware of is ultrasound imaging. By itself, the term "ultrasound" just refers to sounds with frequencies high enough to be outside of the range of human hearing. Very high ultrasound frequencies, on the order of 1-18 MHz, are used for medical ultrasound imaging. The basic principle is to emit sonic waves with a known frequency and to use the amount of time needed for them to bounce back to the probe to image structures in the body. This is similar to how bats and other creatures use echolocation to navigate in the dark, an effect that has been utilized by humans in sonar technology.

The Doppler effect, though, is specifically applied in a technique known as Doppler ultrasonography, where frequency shifts are utilized to determine whether blood (or any other component of the body) is flowing towards or away from the transducer. In such a setup, the transducer serves as a stationary detector for the wave bounced back from the blood, and the blood serves as a moving source. (This may seem counterintuitive at first, because the transducer also serves as a source in the first stage of the process, but the part that actually conveys information about the blood is the second stage, when the sonic wave is reflected back).

MCAT STRATEGY > > >

There is no way to sugarcoat this: sign conventions with the Doppler equation can be confusing and difficult to put into practice on Test Day. Therefore, you need to make sure that whenever you do a Doppler problem, you ground your analysis in a real-world, common-sense assessment of whether the perceived frequency will increase or decrease. Let this serve as a reality check to whatever math you may have to do.

CLINICAL CONNECTIONS

Shock waves have found some interesting medical applications; in particular, in a procedure known as extracorporeal shock wave lithotripsy, they are used to break up kidney stones, making them possible to excrete and thereby avoiding the need for an invasive procedure.

Figure 6. Doppler ultrasonography.

Let's apply the Doppler equation to see how Doppler ultrasonography allows us to determine the velocity with which blood is moving towards or away from the transducer. The full form of the Doppler equation is reproduced below:

Equation 7A.
$$f' = f_0 \frac{(v_{sound} + v_{observer})}{(v_{sound} + v_{source})}$$

However, using the reasoning explained above, $v_{observer}$ equals zero (the transducer is held stationary). We know the speed of sound in the largely aqueous medium of the body. This leaves us with two unknowns, f' and v_{source}, which are bolded in the modified version of the equation below:

Equation 7B.
$$\boldsymbol{f'} = f_0 \frac{(v_{sound} + 0)}{(v_{sound} + \boldsymbol{v_{source}})}$$

Therefore, if we can measure f', which a Doppler ultrasonography transducer can do, we can straightforwardly calculate v_{source}, or the velocity of the blood moving through a vessel.

5. Standing Waves

So far, we've been talking about waves propagating through media without any real restrictions—that is, about how sound can propagate in all directions through air and water. However, there are some scenarios in which waves propagate through media that are physically constrained in one way or another, and this can result in interesting outcomes. Let's consider a taut string, like you might encounter on a guitar or a violin. If you pluck it, a wave will propagate through the string. What happens when the wave gets to the end of the string? It will be reflected back.

Once the wave is reflected back, it will engage in constructive and destructive interference with the waves traveling down the string. Stable patterns of interference among waves propagating in opposite directions result in what is known as a standing wave. Note that this term is somewhat misleading; a standing wave is not a *single* wave, but rather the stable wave-like product of *multiple* waves. A standing wave will generally be sinusoidal in shape and have areas where there is no displacement (corresponding to what would look like $y=0$ on a standard sine curve graph) and areas with maximal displacement, corresponding to the amplitude of the resultant standard waves. The points of zero displacement are referred to as nodes, and the points of maximum displacement are known as antinodes.

More than one standing wave can exist within a given physical arrangement, but the specific properties of stable standing waves are constrained by the physical properties of the medium through which they propagate. There are two common examples of media that support standing waves that you will encounter on the MCAT: taut strings and pipes, which can in turn be subdivided into whether one or both ends are open.

By definition, the ends of a taut string are held tight and cannot vibrate. This means that the ends of a taut string must correspond to nodes in standing waves. As shown in Figure 7, we can have standing waves with various frequencies and wavelengths along a taut string, but they must satisfy the condition of having nodes at both ends. As Figure 7 shows, we can increase the number of antinodes present in the standing wave arbitrarily: we can have a single antinode, two antinodes, three antinodes, or more. As we increase the number of antinodes, it's as if we're compressing more waves into the same space. This means that the frequency of the waves is increasing and the wavelength is decreasing.

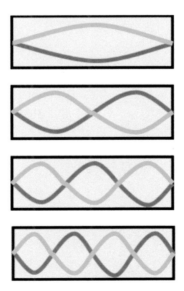

Figure 7. Simple diagram of standing waves.

The standing waveform in a taut string with only one antinode is the lowest-frequency possible standing node, and is defined as the fundamental frequency of the string, and is also known as the first harmonic. Keeping in mind that a wavelength corresponds to *two* antinodes (just as a sine wave passes through peaks of +1 and −1 before repeating), we can see that the length (L) of the string corresponds to half the wavelength (λ) of the fundamental frequency, or λ = 2L. The standing wave that contains two antinodes is defined as the second harmonic of the string, the wave that contains three antinodes is defined as the third harmonic, and so on.

Figure 8 shows the second and third harmonics in addition to the fundamental frequency. Just as we did for the fundamental frequency, where λ = 2L, let's empirically derive formulas for the wavelengths of the harmonics. In the second harmonic, we can see that a single full wavelength is contained, and in the third harmonic, we see that 1.5 wavelengths are included along the length of the string.

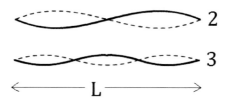

Figure 8. Harmonics and wavelengths along a taut string.

Generalizing these observations, we obtain the following formula for the wavelength of the *n*th harmonic in a taut string:

Equation 8.
$$\lambda = \left(\frac{2}{n}\right)L$$

Since $v = \lambda f$, we can express the wavelength as $\lambda = v/f$. Substituting this into the equation above yields the following equation for the frequency of the *n*th harmonic in a taut string:

Equation 9.
$$f = \left(\frac{n}{2}\right)\frac{v}{L}$$

Let's now move on to discuss standing waves in pipes. In pipes, closed ends support nodes, while open ends are points of maximum displacement, corresponding to antinodes. Based on this observation, we can visualize standing waves and harmonics, and derive the corresponding equations, just as we did for waves on a taut string. In theory, a pipe could have two closed ends. This would be a fairly pointless musical instrument, because very little of the sound would be audible, but if such a contraption were to exist, it would follow the same equations we derived for a taut string, because both ends would be nodes.

In a pipe with two open ends, both ends would be antinodes. The harmonics in such a pipe are shown below in Figure 9. As can be seen, the wavelengths corresponding to each harmonic follow the same pattern, $\lambda = \left(\frac{2}{n}\right)L$, that we saw for wavelengths on a taut string. The only difference has to do with the relative distribution of nodes and antinodes and how they correspond to

MCAT STRATEGY > > >

You should *both* understand the derivation of these equations and memorize them. The point of memorizing them is to save time on Test Day, but you should also be able to replicate the derivation in order to check your work in case of any possible confusion and to build your own confidence about applying the equations.

each harmonic. In a taut string, the *n*th harmonic has *n* antinodes, whereas in an open pipe the *n*th harmonic has *n* nodes. This is just an easily-visualized consequence of the fact that open ends contain antinodes.

The geometry of a pipe with one closed end (which is generally what is meant when you hear the term 'closed pipe') is a little bit more complicated. The closed end corresponds to an antinode and the open end corresponds to a node. The lowest-frequency standing wave that satisfies this parameter will have a wavelength four times the length of the tube—that is, the tube contains the distance from the first node to the first peak of the wave, corresponding to one-fourth of its wavelength. The second harmonic will incorporate two antinodes, corresponding to three-fourths of the wavelength, and the third component will contain one full wavelength and one-fourth of the next one (i.e., five-fourths of a wavelength), and so on, as shown in Figure 9.

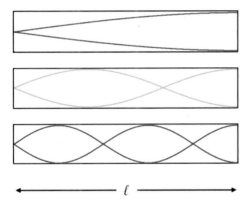

Figure 9. Standing waves in a closed pipe.

These observations can be extended into the following formulas:

Equation 10.
$$\lambda = \frac{4L}{n_{odd}}$$

Equation 11.
$$f = \left(\frac{n_{odd}}{4}\right)\frac{v}{L}$$

An extremely important part of the formulas for closed pipes is that they only work for odd values of *n*! For this reason, we've even incorporated this into the formulas directly. Confusion on this point is a very easy way to miss gettable points, so make sure to incorporate this into your study materials.

6. Must-Knows

> Periodic motion: displacement is y, period of motion is T (in time), frequency (f) is $1/T$ (in Hz)
> – Conservation of energy: at peak, all energy is PE, and at equilibrium point ($y = 0$), all energy is KE; periodic motion involves a constant interplay between KE and PE.
> Transverse waves: motion of particles is perpendicular to direction that the wave is moving in; classic examples include waves in water, as well as light/electromagnetic waves.
> Longitudinal waves: motion of particles is parallel to direction that the wave is moving in; classic example is sound.
> The #1 wave equation: $v = \lambda f$. **If you know nothing else, know this.**
> Interference: when waves overlap, amplitudes add together.
> – Constructive interference: amplitudes in same direction add up for increased overall amplitude.
> – Destructive interference: amplitudes in opposite direction cancel each other out, either totally or partially (damping).
> Velocity of waves is different in different materials.
> Velocity of sound depends on bulk modulus and density: $v_{sound} = \sqrt{\frac{B}{\rho}}$
> – Bulk modulus measures how much pressure is needed to compress a substance by a certain amount.
> – Takeaway point: sound moves fastest in non-compressible materials (solids), slower in liquids (because they are more compressible), and slowest in gas (because it is most compressible). Speed of sound in air is 343 m/s.
> Intensity is defined in terms of power divided by area: $(\frac{W}{m^2})$
> Decibel definition: dB$= 10\log (\frac{I}{I_0})$. Decibels are a logarithmic measure of intensity.
> Doppler effect: waves get "bunched up" or "stretched out" (i.e., frequency increases or decreases) from the perspective of an observer depending on the motion of the observer and source.
> Doppler equation: $f' = f_0 \frac{(v_{sound} + v_{observer})}{(v_{sound} + v_{source})}$
> – $v_{observer} > 0$ if observer moves toward the source; $v_{source} > 0$ if source moves away from the observer
> – Signs with Doppler equation can be tricky: do a reality check based on the physical setup, and whether you expect waves to be bunched up or stretched out, whenever doing a Doppler problem.
> Standing waves: occur when waves reflect back in a constrained medium. **Draw them out.**
> Strings and open pipes: $\lambda = (\frac{2}{n})L$, $f = (\frac{n}{2})\frac{v}{L}$; strings & open pipes have different patterns of nodes and antinodes (nodes on both ends for strings, antinodes on both ends for open pipes).
> Closed pipes: $\lambda = \frac{4L}{n_{odd}}$, $f = (\frac{n_{odd}}{4})\frac{v}{L}$

This page left intentionally blank.

Practice Passage

Air forced out of the lungs causes the vocal cords (Figure 1) to oscillate at various frequencies. Muscles in the larynx can adjust the tension of the vocal cords, thereby producing a periodic source of pressure waves that are harmonic in nature. This source of vibrations is then subject to resonance filtration in the vocal tract, the size and shape of which determines the sound signature of a person's voice.

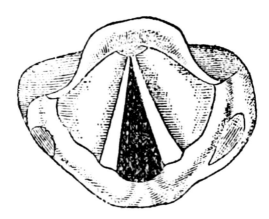

Figure 1. Transverse view of open human vocal cords

Changing the shape of the mouth changes the pitch of the loudest resonance frequency. If a person sings a particular vocal note with their mouth partially open and then opens their mouth completely, the pitch of the sound drops to a lower resonance, while tension in the vocal cords remains unchanged. If the mouth is held in this position and the tongue is moved forwards or backwards within the mouth, the length of the vocal tract can be altered, producing lower and higher pitched sounds, respectively.

Almost all human speech falls within a range of 200 Hz to 8 kHz, which complements the range of human hearing, 20 Hz to 20 kHz. Voice pitch is determined primarily by the resonance amplification of the harmonic overtones, rather than of the fundamental harmonics. Thus, there are few people that can sing bass in the choir, because their vocal tracts are not large enough to act as a resonance chamber for the lowest-frequency vibrations produced by the vocal cords. In fact, a closed tube resonator whose length is about the same as the size of the human vocal tract (17 cm), will produce overtone frequencies that closely approximate the optimal sensitivity range of human hearing, as shown in Figure 2.

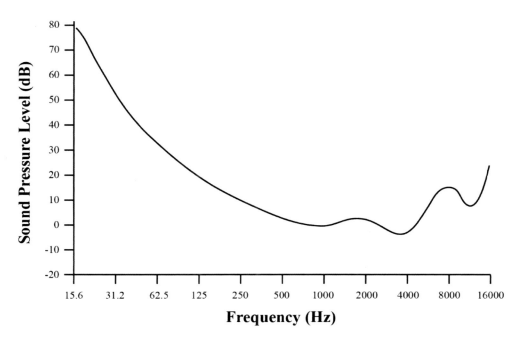

Figure 2. Minimum equal loudness for the range of human hearing

(Note: The speed of sound in air is 334 m/s)

1. What is the wavelength of the highest-pitch sound that the average person can hear?
   A. 17 mm
   B. 27 mm
   C. 17 m
   D. 27 m

2. What is the period of the fundamental vibration whose frequency is 500 Hz?
   A. 2 ms
   B. 5 ms
   C. 200 s
   D. 500 s

3. If the human vocal tract acts like a resonator closed at one end, which of the following frequencies represents a possible overtone?
   A. 500 Hz
   B. 1000 Hz
   C. 1500 Hz
   D. 2000 Hz

4. What happens to the length of the vocal tract, acting as the resonance filter, as a person moves their tongue towards the back of their mouth?
   A. The length of the vocal tract decreases, as the frequency of the sound increases.
   B. The length of the vocal tract decreases, as the frequency of the sound decreases.
   C. The length of the vocal tract increases, as the frequency of the sound increases.
   D. The length of the vocal tract increases, as the frequency of the sound decreases.

5. Which of the following frequencies have a minimum pressure for the perception of hearing that is 100 times greater than the lowest threshold of human hearing?

I. 125 Hz

II. 2 kHz

III. 15 kHz

A. I and II only

B. II and III only

C. I and III only

D. I, II, and III

6. During professional voice recording, the walls of the recording room are coated with a material in order to lower the vocal vibrations in the room that do not hit the microphone to 0 as quickly as possible. This type of signal attenuation is known as:

A. Underdamping

B. Critical damping

C. Overdamping

D. Viscous damping

7. A dog whistle produces sound with two high pitches. These high frequency tones interfere with each other and produce a third frequency, called the difference tone, which is perceived by the human ear.

PIPE	FREQUENCY
1	26.5 kHz
2	24.5 kHz

What will be the frequency of this third tone?

A. -51 Hz

B. -2 Hz

C. 2 kHz

D. 51 kHz

Practice Passage Explanations

Air forced out of the lungs, causes the vocal cords (Figure 1) to oscillate at various frequencies. Muscles in the larynx can adjust the tension of the vocal cords, thereby producing a periodic source of pressure waves that are harmonic in nature. This source of vibrations is then subject to resonance filtration in the vocal tract, the size and shape of which determines the sound signature of a person's voice.

Key terms: vocal cords, frequencies, pressure waves

Cause and effect: Δ cord tension → vibrations → sound of voice

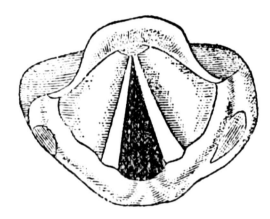

Figure 1. Transverse view of open human vocal cords

Changing the shape of the mouth changes the pitch of the loudest resonance frequency. If a person sings a particular vocal note with their mouth partially open and then opens their mouth completely, the pitch of the sound drops to a lower resonance, while tension in the vocal cords remains unchanged. If the mouth is held in this position and the tongue is moved forwards or backwards within the mouth, the length of the vocal tract can be altered, producing lower and higher pitched sounds, respectively.

Key terms: pitch, tongue, length of vocal tract

Cause and effect: Δmouth shape → Δpitch; tongue moved → pitch change

Almost all human speech falls within a range of 200 Hz to 8 kHz, which complements the range of human hearing, 20 Hz to 20 kHz. Voice pitch is determined primarily by the resonance amplification of the harmonic overtones, rather than of the fundamental harmonics. Thus, there are few people that can sing bass in the choir, because their vocal tracts are not large enough to act as a resonance chamber for the lowest-frequency vibrations produced by the vocal cords. In fact, a closed tube resonator whose length is about the same as the size of the human vocal tract (17 cm), will produce overtone frequencies that closely approximate the optimal sensitivity range of human hearing, as shown in Figure 2.

Key terms: resonance amplification, speech range, hearing, closed tube resonator

Cause and effect: some overtones of the fundamental frequencies of the vocal cords can be amplified by resonance; similar to a closed tube resonator

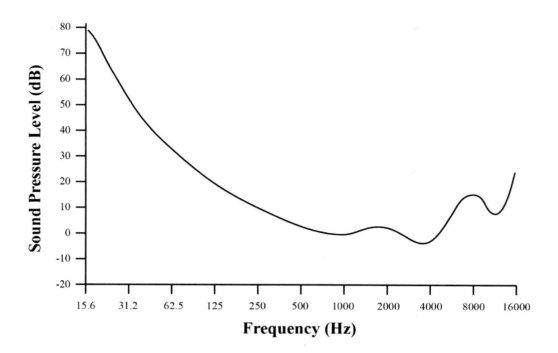

Figure 2. Minimum equal loudness for the range of human hearing

(Note: The speed of sound in air is 334 m/s)

Figure 2 shows the ear is most sensitive to pressure waves having a frequency ≈ 4000 Hz; dB = 10 log [I/Io] where I is the intensity and $I_0 = 10^{-12}$ W/m²

1. A is correct. From the information provided in the passage, the highest frequency that an average person can hear is 20 kilohertz, or 2×10^4 s^{-1}. The equation relating frequency (f), wavelength (λ) and the speed (v) of sound is v = f λ, with the speed of sound in air being 343 m/s. Inserting these values into the equation in scientific notation gives:
$3.4 \times 10^2 = 2 \times 10^4 \lambda$
$(3.4/2) \times 10^{-2} = \lambda$
1.7×10^{-2} m = 17 mm = λ

2. A is correct. Period and frequency are inversely related. The frequency unit of hertz (Hz), is the same as a reciprocal second (s^{-1}), therefore, $1/500 = 1/5 \times 10^{-2} = 0.2 \times 10^{-2} = 2 \times 10^{-3}$ s.

3. C is correct. For a closed tube resonator of length L, the wavelengths (λ) of harmonic vibrations corresponds to λ = (4/n) L, where n = 1, 3, 5, etc. or the odd harmonics. Therefore, the wavelength for the fundamental is when n = 1 and from information in the passage the length of the vocal tract is 0.17 m, giving a wavelength of λ = 4(0.17) = 0.68 m. The frequency is equal to the speed of sound divided by the wavelength, $f = v/λ = 334/0.68 \sim 3.3/6.8 \times 10^3 \sim 0.5 \times 10^3 \sim 500$ Hz. Overtones can be the fundamental multiplied by any odd integer (so 1500 Hz, 2500 Hz, 3500 Hz, etc. would all be possible overtones).

    A, B, D: Choice A is the fundamental and can be eliminated. If you multiply the frequency of the fundamental by the next possible overtone, n = 3, you get 1500 Hz. The even numbered n values are not observed for a closed tube resonator.

4. A is correct. As stated in the passage, if the tongue is moved either forwards or backwards within the mouth, the length of the vocal tract can be systematically changed, producing lower and higher pitched sounds, respectively. The latter corresponds to the situation in the question, producing a higher pitched sound, which also corresponds to a higher frequency.

    B, C: Wavelength and frequency are inversely related so they could not both increase or both decrease.

    D: To increase the length of the vocal tract, the tongue would need to be moved towards the front of the mouth.

5. C is correct. Figure 1 shows the lowest dB level the human ear can detect is just under 4 kHz, with a corresponding dB level on the y-axis of about 0 dB.

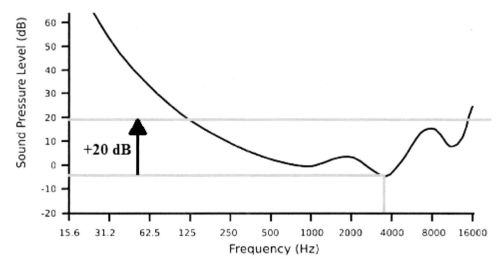

Since dB = 10 log (I/I$_0$), and we are looking for a pressure 100 times greater than that found at 4 kHz, I/I$_0$ = 100, and dB = 10 log 10^2 = 20. Thus, we are looking for frequencies that have dB values of approximately 20. This fits 125 Hz and near the end of the curve, just under 16 kHz, matching RN I and RN III.

II: The dB scale at 2 kHz is just under 10 dB.

6. B is correct. Critical damping just prevents vibration or is just sufficient to allow the object to return to its rest position in the shortest period of time.

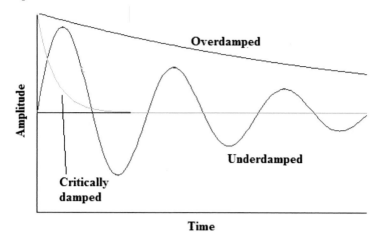

A: The vibrations of an underdamped system will slowly decrease to zero.
C: Overdamping will cause the vibrations to approach zero amplitude more slowly than for critical damping, but faster than underdamping.
D: Viscous damping is caused by such energy losses as occur in liquid lubrication between moving parts or in a fluid forced through a small opening

7. C is correct. Beats are caused by the interference of two waves at the same point in space. The beat frequency is equal to the difference between the frequencies of the two tones. In this case the frequency difference = $|F_2 - F_1|$ = $|26.5 - 24.5|$ = 2 kHz.

Independent Questions

1. A wave is plotted on a coordinate system, where it resembles a sine wave. For this wave, the distance between a peak and an adjacent trough is equal to:
   A. the wavelength of the wave.
   B. half the wavelength of the wave.
   C. twice the wavelength of the wave.
   D. the amplitude of the wave.

2. The legs of a certain jumping insect can be modeled as a single large spring. The spring has a spring constant of 25 N/m and can be assumed to be perfectly elastic. While the spring itself is massless, its end is attached to an object with a mass of 1×10^{-4} kg. The spring is completely compressed, then released, and the mass is observed to have a velocity of 1 m/s when it passes the equilibrium position. Find x, or the distance the spring was compressed.
   A. 4×10^{-1} m
   B. 2×10^{-2} m
   C. 2×10^{-3} m
   D. 4×10^{-6} m

3. The length of a pendulum is increased from 1 m to 16 m. What must happen to its frequency?
   A. It will become one-fourth its previous value.
   B. It will become one-half its previous value.
   C. It will become four times its previous value.
   D. It will become sixteen times its previous value.

4. A sound wave travels from air into a solid medium. All of the following are true EXCEPT:
   A. its wavelength is expected to increase.
   B. its velocity is expected to increase.
   C. its frequency is not expected to decrease.
   D. its frequency is expected to increase.

5. Units that can be used to accurately represent the intensity of a sound wave include which of the following?
   I. Decibels
   II. W/m^2
   III. kg·s^3
   A. I only
   B. I and II
   C. II and III
   D. I, II, and III

6. The sound made by a jackhammer has an intensity of 100 dB, while that heard 100 feet from a jet engine at takeoff is 140 dB. What is the ratio of the intensity of the jet engine to that of the jackhammer?
   A. 4:1
   B. 1000:1
   C. 10000:1
   D. 100000:1

7. In which of the following situations would the observer perceive a higher frequency than that actually produced?
   A. A train blows its horn as it moves at 30 m/s toward the observer, while the observer moves at 30 m/s away from it.
   B. An ambulance horn is played as the ambulance moves at 25 m/s west, while a police car behind it also travels west at 35 m/s.
   C. A tornado siren goes off as the observer walks away from it.
   D. A police car travels at 20 m/s away from a stationary observer.

8. A Doppler ultrasonography apparatus is used to measure the velocity of blood flow in a patient's arm. The transducer is held on the patient's skin and emits a sound wave that hits the blood with a frequency of 2×10^6 Hz. If the velocity of sound through the tissue is 1500 m/s. A clinician observes that the transducer detects a frequency of 1.5×10^6 Hz and wonders whether this may be a measurement error. Assuming the blood flows directly away from the transducer, what velocity of the blood would be implied by this reading?
   A. 2×10^2 m/s
   B. 5×10^2 m/s
   C. 2×10^3 m/s
   D. 5×10^4 m/s

Independent Question Explanations

1. B is correct. The wavelength of a waveform is the distance between two immediately adjacent peaks (or between two immediately adjacent troughs). The distance between a peak and its adjacent trough is thus half this distance, or one-half of the wavelength. In contrast, the amplitude of the wave is the extent of displacement; on a Cartesian coordinate, this is represented by the vertical distance between the x-axis and a peak (or a trough).

2. C is correct. When compressed to a maximum extent, the spring holds all of its energy in the form of elastic potential energy ($PE = \frac{1}{2} kx^2$). In contrast, when passing the equilibrium point of neither compression or extension, the spring's energy is entirely kinetic ($KE = \frac{1}{2} mv^2$). We can thus set these two equations equal to solve for x, or the distance of compression.

$$\frac{1}{2} kx^2 = \frac{1}{2} mv^2$$
$$kx^2 = mv^2$$
$$(25 \text{ N/m})(x^2) = (1 \times 10^{-4} \text{ kg})(1 \text{ m/s})^2$$
$$25x^2 = 1 \times 10^{-4}$$
$$x^2 = (1 \times 10^{-4}) / 25$$

Note that 25 is equal to 2.5×10^1, and 1×10^{-4} can be rewritten as 10×10^{-5} to make division easier:

$$x^2 = (10 \times 10^{-5}) / (2.5 \times 10^1)$$
$$x^2 = 4 \times 10^{-6}$$
$$x = 2 \times 10^{-3} \text{ m}$$

3. A is correct. The equation for the *period* of a pendulum is $T = 2\pi \sqrt{\frac{L}{g}}$, where L represents the length. Increasing the length by a factor of 16, then, must increase the period (T) by a factor of four. However, this question asked about the frequency, not the period! Frequency is the reciprocal of period, so the frequency must change to one-fourth its original value.

4. D is correct. The frequency of a sound wave does not change when it enters a new medium. As such, choice D is the correct answer to this "NOT" question. The remaining statements are true; remember, sound generally travels faster in solids than in air. As such, its velocity is expected to increase as it moves into the solid medium, and since its frequency remains unchanged, its wavelength must increase as well. This is illustrated by the equation $v = \lambda f$.

5. D is correct. Decibels are the units most commonly used for intensity on the MCAT, but the SI units for intensity are W/m^2. A watt (W) is the unit for power, meaning that one watt can be written as one joule per second, or J/s. In turn, a joule is equivalent to one newton times one meter. Thus, watts are equivalent to N·m/s. Since 1 N = 1 kg·m/s^2, 1 W = 1 kg·m^2/s^3. The units for intensity can thus be written as kg·s^3. If this is still confusing, try writing out the units as shown below.

$$\frac{W}{m^2} = \frac{J}{s \cdot m^2} = \frac{N \cdot m}{s \cdot m^2} = \frac{N}{s \cdot m} = \frac{kg \cdot m}{s^3 m} = \frac{kg}{s^3}$$

Thus, all of the Roman numerals represent accurate units for the intensity of sound.

6. C is correct. The two sounds differ by 40 dB. The decibel scale is a logarithmic scale in which each 10-decibel interval represents one order of magnitude, or factor of 10. Thus, a 40-dB difference represents a 10^4 difference in intensity. 10^4 is equal to 10000, so choice C is correct.

7. B is correct. A higher-than-actual frequency will be observed if the source of the sound and the observer are moving closer together *overall*. For option B, picture an ambulance moving down the street in front of a police car, while the police car travels faster behind it. Even though the ambulance is not traveling head-on towards the police car, the two are becoming closer together, and a higher-than-actual frequency will be observed. In all of the other options, either the source and the observer are neither moving apart nor closer together (as in choice A), or they are moving apart overall (choices C and D).

8. B is correct. The Doppler equation is given below:

$$f_{detected} = f_{emitted} \frac{(v_{sound} + v_{observer})}{(v_{sound} + v_{source})}$$

Here, the transducer is the observer (as it detects the returning sound), and the moving blood is the source. Since the transducer is held still, $v_{observer}$ = 0. The source (blood) is moving away from the transducer, so we want to retain the positive sign in the denominator. Converting to scientific notation and plugging in given values yields the following:

$$1.5 \times 10^6 \text{ Hz} = \frac{(2 \times 10^6 \text{ Hz})\,(1.5 \times 10^3 \text{ m/s})}{(1.5 \times 10^3 \text{ m/s} + v_{source})}$$

$$\frac{1.5 \times 10^6 \text{ Hz}}{2 \times 10^6 \text{ Hz}} = \frac{(1.5 \times 10^3 \text{ m/s})}{(1.5 \times 10^3 \text{ m/s} + v_{source})}$$

$$0.75 = \frac{(1.5 \times 10^3 \text{ m/s})}{(1.5 \times 10^3 \text{ m/s} + v_{source})}$$

For the numerator to be 0.75x (or three-fourths) of the denominator, the total denominator must be 2×10^3, meaning that v_{source} must be 0.5×10^3. This value is equal to 5×10^2 m/s, which is the correct answer. This would never be achieved in a real-life setting (note this is faster than the speed of sound in air); in reality, the velocity of blood is closer to 0.1 m/s, though it varies depending on the vessel and location in the body.

This page left intentionally blank.

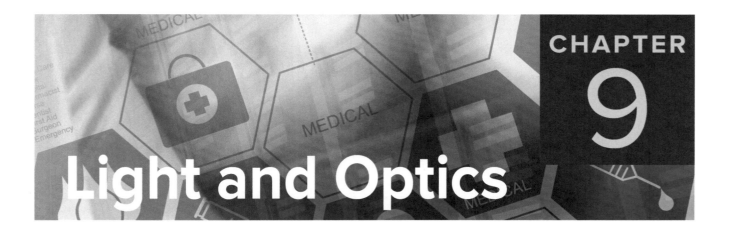

Light and Optics

0. Introduction

In this chapter, we're going to pivot from sound to another extremely important type of wave: light! For all that light is a familiar everyday concept, the physics of light wind up being surprisingly complex. One particularly remarkable fact about light is that it shows both wave-like behavior and particle-like behavior. This phenomenon, characteristic of quantum-scale particles more broadly and known as wave-particle duality, was a revolutionary discovery in early 20th-century physics, and continues to fascinate curious students well into the 21st century. In this chapter, we're mostly going to be focusing on contexts in which light behaves as a wave, while the particle nature of light will be more emphasized in Chapter 10, which deals with atomic and nuclear physics.

1. Electromagnetic Waves

Light is an electromagnetic wave. Electromagnetic waves are transverse waves that have the ability to propagate through vacuum, as well as through other media such as air and water. A distinctive fact about electromagnetic waves is that they have *both* electrical and magnetic components, with amplitude perpendicular to each other and to the direction that the wave is propagating in, as shown in Figure 1.

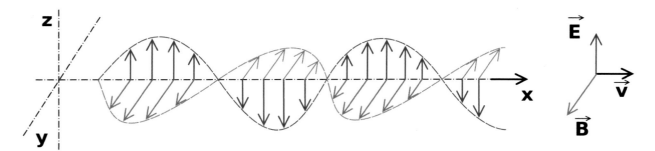

Figure 1. Electromagnetic waves.

Figure 1 is a useful depiction of a *single* electromagnetic wave, but it doesn't give an accurate sense of how the electromagnetic waves behave in tandem. Naturally occurring light is generally randomly polarized. This means that the electric and magnetic fields associated with light waves can be pointing in any direction perpendicular to velocity and perpendicular to each other. One way of visualizing this would be to take the y- and z-axes in Figure 1 and imagine spinning them around. Randomly polarized light can be linearly polarized by a polarizing filter, as shown below in Figure 2.

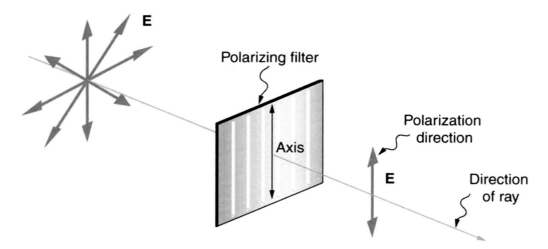

Figure 2. Linear polarization.

Light can also undergo circular polarization. This describes a state of polarization in which the direction of the electric and magnetic fields rotates steadily over time, as shown in Figure 3. Depending on the directionality of the rotation, circular polarized light can be considered either right-handed (clockwise) or left-handed (counterclockwise). In Figure 3, clockwise polarization is shown on top, while counterclockwise polarization is shown on the bottom. For the MCAT, you won't need to be able to immediately differentiate one pattern versus the other, but you should be aware that circular polarized light can have two different directions of rotation.

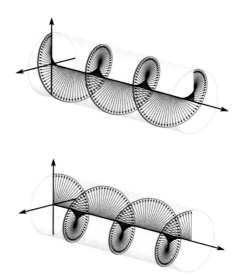

Figure 3. Circular polarization.

The polarization of light is very important for a range of practical purposes. You may be familiar with polarized sunglasses, which reduce glare. Additionally, the fact that circular polarized light can be either clockwise or counterclockwise has been utilized to develop a form of spectroscopy known as optical dichroism, in which the tendency of a molecule to differently absorb clockwise and counterclockwise polarized light is utilized to obtain information about its chirality.

Electromagnetic waves (which are collectively sometimes referred to as electromagnetic radiation) propagate through vacuum at the speed of light (c), 3.00×10^8 m/s. This is one of the very few physical constants that you should know for the MCAT. One important fact about the speed of light is not just that it is very fast (approximately 186,000 miles *per second*), but that it is the fastest speed possible for all forms of conventional matter in the universe.

Visible light only corresponds to a very small subset of electromagnetic radiation. The entire electromagnetic spectrum is shown below, in Figure 4.

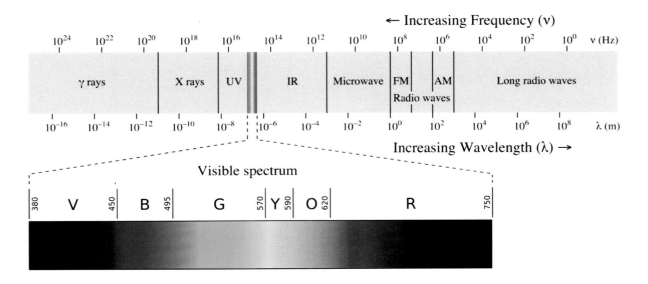

Figure 4. Electromagnetic spectrum.

The electromagnetic spectrum is worth covering in detail before we move on to discuss the specific optical properties of light, because misconceptions about electromagnetic waves have a way of costing students very gettable points.

The first thing to notice about electromagnetic waves is how many "things" that you might not have thought of as being similar to light fall into this spectrum, incorporating everything from radio waves to the infrared waves used in night-vision detectors to the X-ray waves used in medical imaging. A subsidiary point is that the range of variation incorporated in Figure 4 is tremendous: for instance, the wavelengths of electromagnetic radiation alone vary from 10^{-16} meters, which is somewhat smaller than the radius of a proton, to 10^8 meters, which is slightly less than 20 times the radius of the Earth.

A second point to note is that frequency and wavelength are inversely related. This follows from our master equation governing waves, $v = \lambda f$, which is often rewritten for the purposes of light/electromagnetic radiation as $c = \lambda f$. This will be discussed in more detail later in Chapter 10, but we can also relate the frequency of electromagnetic waves to energy through the equation $E = hf$, where h is a constant known as Planck's constant (6.62×10^{-34} m$^2 \cdot$kg/s). This means that waves with a high frequency, and therefore a small wavelength, are higher-energy. This point is so important that it is summarized below in Table 1.

HIGH-ENERGY WAVES	LOW-ENERGY WAVES
High frequency	Low frequency
Short wavelength	Long wavelength

Table 1. Energy, frequency, and wavelength of electromagnetic radiation.

The equations $c = \lambda f$ and $E = hf$ can be combined to give an expression for energy in terms of wavelength. Both forms of the equation for E are shown below:

Equation 1:.
$$E = hf = \frac{hc}{\lambda}$$

The visible light spectrum is often described in terms of wavelength, with units of nanometers. It ranges from approximately 400 nm to approximately 750 nm. In scientific notation, this is equivalent to a range from 4.0×10^{-7} m to 7.5×10^{-7} m. (If these conversions are unfamiliar, now might be a great time to practice!). For the MCAT, you don't need to know the specific wavelengths of each color of light, but you should know the overall range of the spectrum of visual light, you should know that violet light is on the low end of the spectrum (in terms of wavelength) and that red light is on the high end of the spectrum (in terms of wavelength), and you should know the general order of the colors along the visible light spectrum.

You should also be aware of where other types of electromagnetic radiation, especially ultraviolet (UV) and infrared (IR) radiation, fall along the spectrum. Being aware that X-rays are even higher-energy than UV rays and that microwave radiation is even lower-energy than IR radiation is also a good idea. The names *ultraviolet* and *infrared* themselves give you important clues about how these forms of radiation work: UV rays are even higher-energy than violet light (hence *ultra-violet*) and IR rays are even lower-energy than red light (hence *infra-red*).

Devices known as spectrometers are used to measure the degree to which a substance—often in solution—absorbs different wavelengths of light (or UV/IR radiation). This can be useful for tracking the progress of a reaction or for monitoring the purity of a solution. In its most simple terms, the idea is similar to how colorimetric pH indicators are used to monitor the progress of a titration: if the product of a reaction is differently colored than the reactants, then we can use color changes to assess whether

MCAT STRATEGY > > >

The relationship of energy to frequency and wavelength in electromagnetic waves is one of the most important physics relationships for the MCAT. You should practice with this until the idea that high energy = high frequency = short wavelength is absolutely reflexive, because the MCAT loves to test it in various ways.

MCAT STRATEGY > > >

Whether you prefer to memorize both equations for *E* or to derive one from the other is entirely a question of preference, but you should be ready to analyze the energy of electromagnetic waves in terms of either frequency or wavelength on Test Day. From a theoretical physics perspective, the equation involving *f* is fundamental and the equation involving *λ* is derived from it, but from an MCAT perspective, these equations are equally important.

the reaction has been carried out, and to what extent. The difference is that our eyes are relatively imprecise instruments for doing so, whereas a spectrometer allows us to quantitatively determine exactly what is going on in terms of light absorption.

However, you should be very careful about relating absorbance findings to the apparent color of a substance. The apparent color of substances is caused by the wavelengths of light that they *don't* absorb: these are the light waves that are reflected by a substance and are perceived by our eyes. More details about visual perception are presented in Chapter 2 of the Psychology and Sociology textbook. For the purposes of this chapter, and for MCAT physics in general, you don't need to be able to make a perfect prediction of exactly what color something will have based on an absorbance spectrum, but you should know that an absorbance peak for a given wavelength of light means that the substance will *not* appear to be of that color.

> **MCAT STRATEGY > > >**
>
> The mnemonic ROYGBIV, pronounced as if it was a name ("ROY G. BIV") is often used to remember the order of the colors: red, orange, yellow, green, blue, indigo, violet.

> **> > CONNECTIONS < <**
>
> Chapter 2 of Psychology

2. Wave Behavior: Reflection, Refraction, and Diffraction

In this section, we'll cover some aspects of how light waves behave when interacting with various media and surfaces; in particular, we'll review the deceptively similar-sounding terms of reflection, refraction, and diffraction. These concepts will form the basis of our analysis of mirrors and lenses later in the chapter. However, before we get started, there's one background point that it's important to clarify. Throughout this section, we'll be talking about light and illustrating these phenomena using light waves, but reflection, refraction, and diffraction are actually applicable to *all* waves, including sound waves.

Reflection and refraction both refer to what happens when a wave traveling through one medium encounters another medium. There are two possibilities: either the wave bounces off the new medium (reflection) or it continues to travel into the new medium, but along a slightly different path (refraction).

Reflection is fairly simple to analyze. When a light wave bounces off a reflective surface, such as a mirror, it is reflected symmetrically. More formally, we can say that the angle of incidence and the angle of reflection are identical but opposite. This is shown in Figure 5.

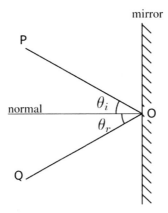

Figure 5. Reflection.

Note that when we discuss optics, we define all angles with reference to the so-called "normal" line, which is a line perpendicular to the optical interface. This doesn't matter very much for simple reflection, as shown in Figure 5, but it will matter very much for more complicated scenarios.

In contrast, refraction occurs when a wave travels from one medium into another. As we discussed in Chapter 8, the propagation speed of a type of wave is specific to the medium that it is traveling through. This includes electromagnetic waves, which means that when a light wave goes from one medium to another, it changes speed. Since the speed of light in a vacuum is the maximum speed at which normal matter is capable of traveling in the universe, it's convenient to define the speed at which light passes through a medium with reference to the speed of light in a vacuum. More specifically, the refractive index (n) of a given material is defined as follows:

Equation 2.
$$n = \frac{c}{v_{material}}$$

That is, the refractive index is the speed of light in a vacuum divided by the speed of light in a given medium. This value will always be greater than 1, since nothing is faster than c. Essentially, the refractive index of a given material measures how much faster light travels in a vacuum than in that material. For example, window glass has a refractive index of 1.52. This means that light travels 1.52 times faster in a vacuum than through window glass. For reference, although you don't need to memorize these values, the refractive index of water is 1.33 and the refractive index of diamond is 2.42. The speed of light in air is very close to the speed of light in vacuum, so for MCAT purposes the refractive index of air can be assumed to be 1 (in other words, we assume that the difference between the speed of light in air and the speed of light in vacuum is negligible).

When light passes from one medium to another and changes speed, it bends. A law known as Snell's law relates the refractive index—that is, how much the speed of a light wave changes—to how much it bends.

Equation 3B.
$$n_1\sin(\theta_1) = n_2\sin(\theta_2)$$

A simple example of refraction is shown below in Figure 6.

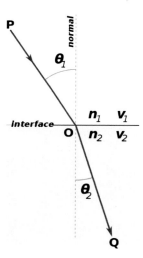

Figure 6. Refraction.

On one hand, the math involved in Snell's law is fairly straightforward, but on the other hand, it's worth investing some effort into developing intuitions about how the angle θ changes with the refractive index. We can rearrange Snell's law to focus on θ as follows:

Equation 3B.
$$\sin(\theta_2) = (\tfrac{n_1}{n_2})\sin(\theta_1)$$

Since the sine of θ increases (although non-linearly) as the angle increases from 0° to 90°, this reformulation of Snell's law tells us that θ_2 is greater than θ_1 if the ratio of $\frac{n_1}{n_2}$ is greater than 1. Another way of saying this, even more simply, is that the angle of the light ray to the normal will increase if the light wave is speeding up as it goes from one medium to the other, and conversely, that the angle to the normal will decrease if the light wave is slowing down. The latter scenario is shown in Figure 6, as light moves from air to water.

> **MCAT STRATEGY > > >**
>
> Snell's law is an example of where it's extremely important to remember that all angles in optics are defined *to the normal*.

An important special case occurs when light is moving into a medium with a smaller index of refraction (that is, when $n_2 > n_1$, or when light is speeding up as it moves into the new medium). A classic example of this is when light is moving from water to air. As this happens, Snell's law tells us that the angle θ with the normal will increase—in other words, the ray of light will be bent further away from the normal. As the angle of the incident ray (θ_1) increases, there will come a point where the angle of the refracted ray (θ_2) reaches 90°. This is known as the critical angle. The next question we might ask would be what happens if we increase the angle of the incident ray even more. As we go beyond the critical angle, the light can no longer refract at all. Instead, all of the light rays are reflected within the original medium. This is known as total internal reflection, and is illustrated schematically in Figure 7.

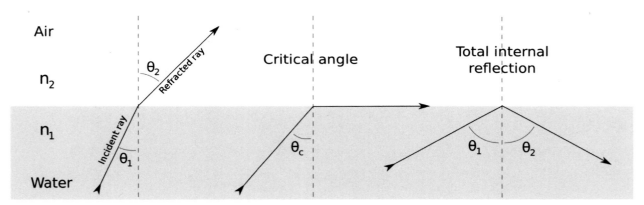

Figure 7. Total internal reflection.

Total internal reflection has many applications in communications and optics, but can also be appreciated in everyday contexts. For example, in a swimming pool, you may notice that when you are just barely submerged in the water and open your eyes underwater, the surface of the water seems to have a mirror-like, shimmering appearance. This is due to total internal reflection.

Another important phenomenon related to refraction is exemplified by how a prism can break up light into its component wavelengths of different colors, as shown below in Figure 8. This phenomenon is known as dispersion.

Figure 8. Dispersion of light in a prism.

The reason why dispersion takes place is because the speed of light in a non-vacuum medium varies depending on wavelength. That is, while the speed of light *in a vacuum* is constant, that is no longer the case for light that is moving through a material such as glass. Interestingly, the speed of a light through a material is related to its wavelength. Light with a relatively long wavelength (that is, red light) is not slowed down as much when it enters a prism as light with a relatively short wavelength (that is, purple light). Since shorter-wavelength light is slowed down more, it bends more. This produces the pattern of dispersion through a prism shown in Figure 8.

The final type of wave behavior that we will be concerned about takes place when a wave encounters an obstacle or an aperture. Apertures are the most common example of this setup for the MCAT, and involve a scenario in which a wave hits a barrier that has a small opening. The waves that hit the barrier are simply reflected back, but those that go through the opening don't simply travel straight through it—instead, they expand outwards. This is known as diffraction, and is shown below in Figure 9.

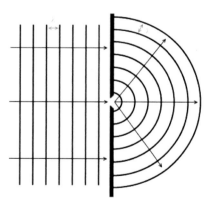

Figure 9. Diffraction.

Diffraction is most noticeable when the aperture is relatively small (where "small" is usually understood as corresponding more or less to the wavelength of the incident wave). If the aperture is large, waves at the center of the aperture will appear to travel through it mostly undisturbed, while the effects of diffraction will be most noticeable at the edges of the aperture.

This is the case for all of the phenomena we have discussed so far in this chapter, but it is worth emphasizing that diffraction is a phenomenon characteristic of all waves. Figure 10 shows a lovely example of the diffraction of ocean waves through a breakwater.

Figure 10. Diffraction of ocean waves.

One of the reasons why experiments involving the diffraction of light are so important is that they played a major role in confirming, beyond a shadow of a doubt, that light shows wave behavior. Moreover, as we'll see below, some experiments with light also provide evidence indicating that light behaves as a particle. This theme of wave-particle duality is a fundamental component of quantum mechanics, which we will discuss in Chapter 10.

Let's now consider what happens when we set up a wall parallel to the aperture and observe what happens as the waves impact that wall. Diffraction sets up an interference pattern in the waves. Some waves will reach the wall in phase with each other, allowing constructive interference to take place, while in some locations on the wall, the waves will arrive out of phase with each other, resulting in destructive interference. Areas of constructive interference manifest as intensity peaks, while areas of destructive interference manifest as areas of darkness. Diffraction patterns vary depending on the arrangement of the aperture(s); the simplest setup, single-slit diffraction, is shown below in Figure 11.

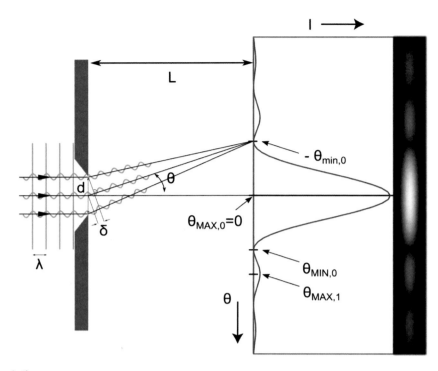

Figure 11. Single-slit diffraction.

As you can see in Figure 11, single-slit diffraction is characterized by a massive intensity peak at the center of the diffraction pattern, followed by alternating areas of gradually weaker intensity peaks and areas of darkness as you move up or down from the center. It is generally considered most useful to characterize single-slit diffraction patterns in terms of locating the minima, or areas that exhibit destructive interference. The following equation gives the location of the mth minimum for light waves with wavelength λ in a single-slit setup with an aperture of length A:

Equation 4.
$$A\sin(\theta) = m\lambda$$

MCAT STRATEGY > > >

You can remember that *single*-slit diffraction gives rise to a *single* massive intensity peak at the center of the wall onto which the light is projected.

Since for a given wavelength of light, the term $m\lambda$ will be constant (or, more accurately, a series of constants depending on the numerical values of m), this means that A and $\sin(\theta)$—and therefore θ itself—are inversely related. In other words, a wider aperture will produce narrower, more closely separated areas of intensity, and vice versa.

Diffraction setups are not limited to single slits. Another famous example of diffraction patterns occurs in a double-slit arrangement. A schematic version of a two-slit diffraction setup is shown below in Figure 12.

Figure 12. Double-slit diffraction setup.

Some assumptions are generally made when analyzing double-slit diffraction, although the details are not extremely important for the MCAT. For instance, we assume that the width of each of the two apertures (the variable we called *A* when analyzing single-slit diffraction) is negligible compared to the distance between them (*D*), and we also assume that the optical screen is separated from the screen with two slits by a much greater distance than *D*.

As can be seen in Figure 12, double-slit diffraction is characterized by a much more even distribution of minima and maxima than single-slit diffraction. The formula for the *n*th maximum is given as follows, and somewhat confusingly, is similar to the formula for the *minima* given above for single-slit diffraction:

Equation 5.
$$D\sin(\theta) = n\lambda$$

This equation implies that maxima occur at whole-number multiples of the wavelength (λ), so it is not surprising that the minima occur at half-wavelengths. The formula for the *n*th minimum in double-slit refraction is given below:

Equation 6.
$$D\sin(\theta) = \left(n + \tfrac{1}{2}\right)\lambda$$

The difference between these two equations may seem confusing, but the mathematical formalism in question is just a fancy way of saying that maxima occur at whole-number multiples of the wavelength and that minima are evenly spaced in between. One important difference between the equations governing double-slit interference and the equation we used to analyze single-slit interference is that for single-slit interference, we care about *A* (the size of the aperture), whereas for double-slit interference, we care about *D*, the distance between the apertures.

The double-slit experimental setup shown in Figure 12 is surprisingly old. The same basic arrangement was used in an experiment conducted by the physicist Thomas Young in 1803, over a century before the principles of quantum mechanics were finally articulated. Since diffraction patterns are characteristic of waves, this experiment provided key evidence in support of the hypothesis that light has a wave nature. Interestingly, this experiment has also provided evidence for the particle nature of light. This seems paradoxical, but it can be experimentally confirmed that if photons are permitted to move one-by-one through the slits, they will impact the optical screen as particles that show a probabilistic distribution, gradually building up to form coherent patterns of maxima and minima. This basic principle is shown in Figure 13, which illustrates the results when this experiment was performed by a Japanese physicist, Akira Tonomura, using electrons.

Figure 13. Double-slit diffraction with electrons.

There is no need to limit ourselves to one or two slits. Combining thousands (or more) tiny slits into a small area results in what is known as a diffraction grating. Diffraction gratings are used in a wide range of optical instruments and produce difficult-to-predict optical patterns due to the emergence of very complex interference patterns. An everyday example is provided by the grooves on a DVD. If you hold the data-containing side of a DVD up to the light and move it around, changing the angle, you will see an interplay of colors due to complex diffraction patterns.

Although real-world diffraction patterns can be complex, the diffraction from X-rays incident on crystalline structures has been analyzed to obtain information about the three-dimensional structures in question. Figure 14 shows the results of X-ray diffraction (also known as X-ray crystallography) applied to a sample of Martian soil in 2012. This image allowed scientists to determine that the soil it was taken from had a chemical composition similar to some volcanic soils in Hawaii. You might look at Figure 14 and wonder how on earth it is possible to induce such specific information from such an abstract-looking image, and that's precisely the point: X-ray diffraction analysis is a highly-specialized technique requiring high-powered quantitative analysis.

Figure 14. X-ray diffraction of Martian soil sample.

X-ray diffraction played a crucial role in the discovery of DNA, its structure, and its role in transmitting genetic information. An X-ray diffraction image of the DNA obtained in 1952 by Raymond Gosling under the supervision of Rosalind Franklin was used by James Watson and Francis Crick as a crucial piece of evidence supporting the double-helix structure of DNA.

> > CONNECTIONS < <

Chapter 3 of Biology

Thin-film interference is a phenomenon commonly confused with diffraction. It occurs when light waves reflect off both the top and bottom boundaries of a substance that forms a thin film. Common examples include thin films formed by soap in air, or by layers of oil or gasoline on water. The basic mechanism is shown below in Figure 15.

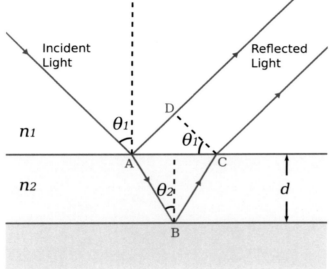

Figure 15. Thin-film interference.

Figure 15 shows what happens with light waves that are incident upon a single point of a thin film, but in reality, light waves will be incident along *every* point. This results in overlapping waves, which means that interference patterns will occur. The shimmering colors that you see on soap bubbles or films of gasoline/oil on water are everyday examples of thin-film interference in action. Thin-film interference is similar to diffraction grating analysis in that both involve interference generating patterns of light, but the underlying mechanism is different; thin-film interference is fundamentally about a combination of reflection and refraction, while diffraction is an entirely distinct property of waves.

Now that we've covered the basic properties of waves, with a particular focus on light, we can move on to explore mirrors and lenses.

MCAT STRATEGY > > >

For all that mirrors and lenses are what students often first think of as examples of optics, a thorough understanding of reflection and refraction provides the foundation for mirrors and lenses. Trying to analyze mirrors and lenses without that foundation will prove surprisingly difficult, so make sure that you understand the principles of reflection and refraction well.

3. Mirrors

Mirrors are substances from which light rays only reflect, without any significant absorbance or refraction. There are three geometrical types of mirrors that you need to be aware of for the MCAT: plane (linear) mirrors, convex mirrors, and concave mirrors. In this section, we'll first review some basic terminology and principles, outline what happens with mirrors of different geometries, and then provide a detailed review of the optical formalism you need to know to predict what kind of images will be formed by mirrors in terms of location, type, and magnification.

> ## MCAT STRATEGY > > >
>
> "Concave" and "convex" are two very similar-sounding words that are easy to confuse. One way to remember which is which is that a *cave* in a cliff wall would involve a *concave* opening.

The first principle of geometric optics—and one that is often skipped over—is that visible objects can be treated as sources of light waves. The light waves generally don't *originate* with the objects (unless we are talking about objects like light bulbs, candles, or the sun), but sufficient light waves are reflected from objects in more or less random directions that we can make this approximation. When the light rays emanating from an object are reflected from a mirror, we can perceive them as an image. A real image is formed in the plane in which the reflected light waves converge again, and a virtual image is formed when the reflected light waves don't actually converge in a physical plane, but our perceptual apparatus reconstructs an image based on where it appears they were coming from.

The simplest example of a mirror is a plane mirror. A ray of light that hits a plane mirror perpendicularly will be bounced back in the same direction, and for rays of light that hit a plane mirror on an angle, they will reflect at the same but opposite angle to the normal, as we saw in Figure 5. Curved mirrors come in two forms: concave mirrors have an inward curve, and convex mirrors have an outward curve. As shown below in Figure 16, convex mirrors scatter incident light rays outwards and concave mirrors cause incident light rays to converge on each other.

Figure 16a. Plane mirror.

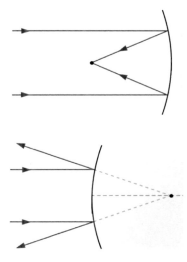

Figure 16b. Convex mirror and concave mirror.

We now have the information to come to a less-than-obvious conclusion: plane mirrors and convex mirrors *must* form virtual images. We can see this based on Figure 16, which shows that parallel light rays that hit a plane or convex mirror will never intersect with each other after they're reflected. Instead, when we perceive the parallel or diverging light rays reflected by plane and convex mirrors, respectively, our brains "work backward" to determine what their source *would* have been, and this is what we perceive as a virtual image.

We can also use the information that we have about mirrors to conclude that concave mirrors are capable of forming real images, because they cause physically real light waves to converge on each other. However, it turns out that the details of what happens with concave mirrors are somewhat complex, so in order to fully understand them, we have to carefully work through the details of how to predict what images a mirror will form.

Let's start with the simplest case: that of a plane mirror. As we can see in Figure 17, our eyes will reconstruct a virtual image that is on the other side of the plane mirror, the same size as the object, and with the same orientation as the object.

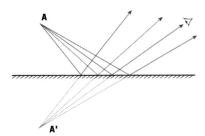

Figure 17. Virtual image in a plane mirror.

In order to extend our analysis to curved mirrors, we have to introduce some additional terminology. We can visualize curved mirrors as being pieces of the circumference of some imagined sphere. That sphere has a radius (r). We can also define a point known as the focal point (f). Imagine parallel rays hitting a curved mirror, as shown above in Figure 16. The point at which the reflections of these parallel incident rays converge is defined as the focal point. In a concave mirror, the focal point is on the same side as the object, whereas in a convex mirror, the focal point is where the virtual rays would meet on the other side of the mirror. Interestingly, the focal point occurs at half of the radius: $f = r/2$. This is shown below in Figure 18.

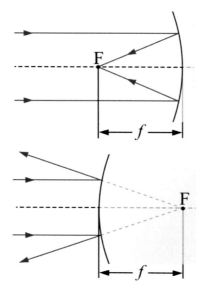

Figure 18. Focal points in concave and convex mirrors.

It's not that important whether you prefer to solve optics problems mathematically or graphically, but you should be prepared to do both. Mathematical solutions have the advantage of being relatively quick because they don't require you to waste time drawing diagrams, but it's often useful to supplement them with a quick diagram as a reality check. At the same time, depending on what a question asks, a quick diagram might be more efficient than wrangling equations.

Returning to plane mirrors, they can be considered as spherical mirrors with an infinite radius, meaning that their focal point is likewise defined as extending out to infinity and therefore not existing to any meaningful extent. The distance of the object (o) is intuitively enough the location of an object relative to the mirror, and the distance of the image (i) is where the image of that object is formed. Perhaps counterintuitively, the image is not generally formed at the focal point. There are two ways that you can determine the location of an image: by using an equation, or by tracing ray lines. We will explore both these methods.

Just as $v = \lambda f$ was in a sense our master equation for waves, an equation known as the thin lens equation is our master equation for optics. As we will see in section 4, it can be usefully applied to lenses, but it also applies to mirrors. The only difference has to do with sign conventions. The thin lens equation relates f, o, and i as follows:

Equation 7.

$$\frac{1}{o} + \frac{1}{i} = \frac{1}{f}$$

The sign conventions are straightforward when applying this to mirrors: positive values correspond to being in front of the shiny part of the mirror, and negative values correspond to being behind the mirror. Therefore, concave mirrors have a focal length (f) > 0, and convex mirrors have a focal length (f) < 0. Magnification can be defined in terms of i and o as follows:

Equation 8.

$$m = -\frac{i}{o}$$

This is a fairly simple equation, and is equivalent to stating that the magnification is equal to the ratio of the size of the image to the size of the object, which is intuitively straightforward. The reason why talking about the distance of the image/object from the mirror is equivalent to talking about the size of the image is that light rays move linearly. More specifically, as an image becomes farther away from the mirror, it gets bigger. (If this seems unclear for the time being, review magnification in light of the ray diagrams presented below.) The final point to make with magnification is the sign convention: a negative value means that the image is inverted compared to the object, which corresponds to it being real, as we will see below (although this point also follows from the sign conventions we outlined above).

For ray diagrams, we want to trace two specific rays in most cases. One ray extends parallel from the top of the object, and when it is reflected, will travel through the focal point of the mirror (either in a real or virtual manner). This follows from the definition of the focal point that we presented above. The second ray is drawn from the top of the object, but at an angle such that either it intersects the focal point (or, if the object is closer to the mirror than the focal point, such that it can be extended backwards to the focal point). This second ray will be reflected from the mirror in a line parallel to the normal. Having drawn these rays, the image can be found very simply: it will be wherever these two rays intersect, and they will intersect at a point that tells you how large the image is.

> ### MCAT STRATEGY > > >
>
> This method of ray tracing is much simpler than you will find in many textbooks—in a nutshell, you will draw one ray that's parallel to the normal as it approaches the mirror and another ray that's parallel to the normal as it's reflected from the mirror. That's it! However, to apply this method successfully, you do have to be flexible about virtual ray lines, in addition to understanding the fundamentals of what terms like "focal length" refer to.

In some cases, it might not be convenient to draw a ray traveling through the focal point (the second ray discussed above); if you run into that situation, you can alternately draw a ray that travels from the top of the object to hit the center of the mirror, at which point it will reflect symmetrically. The image will be found where either the real or virtual path of that ray intersects with that of the first ray.

With all of the above in mind, we can now translate our intuitive understanding of how the different types of mirrors function into a more rigorous understanding.

For a plane mirror, the focal distance is defined as infinity, and we can approximate $1/\infty$ as 0. Therefore, we can apply the thin lens equation as follows:

Equation 9A. $$\frac{1}{o} + \frac{1}{i} = \frac{1}{f} \rightarrow \frac{1}{o} + \frac{1}{i} = \frac{1}{\infty} \rightarrow \frac{1}{o} + \frac{1}{i} = 0$$

Equation 9B. $$\frac{1}{o} = -\frac{1}{i}$$

This means that $o = -i$. Substituting this into the magnification equation, we get:

Equation 10. $$m = -\frac{i}{o} = -\frac{i}{-i} = 1$$

This is just confirming what we already know: the image formed by a plane mirror is virtual, upright, at the same distance as the object, and does not show any magnification. Nonetheless, working through the equations to see how these facts are expressed mathematically is a useful exercise. It may also be worth noting that our method of ray tracing breaks down here, because we don't have any useful way of drawing a focal point at infinity. If we were to try to do this, we'd just get a bunch of parallel lines bouncing back from the mirror.

Next, let's turn to convex mirrors, for which $f < 0$. Where will the image be? We can solve for this by rearranging the thin lens equation as follows:

Equation 11. $$\frac{1}{i} = \frac{1}{f} - \frac{1}{o}$$

We can safely assume in the context of mirrors that $o > 0$ (i.e., that we're dealing with objects placed in front of mirrors, not behind them). Since $f < 0$ and $o > 0$, we can see that $\frac{1}{i} < 0$, because we're subtracting a positive number from a negative number, and therefore that $i < 0$, meaning that the image will be virtual.

Turning to the magnification equation, let's make the fact that $i < 0$ more explicit by referring to it as $-i$. This gives us $m = -\frac{-i}{o}$, or $m = +\frac{i}{o}$ because the two negative signs cancel out. Unlike plane mirrors, we can't conclude anything about the magnification in absolute terms, which will depend on the actual values of i and o. However, we can see that it will be positive, meaning that the image will be upright.

We can confirm the reasoning above by using a ray diagram, as shown below in Figure 19. Note that in Figure 19, we drew a ray hitting the center of the mirror and reflecting symmetrically, which is an alternate possibility that we discussed above.

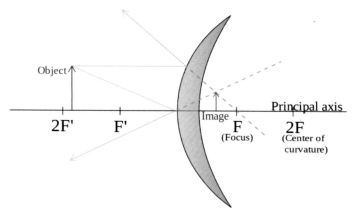

Figure 19. Ray diagram of a convex mirror.

Next, let's turn to concave mirrors, for which $f > 0$. As with convex mirrors, we can rewrite the thin lens equation to solve for i:

Equation 12.
$$\frac{1}{i} = \frac{1}{f} - \frac{1}{o}$$

As before, let's assume that $o > 0$ (i.e., that the object is in front of the mirror). Since $f > 0$ and $o > 0$, solving for i involves subtracting a positive number from another positive number. The outcome of this will depend on the specific values of f and o. Let's work through our options, using specific numbers: in particular, we'll use various combinations of 2 and 20, because picking sharply different numbers will make the outcomes in terms of positive, negative, and zero easier to see. (Note that the units don't matter here, as long as they're consistent). There are three cases we need to analyze: $o > f$, $o = f$, and $o < f$. Visually, these possibilities correspond to starting with an object located far from the mirror and moving it closer.

1. $o > f$. This means that the object is more distant than the focal point. In this case, let's say that $o = 20$ and $f = 2$. The term $\frac{1}{f} - \frac{1}{o}$ then becomes $\frac{1}{2} - \frac{1}{20}$, which is clearly greater than 0. This means that i is positive, and that we have a real image. The magnification formula will yield a negative sign, indicating that the image is inverted.

2. $o = f$. This means that the object is placed at the focal point. Let's say that o and f are both 2 here. The term $\frac{1}{f} - \frac{1}{o}$ then becomes $\frac{1}{2} - \frac{1}{2}$, which equals zero. Using the approximations common in optics, if $\frac{1}{i} = 0$, then i would be considered infinite by convention. This means that no image is formed. The magnification formula would yield a meaningless value here as well.

3. $o < f$. This means that the object is closer to the mirror than the focal point. In this case, let's say that $o = 2$ and $f = 20$. The term $\frac{1}{f} - \frac{1}{o}$ then becomes $\frac{1}{20} - \frac{1}{2}$, which is less than 0. This means that i is negative, indicating that the image is now virtual, and the magnification formula will show that the image is upright, because the two negative signs (one in the formula itself, one in i) will cancel out, as we saw for convex mirrors.

These three cases can also be explored using ray diagrams, as shown below.

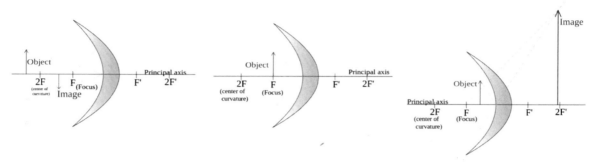

Figure 20. Three cases of a concave mirror.

Table 2 summarizes what we have discussed regarding real and virtual images.

	REAL IMAGES	VIRTUAL IMAGES
Formed by	Real rays	Back-traced rays
Located	In front of the mirror	Behind the mirror
Orientation	Inverted	Upright
Sign of i	Positive	Negative
Type of mirror	Concave, only if $o > f$	Plane, convex, concave if $o < f$

Table 2. Real and virtual images.

The content of Table 2 and the thin lens equation ($\frac{1}{o} + \frac{1}{i} = \frac{1}{f}$) should be automatic on Test Day; a thorough understanding of these two pieces of information and everything that they imply will allow you to answer questions about mirrors quickly and accurately.

4. Lenses

Lenses are our final major topic in this chapter. Although you may remember lenses as being a very complicated and demanding subject in physics class, given what we have already covered about the nature of light and mirrors, extending these principles to lenses at the level expected of you for the MCAT will be relatively straightforward.

The basic difference between lenses and mirrors is that light passes through lenses, which are typically made of glass. Light is refracted both upon entering a lens and upon exiting a lens, and lenses differ in terms of whether they cause the refracted rays to converge or diverge. As shown in Figure 21, convex lenses cause rays to converge, while concave lenses cause them to diverge.

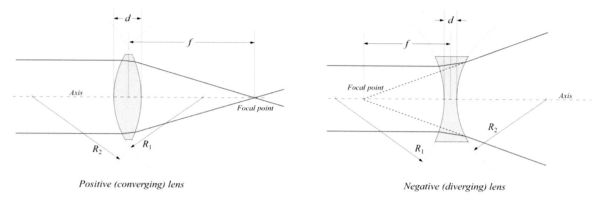

Positive (converging) lens   Negative (diverging) lens

Figure 21. Convex and concave lenses.

The lenses illustrated in Figure 21 contain a term (d) referring to the thickness of the lens. However, we often assume that this thickness is negligible, resulting in so-called thin lenses. If we make that assumption, unsurprisingly, it turns out that we can define the focal length in the same way and apply the thin lens equation. We saw it before in section 3, but it is repeated below:

Equation 13.
$$\frac{1}{o} + \frac{1}{i} = \frac{1}{f}$$

In almost all circumstances on the MCAT, you will be able to apply the thin lens equation. However, if we do have to account for the thickness of the lens, the index of refraction of the lens becomes important. A historically important equation known as the lensmaker's equation allows the focal length (f) to be determined in terms of the index of refraction of the lens (n) and the radii of curvature of each face of the lens (r_1 and r_2):

Equation 14.
$$\frac{1}{f} = (n - 1)(\frac{1}{r_1} - \frac{1}{r_2})$$

Understanding the sign conventions of how the thin lens equation is applied to lenses is very important. The basic commonality in the sign conventions as applied to mirrors and lenses is that real images are formed by real light rays, and that we use positive signs to refer to real images. The main difference is that light rays pass through lenses but are reflected by mirrors, meaning that real images will be on the other side of the lens from the source of light, while virtual images will be on the same side. Based on this convention, f will be positive for convex (converging) lenses, while it will be negative for concave (diverging lenses). This is also a point of similarity between lenses and mirrors.

Since lenses are used for a wide range of practical applications, it's helpful to have a measure of how "powerful" a lens is, or how much it bends light. The power of a lens (P) is defined as the inverse of the focal length in meters.

Equation 15.
$$P = \frac{1}{f}$$

The units of power are diopters (m^{-1}), and they are often used by optometrists (if you wear prescription glasses, it's likely that your prescription is given in terms of diopters, although units are not always provided in clinical use). Note that diopters are a bit of an exception in optics in that we have to take specific care to get the units right. In general, when you use the thin lens equation, it doesn't matter what units you use (e.g., centimeters or meters) as long as you're consistent, but with diopters your focal length *must* be in meters.

Diopters follow the same sign conventions as f, so a positive value corresponds to a converging lens and a negative value to a diverging lens. Since the definition of diopters seems to be so simple, you might ask why it's used. The idea with diopters is that having a unit corresponding to the *inverse* of the focal length gives a direct measurement of how much a lens bends light. A lens with a very small focal length by definition must bend light considerably; it will have a large value in diopters, which directly indicates that the lens is powerful.

We've been treating lenses as more or less ideal objects, and like most forms of idealization, this does not entirely hold true in reality. In particular, rays may not meet up perfectly after refracting through a spherical lens or being reflected by a spherical mirror. This is known as spherical aberration, because it is characterized in a difference in the refraction patterns of light rays that hit close to the center of a spherical lens compared to those that hit on the edges. A not-to-scale version of this is shown in Figure 22, which shows an ideal lens on top and a lens displaying significant spherical aberration on the bottom.

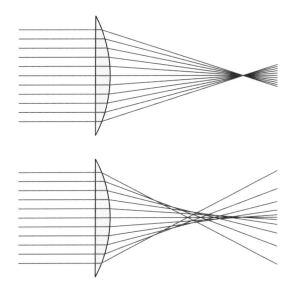

Figure 22. Spherical aberration.

Spherical aberration is a major concern in astronomy, where telescopes are made with multiple spherical lenses and very high precision is necessary.

It is also possible to build systems consisting of more than one lens. In fact, this is common in microscopes and in telescopes. In such systems, the image generated by one lens serves as the object of another lens, which in turn generates a second image. The total magnification of such systems is calculated by multiplying the individual magnifications of each lens, which may be familiar to you from biology lab assignments.

Arguably the most important optical instrument in our daily experience is the human eye itself. Light is first refracted by the cornea, a tough but sensitive anatomical structure that is the eye's outermost covering. The cornea acts as a lens with a fixed focal length; that is, it refracts light considerably, but its activity as a lens cannot be modified. The lens of the eye is located a bit more deeply. It is a more flexible structure that can be controlled to modify how light is focused. The lens works to ensure that images are focused onto the retina at the back of the eye, at which point the images are processed by our nervous system.

In many people, the focusing system of the lens does not work completely correctly. In so-called nearsighted individuals (a condition known as myopia), the lens refracts light too much, making the image focus in front of the retina. In this condition, individuals can see near objects clearly, but not far objects. Nearsightedness is corrected by using a diverging lens, in the form of glasses or a contact lens, to spread out the light waves just enough to hit the retina correctly. This is shown in Figure 23.

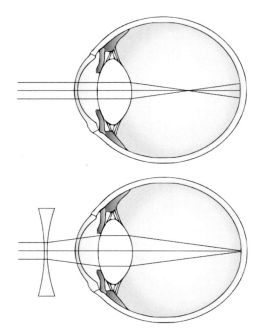

Figure 23. Nearsightedness and its correction using a diverging lens.

Farsightedness is the opposite condition, in which the lens does not bend light sufficiently, meaning that the image would be formed behind the retina. In this condition, an individual can see far-off objects clearly, but near objects may seem blurry. It is treated by using a converging lens that makes the light rays converge closer, on the retina itself. This is shown in Figure 24 below.

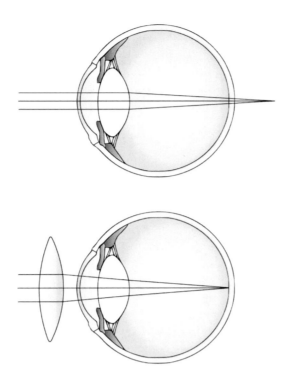

Figure 24. Farsightedness and its correction using a converging lens.

4. Must-Knows

> Light is an example of an electromagnetic (EM) wave; in EM waves, electric and magnetic components are both perpendicular to propagation direction and to each other; can be polarized.
> EM spectrum: *huge* range of wavelengths; visible light is ~400-750 nm.
> Crucial equation: $E = hf = \frac{hc}{\lambda}$
> The apparent color of an object is due to the light wavelengths it *doesn't* absorb.
> Reflection: when a light wave bounces off of an object; angle of incidence equals angle of reflection.
> Refraction: angle of light in a new medium changes due to change in velocity.
>   – $n = \frac{c}{v_{material}}$ (index of refraction)
>   – Snell's law: $n_1\sin(\theta_1) = n_2\sin(\theta_2)$
>   – In optics, all angles are to the normal (perpendicular to surface)
> As light moves from a medium with a larger index of refraction to one with a smaller angle of refraction (meaning that it is speeding up), total internal reflection can occur past the critical angle.
> Diffraction: when waves move through a barrier with a small opening, they spread out.
>   – Single-slit minima: $A\sin(\theta) = m\lambda$
>   – Double-slit maxima: $D\sin(\theta) = n\lambda$, double-slit minima: $D\sin(\theta) = (n + \frac{1}{2})\lambda$
> Concave mirrors/lenses curve in, convex ones bulge out.
> Thin lens equation: $\frac{1}{o} + \frac{1}{i} = \frac{1}{f}$
> Magnification: $m = -\frac{i}{o}$

> Real and virtual images in mirrors:

	REAL IMAGES	VIRTUAL IMAGES
Formed by	Real rays	Back-traced rays
Located	In front of the mirror	Behind the mirror
Orientation	Inverted	Upright
Sign of i	Positive	Negative
Type of mirror	Concave, only if $o > f$	Plane, convex, concave if $o < f$

> Positive (convex, converging) lenses cause light waves to bend towards each other.
> Negative (concave, diverging) lenses cause light waves to bend away from each other.
> Power of a lens in diopters: $P = \frac{1}{f}$
> In lenses, conventions still hold that real images are formed by real rays and are inverted (at least in single-ray systems), and virtual images are back-traced and upright.

This page left intentionally blank.

Practice Passage

In order for diffraction experiments to yield useful results, there must be a regular repeating pattern associated with material used. To determine the spacing between parallel lines on a diffraction grating, students used a red (λ = 650 nm) laser pointer. When the laser is focused on a horizontally oriented diffraction grating, a vertical series of bright red spots is observed on a screen at distance (L) from the grating (Figure 1). The angle θ can be determined from L and the distance (d) between the bright spots. For constructive interference to occur, the diffracted light rays must travel integer multiples (orders, n) of the wavelength (λ).

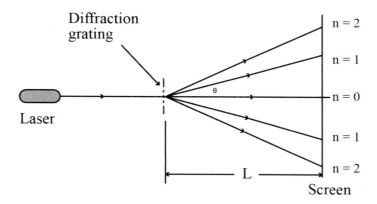

Figure 1. Laser diffraction experiment setup

The Fraunhofer equation is used to calculate the spacing between parallel lines (d) on the diffraction grating.

$$d\sin(\theta) = n\lambda$$

The orientation of the bright spots is always perpendicular to the orientation of the grating. If the grating in the experiment is rotated 90°, horizontally arranged bright spots will result. Babinet's principle states that the observed diffraction pattern will be the same as the diffraction pattern of an aperture of the same shape. Thus, a diffraction grating consisting of two sets of parallel lines intersecting at some angle α would produce two sets of bright spots also intersecting at that same angle.

X-ray diffraction was crucial to the determination of the crystalline structure of DNA. Researchers were able to orient the crystal such that the long axis of the unit cell was perpendicular to the path of the X-ray beam. The helical structure of crystalline DNA is better understood by analogy to the shape of a coiled spring.

Examining a spring held with the principle axis oriented vertically, one would see two sets of parallel lines. Figure 2a is idealized to ignore the curved shapes that would be seen on the ends. The lines form an angle of 2α, where α represents the pitch angle of the helix. A large number of DNA molecules all oriented vertically would result in a series of intersecting diffraction grating lines corresponding to the straight sections of the helix. Diffraction would produce two series of intersecting bright spots (Figure 2b).

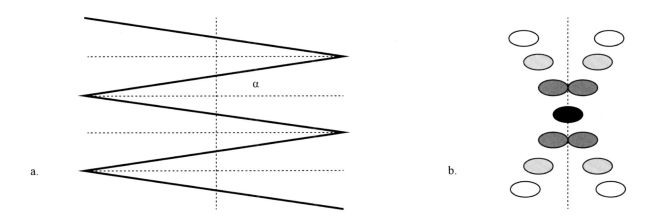

Figure 2 (a) A side representation of a vertically oriented helical coil structure, and (b) the resulting diffraction pattern.

1. A student performed a diffraction experiment using an experimental set-up similar to that shown in Figure 1. If the distance between the laser pointer and the diffraction grating is increased, what happens to the bright spots on the screen?
   A. The distance between the bright spots increases, but the brightness of the spots remains the same.
   B. The distance between the bright spots decreases, but the brightness of the spots remains the same.
   C. The distance between the spots remains the same, and the brightness of the spots remains the same.
   D. The distance between the spots remains the same, but the spots get smaller.

2. A student performed an experiment similar to that shown in Figure 1, but instead of using a red laser, she used a blue laser. How will the spacing between the bright spots using the blue laser compare to the spacing using the red laser?
   A. The spacing gets bigger because the wavelength of blue light is longer than the wavelength of red light.
   B. The spacing gets smaller because the wavelength of blue light is longer than the wavelength of red light.
   C. The spacing gets bigger because the wavelength of blue light is shorter than the wavelength of red light.
   D. The spacing gets smaller because the wavelength of blue light is shorter than the wavelength of red light.

3. X-ray diffraction results from the scattering that occurs when electromagnetic radiation interacts with the electrons of atoms. Which of the following portions of crystalline nucleic acids would scatter x-rays the most?
   A. Phosphate groups
   B. Ribose groups
   C. Purine bases
   D. Pyrimidine bases

4. Which of the following is most likely to be observed in the diffraction pattern shown in Figure 2 if a weight were suspended from the spring?
   A. The pitch angle α would decrease.
   B. The pitch angle α would increase.
   C. The spots would get brighter.
   D. The spots would get less bright.

5. If the experimental apparatus from the passage was moved and the laser fired *in vacuo*, what would be the velocity of the beam if it reflects off the diffraction grating and has a frequency of 100 MHz (Note: Planck's constant = 6.62×10^{-34} kgm^2/s)?

A. 3.0×10^1 m/s

B. 6.5×10^1 m/s

C. 3.0×10^8 m/s

D. 6.5×10^8 m/s

6. If the electric field of the laser used in the experiment is oriented 40° with the horizontal plane, what will be the orientation of the magnetic field of the laser?

A. 50° to the vertical plane

B. 90° to the vertical plane

C. 130° to the horizontal plane

D. 90° to the horizontal plane

7. Students who are testing the apparatus and observe the following bright spot pattern:

Which diffraction grating are they using?

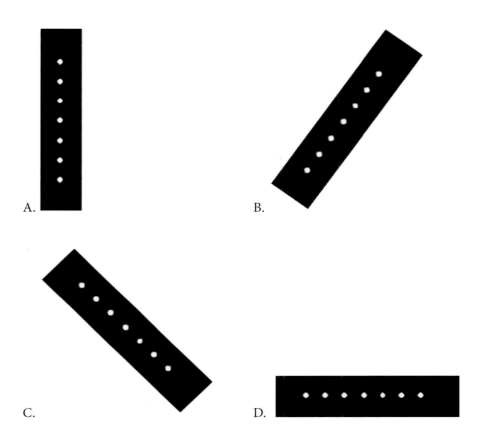

Practice Passage Explanations

In order for diffraction experiments to yield useful results, there must be a regular repeating pattern associated with material used. To determine the spacing between parallel lines on a diffraction grating, students used a red (λ = 650 nm) laser pointer. When the laser is focused on a horizontally oriented diffraction grating, a vertical series of bright red spots is observed on a screen at distance (L) from the grating (Figure 1). The angle θ can be determined from L and the distance (d) between the bright spots. For constructive interference to occur, the diffracted light rays must travel integer multiples (orders, n) of the wavelength (λ).

Key terms: diffraction, spacing, bright spots, constructive interference; red laser

Cause and effect: light hits repeating pattern → diffraction; diffraction pattern dimensions allow for calculation of grating dimensions

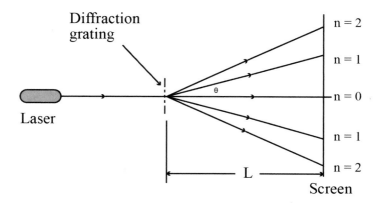

Figure 1 Laser diffraction experiment setup

Figure 1 The figures shows a laser beam passing through a diffraction grating, which causes the production of multiple orders of diffraction (n = 0, 1, 2, etc.) in which the rays are the result of constructive interference.

The Fraunhofer equation is used to calculate the spacing between parallel lines (d) on the diffraction grating.

$$d\sin(\theta) = n\lambda$$

The orientation of the bright spots is always perpendicular to the orientation of the grating. If the grating in the experiment is rotated 90°, horizontally arranged bright spots will result. Babinet's principle states that the observed diffraction pattern will be the same as the diffraction pattern of an aperture of the same shape. Thus, a diffraction grating consisting of two sets of parallel lines intersecting at some angle α would produce two sets of bright spots also intersecting at that same angle.

Key terms: Fraunhofer equation, Babinet's principle, diffraction grating

Cause and effect: bright spots will be perpendicular to grating; $\sin \theta \approx \lambda/d$

X-ray diffraction was crucial to the determination of the crystalline structure of DNA. Researchers were able to orient the crystal such that the long axis of the unit cell was perpendicular to the path of the X-ray beam. The helical structure of crystalline DNA is better understood by analogy to the shape of a coiled spring.

Key terms: X-ray diffraction, DNA, coiled spring

Cause and effect: diffraction of X-rays allowed determination of helical shape, like a coiled spring

Examining a spring held with the principle axis oriented vertically, one would see two sets of parallel lines. Figure 2a is idealized to ignore the curved shapes that would be seen on the ends. The lines form an angle of 2α, where α represents the pitch angle of the helix. A large number of DNA molecules all oriented vertically would result in a series of intersecting diffraction grating lines corresponding to the straight sections of the helix. Diffraction would produce two series of intersecting bright spots (Figure 2b).

Key terms: spring, pitch angle

Cause and effect: X-ray diffraction pattern for DNA → intersection = straight parts of helix; 2 intersecting lines (X) observed

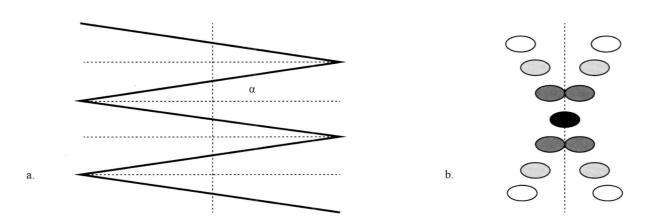

Figure 2 (a) A side representation of a vertically oriented helical coil structure, and (b) the resulting diffraction pattern.

Figure 2 shows the side view of the DNA helix, idealized as a coiled spring hanging vertically; straight portions of the coil can be thought of as intersecting diffraction grid lines, which produce an X pattern of bright spots when the appropriate wavelength passes through the coil perpendicular to the primary axis

1. C is correct. Laser photons are highly coherent photons that do not significantly disperse over short distances. As a result the distance between the laser and the diffraction grating does not have a significant effect on brightness or diameter of the laser beam. Based on Equation 1, the angle of diffraction is unaffected by the distance between the laser and the diffraction grating.
   A, B, D: The distance between the laser and the diffraction grating does not have a significant effect brightness or diameter of the laser beam, eliminating choices A, B, D.

2. D is correct. Blue light has a shorter wavelength than red light, eliminating choices A and B. From Equation 1, there is a direct relationship between the wavelength of light and the sine of the angle of diffraction, causing the spacing between the diffraction spots to decrease.

3. A is correct. The phosphorus atom represents the atom with the greatest number of electrons and would scatter X-rays the most. While it may be tempting to read the question as total # of electrons on the molecule, this is not

the type of grinding work the exam would ask for, and they have not specified which purine or pyrimidine is being referenced, so the question must mean atomic electron ratio.

B, C, D: Carbon, oxygen, nitrogen and hydrogen atoms on ribose and the nucleotides have fewer electrons than phosphorus.

4. B is correct. As the spring is stretched the pitch angle will increase and the spacing between the parallel portions of the helix will increase, but this will not have a significant effect on the brightness of the spots. Choice B is the correct answer.

5. C is correct. *In vacuo* means that the experiment is taking place in the vacuum of space. All light travels with the velocity of c, 3.0×10^8 m/s when in space. Do not be distracted by all the extraneous information.

B: This is the velocity we get if we incorrectly use the equation $v = \lambda f$ in this situation.

6. C is correct. Electromagnetic radiation consists of oscillating electric and magnetic fields, oriented perpendicular (90°) to each other. This will allow us to find the relative angles between each plane and the magnetic field.

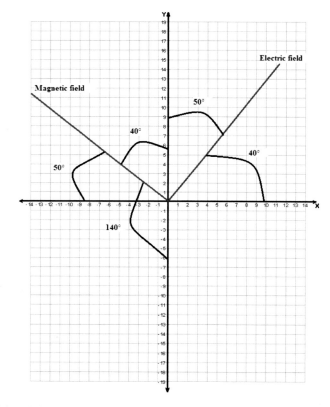

The angle between the field and the horizontal plane is 50° from the horizontal plane in the counterclockwise direction, and 90 + 40 = 130° from the horizontal plane in the clockwise direction.

7. A is correct. Paragraph two tells us that the orientation of the bright spots is always perpendicular to the orientation of the grating, which means the grating must be vertically oriented.

Independent Questions

1. An electromagnetic wave is made to pass through a vertical polarizing filter. The light exiting this filter is then linearly polarized again by passing through a horizontal filter. What percent of the original light will be observed after this second filter?
   A. 0%
   B. 50%
   C. This answer cannot be determined without more information.
   D. Electromagnetic waves cannot be linearly polarized.

2. In comparison to ultraviolet radiation, infrared radiation is characterized by:
   A. a slower velocity.
   B. a higher frequency.
   C. a longer wavelength.
   D. higher energy.

3. The refractive indices of glass and water are approximately 1.52 and 1.33, respectively. A ray of light travels from water into glass at an angle of incidence of 47°. Which of the following is/are true of this situation?
   I. The angle of refraction will be 47°.
   II. The angle of refraction will be smaller than the angle of reflection.
   III. Total internal reflection may occur.
   A. I only
   B. II only
   C. II and III only
   D. I, II, and III

4. A mirror has a focal length of –2 m. Which of the following best describes this mirror?
   A. It is concave and forms virtual images.
   B. It is concave and forms real images.
   C. It is convex and forms virtual images.
   D. It is convex and forms real images.

5. The lens of the eye is a convex lens. When relaxed, the lens has a focal length of approximately 1.7 cm. An ideal, convex synthetic lens is constructed with this same focal length. When an object is placed 17 cm in front of this lens, what will be the magnification of the resulting image? Assume that the thin-lens equation applies.
   A. –9
   B. $-\frac{1}{9}$
   C. $\frac{1}{9}$
   D. 9

6. A concave lens is cut from a sphere with a radius of 40 cm. The power of this lens is:
   A. –5 diopters
   B. –2.5 diopters
   C. 0.05 diopters
   D. 5 diopters

7. Which of the following lenses may be used to correct myopia (nearsightedness)?
   A. A converging lens with a focal length of –0.25 m
   B. A converging lens with a focal length of +0.3 m
   C. A diverging lens with a focal length of –0.22 m
   D. A diverging lens with a focal length of +0.27 m

8. Under what conditions may a convex lens produce a virtual image?
   A. Under all conditions
   B. Under no conditions
   C. Only when the object distance is greater than the focal length of the lens
   D. Only when the object distance is smaller than the focal length of the lens

Independent Question Explanations

1. A is correct. Light, which is an electromagnetic wave, can absolutely be linearly polarized. The filters will "filter out" any light rays that are not pointing in a certain direction. Here, only light moving in the vertical direction will pass through the first filter. This leaves only vertically oriented light remaining after it passes through the first filter, leaving no light traveling in the horizontal direction. Next, light will pass through the second, horizontal filter, which filters out all but horizontal light, filtering out the remaining vertically-oriented light. This results in 0% of the original light will pass through the second filter. In general, two perpendicular linear polarizers will filter out all light that is incident on them.

2. C is correct. Be sure to know your electromagnetic spectrum! Infrared radiation is lower-frequency, and thus lower-energy, than ultraviolet radiation (eliminate choices B and D). Option A can also be eliminated, as both forms of radiation will travel at the speed of light (3.00×10^8 m/s in a vacuum). However, since it has a *lower* frequency, infrared radiation does have a higher/longer wavelength than UV light; remember, frequency and wavelength are inversely proportional.

3. B is correct. Here, the light is traveling from a material with a lower refractive index (water, n = 1.33) to one with a higher index (glass, n = 1.52). In this case, light will refract toward the normal, meaning that the angle of refraction will be smaller than the angle of incidence. We also know that the angle of *reflection* is equal to the angle of incidence. This information is summarized below:

    angle of incidence = angle of reflection = 47°

    angle of refraction < 47°

    This proves Roman numeral I false and Roman numeral II true. Finally, statement III is false; total internal reflection occurs only when traveling from a material with a higher refractive index to a material with a lower one.

4. C is correct. Since this mirror has a negative focal length, it must be convex (eliminate choices A and B). Convex mirrors always form virtual images.

5. B is correct. To find the magnification, we first must find the image distance, for which we can use the thin-lens equation:

    $$\frac{1}{o} + \frac{1}{i} = \frac{1}{f}$$

    $$\frac{1}{17\ cm} + \frac{1}{i} = \frac{1}{1.7\ cm}$$

    $$\frac{1}{i} = \frac{1}{1.7\ cm} - \frac{1}{17\ cm}$$

    Don't panic when you see this math; it's no coincidence that these denominators look similar! Finding a common denominator yields the following:

    $$\frac{1}{i} = \frac{10}{17\ cm} - \frac{1}{17\ cm} = \frac{9}{17\ cm}$$

    $$i = \frac{17}{9}\ cm$$

    The magnification can then be calculated as follows; note that our answer is negative because this convex lens will produce an inverted image.

    $$m = -\frac{i}{o} = -\frac{\frac{17}{9}}{17} = -\frac{1}{9}$$

6. A is correct. The question stem tells us that the radius of curvature (r) of the lens is 40 cm. Radius of curvature is equal to twice the focal length, so the focal length here is 20 cm. But wait! This lens is concave, making it a diverging lens; thus, it must have a negative focal length. The focal length is thus −20 cm, or −0.2 m.

    $$P = \frac{1}{f} = \frac{1}{(-0.2\ m)} = -5\ diopters$$

7. C is correct. Myopia refers to a condition in which the lens of the eye focuses light before it reaches the retina, resulting in an image that forms before it reaches the photoreceptors in the back of the eye. This condition can be corrected using a diverging lens which will increase the image distance and allow the image to focus later (eliminate choices A and B). Diverging lenses always have negative focal lengths, making choice C the correct answer.

8. D is correct. Convex lenses are converging; as such, they usually produce real, inverted images. The only case in which a convex lens would produce a virtual image is when the object is very close; specifically, when the object distance is less than f, the focal length of the lens.

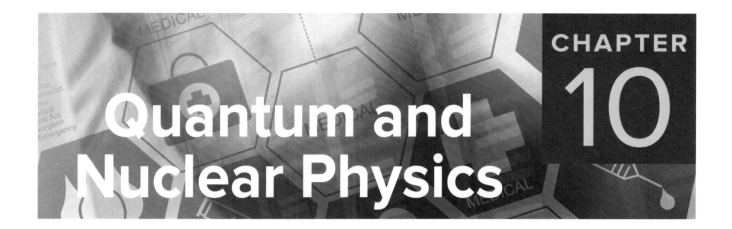

0. Introduction

In this chapter, we'll be focusing on atoms, which are the building blocks of molecules, and their structure. In terms of finishing off your physics preparation for the MCAT, this chapter has two main goals: first, to cover some high-yield, frequently-tested content such as the photoelectric effect, emission/absorption spectra, and radioactive decay; and second, to provide you with a deeper grounding in some of the foundational principles of general chemistry. The structure of the atom, in particular, is a topic that bridges physics and general chemistry.

1. Models of the Atom, Heisenberg Uncertainty Principle

Having identified atoms as the building blocks of molecules, we're now faced with a question that is easy to articulate but is surprisingly difficult to answer well: what are atoms made of? There are three kinds of subatomic particles that you need to be familiar with for the MCAT: protons, neutrons, and electrons. Protons and neutrons, in turn, have smaller subcomponents known as quarks, but the details are irrelevant for the MCAT.

Protons, neutrons, and electrons all have important properties in terms of mass and charge, as summarized below in Table 1 (which you may remember from Chapter 6):

	PROTON	**NEUTRON**	**ELECTRON**
Mass	1.672×10^{-27} kg (1 Da, 1 amu)	1.674×10^{-27} kg (1 Da, 1 amu)	9.019×10^{-31} kg (5.486×10^{-4} Da/amu)
Charge	1.602×10^{-19} C (+1 e)	0 C (0 e)	-1.602×10^{-19} C (−1 e)

Table 1. Mass and charge of subatomic particles.

Protons and neutrons have a mass of 1 dalton (Da) or 1 atomic mass unit (amu) (these terms are not technically defined in the same way, but for MCAT purposes they're basically equivalent). The elementary unit of charge (e) is used to refer to the magnitude of charge possessed by a single proton or a single electron. Protons have a charge of +1 e, electrons have the opposite charge (-1 e), and neutrons have no charge. Although electrons have mass, their mass is very small. With this in mind, you can think of the mass of an atom as being due to its neutrons and protons, and the charge of an atom as being due to its protons and electrons.

Protons, neutrons, and electrons are not distributed randomly throughout an atom. Atoms have a dense core of protons and neutrons that is known as the nucleus, and the nucleus is surrounded by electrons. As we will see, different models of atomic structure describe the arrangement of electrons differently, but a way of thinking about it that is both simple and reasonably correct is to think of the nucleus as being surrounded by a structured cloud of electrons.

As always when introducing a new kind of object, it's important to characterize its size so that we can get a sense of the scales involved. Atoms are very small, with radii generally on the order of 50-200 pm (that is, between 5×10^{-11} m and 2×10^{-10} m). Atomic sizes are sometimes described using units of angstroms (Å), with 1 Å defined as equal to 1.0×10^{-10} m. However, nuclei are *extremely* tiny, with radii on the order of 1-10 fm ($1\text{-}10 \times 10^{-15}$ m). To translate this discrepancy onto a macroscopic scale, let's imagine that the earth (radius, 6.37×10^{6} m) was an atom. A nucleus would then have a radius on the scale of 10^2 meters, which might correspond to the height of many large buildings (although only about one-quarter of the Empire State Building) or the 100-yard dash that is familiar to many students from track and field or gym class. Another way of putting it would be that if we were to include a to-scale model of an atom on a page of this textbook, you'd need at least a magnifying glass to see the nucleus.

The basic features of an atom may be very familiar from science classes stretching back as far as high school or even earlier, to the point that we can easily forget that this model is really *weird*. In particular, it's difficult to reconcile this model of an atom with the principles of electromagnetism that we spent multiple chapters painstakingly working through earlier in this book. We have two basic questions to answer here: (1) why do protons, which are positively charged, stick together and not just fly apart; and (2) since protons and electrons have opposite charges and are therefore attracted to each other, why don't they crash into each other?

MCAT STRATEGY > > >

In general, it's important to ask 'why' when studying physics, but this is especially important for atomic and nuclear physics. When studying for the MCAT, you always want to anticipate passage-based questions that might frame the material in a surprising or unexpected way, meaning that you have to deploy critical thinking skills—even for physics!

These questions might sound superficial and silly, and are the kind of questions that you might hesitate before asking a professor or a tutor, but it turns out that they're easy to ask but very hard to answer. In fact, developing satisfactory answers to these two questions was one of the major accomplishments of early 20th-century physics, and the answers to these questions contain most of the important principles of quantum mechanics.

As mentioned previously, there are four fundamental forces in nature: electromagnetism, gravitation, the strong nuclear force, and the weak nuclear force (in fact, physicists have managed to unify the weak nuclear force and electromagnetism into something called the electroweak interaction, but this goes beyond the level of the MCAT). As the names imply, the strong nuclear force and weak nuclear force are important for understanding the nucleus. The strong nuclear force is an interaction between protons and neutrons that keeps protons together in the nucleus. The weak nuclear force is not especially important for the MCAT, but it does play a role in beta decay, which we will analyze below in section 3.

The fact that the strong nuclear force holds protons together in the nucleus of an atom doesn't mean that electromagnetic interactions cease to be relevant; it just means that the strong nuclear force is stronger than electromagnetism on that particular scale. To take a rough analogy from the macroscopic world, if I lift a bag of groceries up from the ground and hold it there, it's not like I've nullified the existence of gravity—instead, the correct way to analyze this would be to say that the force exerted by my arms exceeded the force of gravity, such that I did work against the force of gravity by lifting the bag up and that the bag now has a certain amount of potential energy due to that work. Similarly, since the strong nuclear force holds protons together despite the repulsive force among them that exists due to electromagnetism, a certain amount of potential energy is present in the nucleus of every atom.

This potential energy is known as the binding energy of a nucleus, and this energy is what makes nuclear power and nuclear bombs so powerful. To get a sense of this power, we need to take advantage of what is probably the most familiar and least-understood physics equation in existence: $E = mc^2$. This equation refers to a principle known as mass-energy equivalence that was discovered by Albert Einstein in 1905. The binding energy of a nucleus provides a relatively straightforward example of this principle in action, and analyzing it will help us get a sense of how intense the binding energy of a nucleus is.

Equation 1. $$E = mc^2$$

If we attempt to calculate the mass of a helium nucleus, which contains two protons and two neutrons, using the values in Table 1, we'll get a value of 6.692×10^{-27} kg. The actual experimentally determined value is 6.645×10^{-27} kg. If you were doing a chemistry lab, this is the moment where you might shrug your shoulders, do a percent error calculation, write it up, and move on, but this discrepancy, technically referred to as the mass defect of helium, is empirically very robust. At first glance, this would appear to be a violation of the conservation of mass, but the principle of mass-energy equivalence allows us to deduce that the mass defect corresponds to the binding energy, which we can then calculate using $E = mc^2$.

In the example above, the mass defect is 0.047×10^{-27} kg. Substituting this into $E = mc^2$, we get $E = (0.047 \times 10^{-27}$ kg$)(3.000 \times 10^8$ m/s$^2)^2 = 4.23 \times 10^{-12}$ J. This is still a tiny amount, but note that it is *fifteen* orders of magnitude larger than the mass of an individual proton or neutron. Let's try to apply this to a more macroscopically accessible quantity; say, one mole of H_2, which by definition (Avogadro's number) contains 6.02×10^{23} H_2 molecules or 1.204×10^{24} H atoms (taking into account the fact that helium is a diatomic gas in its natural state). This means that the total mass defect in a mole of H_2 would correspond to $(4.23 \times 10^{-12}$ J/H nucleus$)(1.204 \times 10^{24}$ H nuclei$) = 5.09 \times 10^{12}$ J. This is a ludicrous amount of energy, corresponding to ~1/60 of the energy released by the atomic bomb dropped on Hiroshima in World War II—from only four grams of helium!

As a brief note about units, it is often inconvenient to use joules to talk about energy on the subatomic scale, because we would have to use very, very small numbers. For that reason, you may sometimes see a unit known as the electron-volt (eV), which is defined as the energy equivalent to the work needed to move an electron through an electric potential difference of 1 V. Its conversion to joules is 1 eV $= 1.602 \times 10^{-19}$ J. The energy contained in the mass defect of helium was on the order of millions of electronvolts, or MeV, which is a unit that is sometimes encountered (along with the other SI prefixes) when discussing nuclear reactions.

Our second question—about why it is that protons and electrons don't crash into each other—requires us to more thoroughly understand the nature of electrons. The Bohr model of the atom, developed in 1913, suggested that electrons orbit around the nucleus in one of a limited number of stable-energy orbital levels, corresponding to discrete amounts of energy. As we'll see below in section 2, in our discussion of the photoelectric effect, the Bohr model can still be useful in certain circumstances, but it is obsolete. In particular, the idea that electrons "orbit" the nucleus is not correct. Such a model would indeed eventually lead to difficulties involving orbital momentum, electrostatic interactions, and whether the electrons would collapse into the nucleus.

Figure 1. Bohr model of the atom.

Recall that in Chapter 9, we discussed the wave-particle duality of light. It turns out that light is not the only substance to show wave-particle duality. Electrons show some behavior, such as diffraction patterns, that can only be understood in terms of waves, and this understanding is critical for correctly understanding the microstructure of the atom. Moreover, wave-particle duality applies to matter in general. The de Broglie equation gives the wavelength of a piece of matter as $\lambda = \frac{h}{mv}$. Planck's constant, h, is a very tiny number (6.62×10^{-34} J·s), meaning an object does not have to be very heavy at all for its wavelength to become so small as to be virtually meaningless. For the purposes of the MCAT, electrons and light are the only substances for which wave-particle duality is important.

The story gets even stranger, though. Electrons are not just waves, but can be thought of as probability waves. We don't *know* where a given electron is at a moment in time, but we can assign probabilities to it being in specific locations. The areas across which a probability wave is dispersed for a given electron are known as orbitals. Orbitals are discussed more in Chapter 1 of the Chemistry and Organic Chemistry textbook, but we can summarize some key points relevant to physics:

Orbitals have distinct, quantized energy states (n; n = 1, 2, 3, 4, …, although in real-world applications it's rare to encounter values of n greater than 6), with higher numbers corresponding to being further away from the nucleus and having a higher energy state (this is because electrons "want" to be close to the nucleus).

Only one electron can have a given quantum state in an atom at the same time. By "quantum state" we mean a full specification of which energy level, angular momentum quantum number, magnetic quantum number, and spin a given electron has. (For a full review of these concepts, see Chapter 1 of the Chemistry and Organic Chemistry textbook). This is known as the Pauli exclusion principle. It is extremely fundamental for quantum mechanics, but for MCAT purposes, it's mostly useful as a piece of background information that helps explain why arbitrary amounts of electrons can't just be mashed close together to the nucleus as if they were a compressible gas.

> > **CONNECTIONS** < <

Chapter 1 of Chemistry

However, the Pauli exclusion principle doesn't mean that a given electron is fixed to whatever orbital location it is in. The lowest-energy (and therefore default) state that an electron is in is known as its ground state, which can be thought of as the closest possible location to the nucleus. If an electron absorbs energy, however, it can be promoted to a higher-energy state, which is known as an excited state. In the next section, we will see how this applies to a fascinating phenomenon known as the photoelectric effect.

There is one more major theoretical principle in quantum physics that we need to cover at this point: the Heisenberg uncertainty principle. This principle states that the more precisely we can establish the position of a particle, the less precisely we can establish its momentum, and vice versa. A common misconception holds that this has to do with the precision of our measurement techniques, but this is not the case; this uncertainty is a basic property of our universe, not a technological limitation. The Heisenberg uncertainty principle can be formalized as follows:

Equation 2.
$$\sigma_p \sigma_x = \frac{h}{4\pi}$$

In this equation, σ indicates the standard deviation and p indicates momentum (definable as mass multiplied by velocity), such that σ_x refers to the standard deviation of position (i.e., how precisely we know where a particle is) σ_p refers to the standard deviation of momentum (i.e., for a particle with a given mass, the uncertainty in its velocity). As we have seen before, h is Planck's constant (6.62×10^{-34} J·s). This principle is famously counterintuitive, and it actually provides an answer to the second question we articulated above: why don't electrons collapse into the nucleus? Let's use the Heisenberg uncertainty principle to calculate what would happen if we tried to limit an electron to the radius of a nucleus (~1×10^{-15} m). We can rewrite this equation using Δ instead of σ to indicate that we're interested in concrete intervals, set Δx to be equal to 1×10^{-15} m, and substitute in the mass of an electron (9.02×10^{-31} kg):

$$\Delta_x \Delta_p = \frac{h}{4\pi}$$

$$(1 \times 10^{-15} \text{ m})\Delta mv = \frac{h}{4\pi}$$

$$\Delta v = \frac{6.62 \times 10^{-34} \text{ J·s}}{(4\pi)(1 \times 10^{-15} \text{ m})(9.02 \times 10^{-31} \text{ kg})}$$

$$\Delta v = 5.84 \times 10^{10} \text{ m/s}$$

Not only is this uncertainty ridiculously huge, it's actually larger than the speed of light, suggesting that trying to compress an electron into the tiny, tiny space of a nucleus would yield an uncertainty in its velocity so great that it would be physically meaningless—or in other, simpler words, the Heisenberg uncertainty principle implies that you simply can't confine an electron in such a small space.

Now that we've covered the theoretical basics regarding subatomic structure, in the next sections, we'll explore some concrete applications of these principles.

2. Photoelectric Effect, Absorption and Emission of Light

The photoelectric effect refers to a phenomenon in which a substance (usually a metal) emits electrons in response to a beam of photons being shined onto it. Einstein's 1905 account of the photoelectric effect won a Nobel Prize; this may be surprising since Einstein is typically associated with the theory of relativity, but it's an interesting piece of trivia that helps to underscore the importance of this phenomenon.

The basic idea behind the photoelectric effect is that the energy of incident photons is absorbed by the material and excites electrons to the point that they are ejected from their atoms. An important observation, however, is that the

MCAT STRATEGY > > >

For the MCAT, you don't need to know every step of how to prove why electrons don't collapse into the nucleus. However, you do need to know what the Heisenberg uncertainty principle is, and it is certainly useful to be aware that macroscopic intuitions aren't always helpful on the quantum level, where things *get weird*. The takeaway point here is that you have to apply your knowledge about atomic/nuclear physics systematically, not just go for what seems reasonable on a gut level.

photoelectric effect is frequency-dependent. If the light shined on a substance is below a certain frequency (known as the threshold frequency), absolutely nothing will happen, no matter what you do. However, once the frequency of the light source surpasses the threshold frequency, not only does electron ejection happen, but it becomes proportional to the intensity of the light beam.

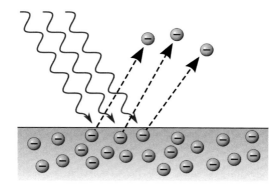

Figure 2. Photoelectric effect.

Two basic insights are needed to explain the photoelectric effect: first, that a certain amount of energy is necessary to excite an electron to the point that it can be ejected from an atom; and second, that each particle of light (known as a photon) hits the metal with an energy dependent on the frequency of the wave. Thus, if the photon doesn't contain enough energy to eject the electron, nothing happens, but if the photons in a light beam have sufficient energy, they will cause electrons to be ejected, and the more photons hit the material, the more electrons will be ejected. As such, this phenomenon provides powerful support for the idea that light can behave as a particle as well as a wave, and for many of the postulates of the quantum mechanics-informed model of the atom that we presented in section 1.

The energy of a photon is given by the following equations:

Equation 3.
$$E = hf$$

Equation 4.
$$E = \frac{hc}{\lambda}$$

We've seen these equations before, but they're worth repeating, because they are quite high-yield for the MCAT. $E = hf$ is the form of the equation that is most closely connected on a conceptual level with the photoelectric effect, because it directly links a photon's energy to its frequency, but the second equation can be easily derived by using the equation $c = \lambda f$.

In a confusing bit of terminology, the minimum amount of energy needed to expel an electron from an atom of a substance is known as the work function of that substance. Since that corresponds to the threshold frequency, we can define the work function as follows:

Equation 5.
$$E_{work \cdot function} = hf_{threshold}$$

Next, we may ask what happens if a metal is hit by a photon carrying more energy than the bare minimum necessary to eject the electron. In that case, the extra energy can go towards the kinetic energy of the electron, the maximum kinetic energy of which corresponds to the energy of the incident photon minus the work function (or the energy that was spent ejecting the electron):

Equation 6A.

$$KE_{max} = E_{incident} - E_{work \cdot function}$$

Equation 6B.

$$KE_{max} = hf_{incident} - hf_{threshold}$$

The photoelectric effect deals with a relatively extreme case of exciting an electron, to the point that it gets completely ejected from the atom. However, it turns out that it's also very productive to analyze how electrons can move among energy levels within an atom. For each atom, a very specific amount of energy is required to excite electrons and move them from one orbital energy level to another (e.g., from $n=1$ to $n=2$, from $n=1$ to $n=3$, and so on).

As we saw above for the photoelectric effect, a specific quantized unit of energy will correspond to a specific frequency of light (and therefore, a specific wavelength). This means that an atom will absorb specific wavelengths of light that correspond to transitions between two orbital energy levels. Perhaps surprisingly, this process also works in reverse: if an electron that has been excited to a higher-energy orbital level drops down to a lower-energy orbital, a photon will be released with an amount of energy that corresponds to the energy gap between those two levels.

Hydrogen is often used as a model atom for absorption and emission, and the wavelength of light corresponding to the energy needed to transition between any two energy levels in a hydrogen atom is given by the Rydberg equation:

Equation 7.

$$\frac{1}{\lambda} = R\left(\frac{1}{n_1^2} - \frac{1}{n_2^2}\right)$$

In this equation, R is the Rydberg constant (1.10×10^7 m^{-1}) and n_1 and n_2 are the two orbital levels in question. It's unlikely that you will be asked to solve a quantitative problem involving the Rydberg equation on the MCAT, and if you do, you don't need to be especially careful with which orbital level you assign as n_1 and which you assign as n_2—you just need to remember that energy (in the form of a photon) will be absorbed if an electron is being excited to a higher energy level, whereas it will be released if an electron is dropping back down to a lower energy level.

A practical takeaway point from the above discussion is that specific elements will absorb and emit specific wavelengths of light (although not necessarily limited to visible light). This can be visualized using a spectrum of light. An absorption spectrum shows you the range of visible light with black gaps corresponding to the wavelengths of light that are absorbed, whereas an emission spectrum is the opposite—a black background on which the emitted wavelengths of light appear. Absorption and emission spectra for hydrogen are shown below in Figure 3. You should be familiar with both, although emission spectra of individual elements are used more frequently in MCAT-relevant contexts because they are easier on the eye and can be converted to grayscale (as on the MCAT itself) without becoming nearly impossible to interpret.

410 nm 434 nm   486 nm   656 nm

Figure 3. Absorption and emission spectra of hydrogen.

Absorption and emission spectra for elements can essentially serve as their fingerprints, and as such have provided key data for astronomical research into the composition of other planets and even stars. The rapidly progressing field of exoplanetology is actively searching for Earth-like planets in other solar systems, and absorption and emission spectra make a major contribution to their conclusions about planets that may be suitable for life.

However, in the organic chemistry and biochemistry-centric world of the MCAT, we need to be aware of how these principles are applied to reactions involving large organic molecules. Organic molecules generally don't show the same kind of extremely tight, discrete banding that we see for elements, because their atomic structure is *much* more complex, but the principles of absorption/emission analysis can still be fruitfully applied in several contexts.

On a very basic level, the use of color-changing indicators in acid-base chemistry is an implementation of absorption spectrum analysis, although the only "analysis" we have to do in such cases is to watch how the color changes. Indicators are molecules defined by the property that their protonation status dramatically changes their absorption properties. Don't forget, though, that the visible color of a substance is defined not by the light rays that it absorbs, but by the light rays it reflects.

Another common application of absorption/emission is ultraviolet (UV) visualization in organic chemistry, which may be especially familiar from thin-layer chromatography. Organic molecules that exhibit conjugation (systems of alternating double bonds) have delocalized electrons that can be excited by the application of UV light. Once they are excited, the electrons drop down to lower-energy levels, releasing lower-energy, higher-wavelength visible light, which is why you may remember seeing glowing blotches show up on TLC plates under ultraviolet light. A similar principle is utilized in fluorescent lights.

Absorption spectra can be plotted in a more nuanced way by shining light at various wavelengths through a substance, usually in solution, and measuring how much of the light gets absorbed. This technique is known as spectrophotometry, and is widely used in laboratory contexts to quantify the outcomes of reactions. Figure 4 below shows an absorption spectrum for two types of chlorophyll, the main compound that makes plants green and plays an important role in plant metabolism.

Figure 4. Absorption spectrum for chlorophyll.

The absorption spectrum for chlorophyll drives home two important points. First, imagine that you were tracking a reaction in which chlorophyll a was being converted to chlorophyll b. The emergence of a sharp peak around 480 nm and a slightly more rounded peak around 630 nm would help indicate that the reaction was taking place. Second, and perhaps even more importantly in terms of sources of potential errors on Test Day, *note that chlorophyll is green*. This is confirmed by the miniscule absorbance in the 500-580 nm wavelength, corresponding to green light—this means that virtually all of the green light is being reflected back at us, which is why chlorophyll has a green color.

3. Radioactivity and Nuclear Decay

The final domain of nuclear physics that you need to be aware of for the MCAT contains the related topics of nuclear reactions, radioactivity, and nuclear decay. The common thread here is that these topics deal with changes that take place involving the nucleus. As this is the last section in the Physics book, you may be tempted to race through it, but resist that temptation. The MCAT does not cover these topics in great theoretical depth, but it is highly likely that you will be tested on this material, at least to some extent, on Test Day. You don't have to know a *lot* for this section, but you do have to know the basic mechanics of nuclear reactions and radioactivity very thoroughly.

Since the basics are so important for success in this area on Test Day, it's worth investing some time in reviewing how the subatomic particles (protons, neutrons, and electrons) are used to classify different types of matter.

The number of protons that an atom has is its atomic number. This criterion essentially determines its identity: an atom with a single proton is hydrogen, one with two protons is helium, one with five protons is nitrogen, one with six protons is carbon, and so on. If you change the number of protons in an atom, you change what element it is.

The protons and neutrons of an atom are added together to make up its atomic weight (recall that the mass of a single proton or neutron corresponds to roughly 1 atomic mass unit, or amu). Some variation generally exists in how many neutrons are present in atoms of a given element. The different forms of an element that result from combining a fixed number of protons with a variable number of neutrons are known as isotopes. The atomic weight given on the periodic table reflects the average atomic weight of a given element in nature, taking into account its isotopes. For example, the atomic weight of carbon is 12.011 amu, which tells you that most carbon atoms have six protons and six neutrons, but some have more. In fact, carbon isotopes with seven neutrons (carbon-13 or ^{13}C; isotopes are named after their atomic weight by convention) and eight neutrons (carbon-14 or ^{14}C) are common enough that they have important applications (which we will discuss more below).

MCAT STRATEGY > > >

You may be used to assuming that an atom will have the same number of protons and neutrons, but that's not necessarily the case, especially as you go higher in the periodic table. As with many things in atomic/nuclear physics, watch out for unwarranted assumptions that you may bring with you, either from the macroscopic world or from some familiar examples. The name of the game is to systematically apply what they give you!

Variation in the number of electrons that an atom has affects the charge of the atom, as the charge can be determined by the number of protons minus the number of electrons (since protons and electrons have the same magnitude of charge, but opposite). In most situations, you can't change the number of protons that an atom has, and even if you can, doing so generates an entirely new element, so for all practical purposes, variations in charge are due to variations in electrons. Virtually all of chemistry, including all chemical reactions, describes electron interactions. In a certain sense, we have two entire textbooks dedicated to electron interactions (the Chemistry and Organic Chemistry textbook and the Biochemistry textbook), but it will not be the main focus of this section.

In the context of nuclear physics, special notation is used to refer to atoms in a way that makes explicit both the atomic number and the isotope. The atomic number is written as a subscript on the left of the atomic symbol, and the atomic weight (indicative of the isotope) is written as a superscript on that side. For example, $_{6}^{12}C$ is the most common isotope of carbon, and contains six protons and six neutrons for a total weight of 12 amu.

Two common types of nuclear reactions are nuclear fusion and nuclear fission. For the MCAT, you do not have to know any specific fusion or fission reactions in depth, but you do need to know what they are in general terms, so read through the following examples with the goal of understanding of the general concepts, the notation, and how to apply conservation of mass to ensure that nuclear reactions are balanced.

For fusion, let's look at the fusion reaction that produces helium in the sun. Due to the binding energy of the helium nucleus (discussed above), producing helium through fusion creates a tremendous amount of energy, although a lot of energy is needed to get the process started by getting protons close enough to each other for the strong nuclear force to kick in and overpower electromagnetic repulsion.

Helium is produced in the Sun by the fusion of deuterium and tritium. Deuterium is an isotope of hydrogen that contains one proton and one neutron (unlike the most common isotope of hydrogen, which only contains a proton and is therefore known as protium). Interestingly, virtually all extant deuterium was produced in the Big Bang. It makes up roughly 1 in each 6,000 hydrogen atoms on Earth, and is known as "heavy hydrogen." When incorporated into water, the result is "heavy water," which has various laboratory and practical applications. Tritium is a radioactive isotope of hydrogen that contains one proton and two neutrons, and can be derived from the radioactive decay of lithium and helium (the details need not concern us). The deuterium and tritium nuclei combine to produce a helium nucleus, emitting one free neutron and generating energy, as follows:

$$_{1}^{2}H + _{1}^{3}H \rightarrow _{2}^{4}He + _{0}^{1}n + \text{energy}$$

Note that the symbol n is used to indicate a neutron; p is used to indicate protons, e^- is used to indicate electrons, and e^+ is used to indicate positrons, a species of particle with the mass of an electron but a positive charge. Another important point to note here is that we can balance the equation similarly to how we balance a chemical equation: the number of mass-containing particles need to add up. In this case, the protons and neutrons both add up, but in other reactions we will see the interconversion of protons and neutrons; even in that case, we need to account for what happens to every reactant. If relevant, we also need to account for charge.

An example of nuclear fission is what happens with a neutron hits a ^{235}U nucleus. It causes the nucleus to break down into ^{92}Kr and ^{141}Ba, releasing three neutrons. We can write out this reaction as follows:

$$^{235}_{92}\text{U} + {}^{1}_{0}n \rightarrow {}^{92}_{36}\text{Kr} + {}^{141}_{56}\text{Ba} + 3\ {}^{1}_{0}n$$

As with the fusion reaction we saw before, we should track the protons and atomic weights to make sure that everything balances.

Radioactive decay refers to the spontaneous breakdown of certain isotopes, in which unstable nuclei eject mass (and therefore energy) or photons as radiation. Radioactive decay can be classified according to the type of particles emitted as alpha decay, beta decay, or gamma decay. Nuclear physicists have invested a tremendous amount of time and resources into predicting and explaining which nuclei undergo which types of decay, but you don't have to worry about this at all. For the MCAT, you only need to be able to do two things: first, and most importantly, distinguish among the various types of decay; and second, use the principle that more massive particles interact more readily with matter, making them both more dangerous and more easily shielded against.

In alpha decay, an alpha (α) particle is emitted. Alpha particles are simply helium nuclei, with two protons, two neutrons, and a +2 charge. As such, they're relatively massive (at least on the scale of nuclear physics) and interact easily with matter. This means that they can be quite dangerous if ingested into the body, but also that they can easily be shielded against (even a piece of paper can do the trick). The summary equation for alpha decay is given below. Note that by convention, Z is used for the atomic number and A for the atomic weight.

Equation 8.
$$^{A}_{Z}\text{X} \rightarrow {}^{A-4}_{Z-2}\text{Y} + {}^{4}_{2}\alpha$$

As the name suggests, in beta decay, a beta (β) particle is released. Beta decay actually comes in two forms: beta-minus (β⁻) and beta-plus (β⁺) decay. A key point to recognize here is that a β⁻ particle is actually just an electron, and a β⁺ particle is a positron (also sometimes written as e^+), which is a particle with the same mass as an electron but a positive charge. In beta-minus decay, a neutron is converted into a proton in the nucleus, and a β⁻ particle (an electron) is ejected to maintain charge balance. In beta-plus decay, the idea is the same but the charges are flipped: a proton is converted into a neutron and a β⁺ particle (a positron) is emitted to preserve charge. In both cases, a massless particle known as a neutrino is

> ## MCAT STRATEGY > > >
>
> Remember that in beta-*minus* decay, the emitted particle has a *negative* charge and that in beta-*plus* decay, the emitted particle has a positive charge. You then have to adjust the atomic number of the remaining nucleus to compensate for the charge of the emitted particle.

also ejected, but neutrinos are not relevant for the MCAT. Beta particles are much, much lighter than alpha particles and are also less strongly charged, so they are less likely to interact with matter. This makes them less immediately dangerous but also harder to shield. The summary equations for both types of beta decay are given below:

Equation 9A.
$$^{A}_{Z}\text{X} \rightarrow {}^{A}_{Z+1}\text{Y} + {}^{0}_{0}\beta^{-}$$

Equation 9B.
$$^{A}_{Z}\text{X} \rightarrow {}^{A}_{Z-1}\text{Y} + {}^{0}_{0}\beta^{+}$$

Gamma decay is reminiscent of light emission that we talked about earlier, in that it involves the emission of a gamma (γ) ray, which is a high-energy photon, from an excited nucleus. There are two main differences between gamma decay and light emission: first, gamma decay involves an excited *nucleus*, not an excited electron; and second, gamma rays are well outside of the range of visible light (they're *much* higher energy). An asterisk (*) is sometimes used to represent a high-energy nucleus. With that in mind, we can write the generalized equation for gamma decay as follows:

Equation 10.
$$^A_Z X^* \rightarrow {}^A_Z X + \gamma$$

In a certain sense, the equation for gamma decay is the easiest of them all; gamma rays have no mass or charge (because they're photons), so we don't have to deal with atomic numbers or weights changing. Essentially, you can think of gamma rays just as the manifestation of the energy that is being lost from an excited nucleus. Gamma rays are excellent at penetrating through matter and are high-energy enough to have an effect on health, although less so than alpha or beta particles.

A final reaction is not technically radioactive decay. In what is known as electron capture, a nucleus "grabs" an electron, which changes a proton into a neutron. The idea here is that the positive and negative charges of the proton and electron, respectively, cancel out. In electron capture, the atomic weight stays the same, but the atomic number decreases by one, as shown below:

Equation 11.
$$^A_Z X + e^- \rightarrow {}^A_{Z-1} Y$$

Table 2 below summarizes the main types of radioactive reactions that you need to know for the MCAT.

TYPE	EQUATION	PARTICLE RELEASED	PENETRATION/HARM
Alpha decay	$^A_Z X \rightarrow {}^{A-4}_{Z-2} Y + {}^4_2 \alpha$	Alpha particle ($^4_2 \alpha$ or $^4_2 He$); a helium nucleus	Easy to shield against; very dangerous to ingest/inhale
Beta-minus decay	$^A_Z X \rightarrow {}^A_{Z+1} Y + {}^0_0 \beta-$	Beta-minus particle (an electron)	More easily penetrates matter; moderately damaging/mutagenic
Beta-plus decay	$^A_Z X \rightarrow {}^A_{Z-1} Y + {}^0_0 \beta+$	Beta-plus particle (a positron)	
Gamma decay	$^A_Z X^* \rightarrow {}^A_Z X + \gamma$	Gamma particle (high-energy photon)	Very penetrative; biologically active but the least harmful
Electron capture	$^A_Z X + e^- \rightarrow {}^A_{Z-1} Y$	N/A	

Table 2. Types of radioactive decay.

Strictly speaking, it isn't possible to predict exactly when an individual radioactive isotope will undergo decay, but the timing of radioactive decay within a sample of radioactive material as a whole is very predictable. Radioactive decay occurs via an exponential decay process, in which the amount of remaining radioactive material asymptotically approaches, but technically speaking never reaches, zero. It is usually measured in terms of the half-life, or the amount of time it takes for half of a radioactive sample to decay. The half-life is often denoted as $t_{1/2}$.

Mathematically, we can describe exponential decay as follows. If we want to calculate n, the remaining nuclei that have not yet decayed at a given time t, it turns out that all we need to do is to know the original amount of nuclei (n_0) and multiply it by a certain power of e:

Equation 12.
$$n = n_0 e^{-\lambda t}$$

In this equation, λ is a quantity referred to as the decay constant, which is specific to a given substance and is a mathematical indicator of how quickly it decays. The derivation for this goes well beyond the scope of the MCAT, but the decay constant is related to the half-life as follows: $t_{1/2} = \frac{0.693}{\lambda}$. This equation shows you that a larger decay constant means a shorter half-life, which in turn corresponds to faster decay.

This mathematical formalism is elegant, but for the MCAT, it is much more likely that you will simply need to apply common sense to the analysis of radioactive decay in terms of half-lives. Table 3 below presents a simple chart, using both fractions and percentages, of how much of a sample is left after each successive half-life.

MCAT STRATEGY > > >

You should plan on knowing the material in Table 2 *cold* for Test Day. Radioactive decay is a fairly frequently tested topic, because it has applications in medical imaging and research, and types of decay are one of those topics where questions are very gettable if you know your stuff and very hard to figure out if you don't. In particular, know which type of decay is which and be able to distinguish the equations from each other.

HALF-LIVES	0	1	2	3	4	5
Fraction left	1	$\frac{1}{2}$	$\frac{1}{4}$	$\frac{1}{8}$	$\frac{1}{16}$	$\frac{1}{32}$
Percentage left	100%	50%	25%	12.5%	6.25%	3.125%

Table 3. Amount of a substance remaining after successive half-lives.

Since radioactive decay is exponential, it can be presented graphically as an exponential curve. Such graphs can also be transformed into semi-log plots, in which the y-axis (here, the remaining number of nuclei) is expressed logarithmically, while the x-axis (here, time or the number of half-lives) remains unchanged. This transformation results in a linear graph, which can be useful for various mathematical purposes. Figure 5 contains a comparison of exponential and semi-log graphs that would be typical for radioactive decay.

MCAT STRATEGY > > >

If faced with a half-life problem on Test Day, Rule #1 is to keep it simple, Rule #2 is to keep it simple, and Rule #3 is to keep it simple! Don't get fancy with your math unless you absolutely have to (possible, but very unlikely), don't feel shy about writing out some version of Table 3 on your scrap paper to make sure you don't make a silly mistake, and last but not least, make sure that you are answering what the question is asking (for instance, does it want to know how much is *left* or how much *has decayed*?).

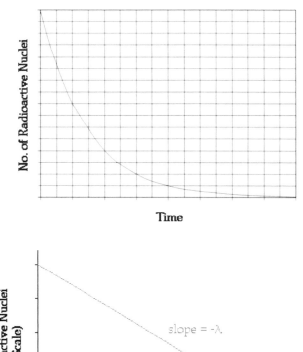

Figure 5. Exponential and semi-log graphs for radioactive decay.

Note that on a semi-log plot, the half-life is determined differently than it is on an exponential graph, as shown in Figure 5.

As a final point in this chapter, it's worth having a general sense of how radioactive decay is applied scientifically. One common application is positron emission tomography (PET scans), in which a radioactive tracer (generally, fluorodeoxyglucose, but the details can vary depending on the purpose of the scan) is injected. The radioactive tracers involved in PET scans have relatively short half-lives, such that sensitive detectors can analyze where the emitted radioactive particles are coming from in the body, and then process that information to create highly detailed medical images.

MCAT STRATEGY > > >

In terms of practical strategies for Test Day, the takeaway point here is to always, always, *always* read the axes carefully and think about how they apply to the problem you're trying to solve. The MCAT loves to penalize students for jumping to conclusions based on graphs without careful consideration of the axes and the units. For example, just because you see a graph of decay with a line on it doesn't mean that the actual process is linear; in such a case, you'd just be looking at a semi-log plot.

A similar principle is applied in biochemical experiments, where it is known as radiolabeling; by incorporating a radioactive atom into the compounds you're interested in, it becomes possible to trace the flow of atoms through a reaction or a biological process. This technique has been used for purposes as diverse as determining how genetic information is transferred (as in the 1952 Hershey-Chase experiment that helped establish that DNA is the genetic material) and elucidating the mechanisms of chemical reactions.

4. Must-Knows

> Components of atoms: protons, neutrons, electrons; protons & neutrons form small nucleus at center of atom, held together by strong nuclear force.
> — Number of protons: atomic number (determines basic identity of element)
> — Number of protons + neutrons: atomic weight (variations are known as isotopes)
> — Number of electrons: ions; involved in chemical properties
> $E = mc^2$ tells us that mass and energy are interchangeable; mass defect in neutrons indicates that atoms hold tremendous potential energy.
> Electrons are modeled as orbiting the atom in the Bohr model, but more accurately are thought of as waves with a certain probability to be in a given location.
> Heisenberg uncertainty principle: $\sigma_p \sigma_x = \frac{h}{4\pi}$, meaning that the more precisely we establish a particle's location, the less precisely we can establish its momentum, and vice-versa.
> Photoelectric effect: if a photon hits an atom with an energy of at least the threshold level ($E_{work \cdot function} = hf_{threshold}$), an electron will be ejected:
> Kinetic energy of ejected electron: $KE_{max} = E_{incident} - E_{work \cdot function}$, $KE_{max} = hf_{incident} - hf_{threshold}$
> Electrons transition between energy levels within atoms, emitting photons whose wavelength can be calculated as: $\frac{1}{\lambda} = R \left(\frac{1}{n_1^2} - \frac{1}{n_2^2} \right)$. Resultant emission spectra are diagnostic of elements and molecules.
> Types of radioactive decay:

TYPE	EQUATION	PARTICLE RELEASED	PENETRATION/HARM
Alpha decay	$^A_Z X \rightarrow ^{A-4}_{Z-2} Y + ^4_2 \alpha$	Alpha particle ($^4_2 \alpha$ or $^4_2 He$); a helium nucleus	Easy to shield against; very dangerous to ingest/inhale
Beta-minus decay	$^A_Z X \rightarrow ^A_{Z+1} Y + ^0_0 \beta-$	Beta-minus particle (an electron)	More easily penetrates matter; moderately damaging/mutagenic
Beta-plus decay	$^A_Z X \rightarrow ^A_{Z-1} Y + ^0_0 \beta+$	Beta-plus particle (a positron)	
Gamma decay	$^A_Z X^* \rightarrow ^A_Z X + \gamma$	Gamma particle (high-energy photon)	Very penetrative; biologically active but the least harmful
Electron capture	$^A_Z X + e^- \rightarrow ^A_{Z-1} Y$	N/A	

> Decay is analyzed in terms of half-lives:

HALF-LIVES	0	1	2	3	4	5
Fraction left	1	$\frac{1}{2}$	$\frac{1}{4}$	$\frac{1}{8}$	$\frac{1}{16}$	$\frac{1}{32}$
Percentage left	100%	50%	25%	12.5%	6.75%	3.375%

This page left intentionally blank.

Practice Passage

Cardiologists often use stress tests to measure the ability of a patient's heart to deliver adequate volumes of blood during physical exertion. In some cases the stress is drug induced, rather than by way of actual exercise. The test compares coronary circulation while the patient is at rest, to circulation during maximum exertion. Abnormal blood flows can indicate heart disease caused by blockages in the coronary arteries, and indicate the possibility of myocardial infarction. Perhaps the most common method for gauging the flow of blood to the heart is by way of nuclear imaging. This is done by injecting a sample of a radioisotope into the patient's blood, followed by imaging using a camera that is sensitive to the nuclear radiation produced.

The radioisotope of choice for imaging purposes has become technetium-99m, which is a gamma emitting metastable isotope having a short half-life of 6.01 hours. The product of the gamma emission is Tc-99, which is also radioactive, undergoing beta decay, with a half-life of 2.1×10^5 years. There are no stable isotopes of technetium, and all must be made in a nuclear reactor by transmutation. A Tc-99m generator that can easily be handled by appropriately trained medical technicians has been developed based on the decay of molybedenum-99, which has a half-life of 66 hours. Molybdenum-99 is produced by neutron activation of the stable isotope, molybdenum-98, which is the most abundant (24.14 %) of the seven naturally occurring isotopes of molybdenum. The generator facilitates transport of the radiopharmaceutical from the source nuclear reactor, to the hospital or clinic where testing will occur. Reactions 1 and 2 summarize the nuclear processes that involve the meta-stable isotope of technetium.

$$\text{Reaction 1} \qquad {}^{99}_{42}\text{Mo} \rightarrow {}^{99m}_{43}\text{Tc} + {}^{0}_{-1}\beta$$

$$\text{Reaction 2} \qquad {}^{99m}_{43}\text{Tc} \rightarrow {}^{99}_{43}\text{Tc} + \gamma\,(140\text{ keV})$$

Technetium is a transition metal which forms a stable pertechnitate ion, TcO_4^-, which has chemical properties similar to permanganate. In lower oxidations states, technetium ions form a variety of complexes with organic ligands that can be tailored to deliver the radioisotope to a particular organ of the body. This has led to breakthroughs in the treatment of parathyroid disorders and breast cancer.

1. Based on information presented in the passage, pertechnitate is expected to be a good:
   A. oxidizing agent.
   B. reducing agent.
   C. acid.
   D. base.

2. Molybdenum's naturally occurring stable isotopes have mass numbers between 92 and 100. If the atomic mass of molybdenum is 95.95 amu, which of the following must be true based on information presented in the passage?
   A. There must be more than one naturally occurring stable isotope of molybdenum with fewer than 54 neutrons.
   B. There must be more than one naturally occurring stable isotope of molybdenum with more than 56 neutrons.
   C. The most abundant naturally occurring isotope of molybdenum has 54 neutrons.
   D. All of the isotopes of molybdenum have 42 neutrons.

3. What is the product of the beta decay of Tc-99?
   A. Ru-99
   B. Ru-98
   C. Mo-99
   D. Mo-98

4. If it takes 24 hours for a technetium generator to be delivered from the nuclear reactor to a cardiologist's laboratory, by what percentage has the amount of Mo-99 decreased in the generator during delivery?
   A. <1%
   B. 22%
   C. 78%
   D. 94%

5. Patients should be informed about the risks associated with any medical procedure. Which of the following pose a significant risk associated with radiopharmaceuticals?
   I. Internal exposure to radiopharmaceuticals can have a carcinogenic effect.
   II. Internal exposure to radiopharmaceuticals can have a mutagenic effect.
   III. Internal exposure to radiopharmaceuticals can have a teratogenic effect.
   A. I only
   B. II only
   C. I and II only
   D. I, II, and III

6. Mass spectrometry is used to separate particles based only on their mass to charge ratio. If, during this process, a uniform magnetic field is used to accelerate the particles of the sample, what must be true of these particles as they enter the magnetic field?
   I. The particles are charged.
   II. The particles are moving at a constant velocity.
   III. The particles have the same velocity.
   A. I only
   B. II only
   C. I and III only
   D. I, II, and III

7. Which of the following graphs correctly shows the total mass of β-particles released from a sample of Tc-99 as the sample decays?

A.
time

B.
time

C.
time

D.
time

Practice Passage Explanations

Cardiologists often use stress tests to measure the ability of a patient's heart to deliver adequate volumes of blood during physical exertion. In some cases the stress is drug induced, rather than by way of actual exercise. The test compares coronary circulation while the patient is at rest, to circulation during maximum exertion. Abnormal blood flows can indicate heart disease caused by blockages in the coronary arteries, and indicate the possibility of myocardial infarction. Perhaps the most common method for gauging the flow of blood to the heart is by way of nuclear imaging. This is done by injecting a sample of a radioisotope into the patient's blood, followed by imaging using a camera that is sensitive to the nuclear radiation produced.

Key terms: stress tests, circulation, nuclear imaging

Cause and effect: coronary artery block → MI; stress tests = flow at rest vs. flow under exertion using radioisotope tracking

The radioisotope of choice for imaging purposes has become technetium-99m, which is a gamma emitting metastable isotope having a short half-life of 6.01 hours. The product of the gamma emission is Tc-99, which is also radioactive, undergoing beta decay, with a half-life of 2.1×10^5 years. There are no stable isotopes of technetium, and all must be made in a nuclear reactor by transmutation. A Tc-99m generator that can easily be handled by appropriately trained medical technicians has been developed based on the decay of molybedenum-99, which has a half-life of 66 hours. Molybdenum-99 is produced by neutron activation of the stable isotope, molybdenum-98, which is the most abundant (24.14 %) of the seven naturally occurring isotopes of molybdenum. The generator facilitates transport of the radiopharmaceutical from the source nuclear reactor, to the hospital or clinic where testing will occur. Reactions 1 and 2 summarize the nuclear processes that involve the meta-stable isotope of technetium.

Key terms: meta-stable isotope, half-life, gamma emission, beta decay, transmutation, neutron activation, radiopharmaceutical

Cause and effect: The meta stable isotope of technetium emits gamma photons which are easily used for imaging; use of technetium generators based on the beta decay of Mo-99 has made it possible to safely do stress tests in clinical settings

$$\text{Reaction 1} \qquad {}^{99}_{42}\text{Mo} \rightarrow {}^{99m}_{43}\text{Tc} + {}^{0}_{-1}\beta$$

$$\text{Reaction 2} \qquad {}^{99m}_{43}\text{Tc} \rightarrow {}^{99}_{43}\text{Tc} + \gamma \, (140 \text{ keV})$$

Reaction 2 shows gamma photon emission, which has 140 keV of energy. Note that the sum of the subscripts on the reactant and product sides are equal

Technetium is a transition metal which forms a stable pertechnitate ion, TcO_4^-, which has chemical properties similar to permanganate. In lower oxidations states, technetium ions form a variety of complexes with organic ligands that can be tailored to deliver the radioisotope to a particular organ of the body. This has led to breakthroughs in the treatment of parathyroid disorders and breast cancer.

Key terms: Transition metal, permanganate, oxidation states, ligands, parathyroid

Cause and effect: Technetium is a transition metal with chemistry similar to that of manganese. As a result it can form coordination complexes with organic ligands that can direct the radioisotope to specific organs for specific imaging purposes

1. A is correct. As stated in the passage, technetium is in the same group of the periodic table as manganese. Like permanganate (MnO_4^-), pertechnitate (TcO_4^-) is expected to be a very good oxidizing agent. Permanganate is essentially a neutral ion with respect to acid/base properties and pertechnitate would be expected to be similar.

2. A is correct. Since Mo-92, Mo-98 and Mo-100 account for three of the seven isotopes, there must be four isotopes remaining. If three of these isotopes were Mo-99, Mo-97 and Mo-96, then the final isotope must be either Mo-93, Mo-94, or Mo-95, all of which have fewer than 54 neutrons, requiring that there is more than one isotope with less than 54 neutrons.
   B, C, D: The passage states that Mo-98 is the most abundant naturally occurring stable isotope of molybdenum. Subtracting the number of protons from the mass number of this isotope gives 56 neutrons. Choice D can be eliminated because isotopes must have different numbers of neutrons. While choice B could be true, it is not required to be true. Since the atomic mass (95.95 amu) is the weighted average of the isotopes of an element. The passage states that there are "seven naturally occurring isotopes of molybdenum", with Mo-98 being the most abundant, at 24.14%. The question indicates that the mass numbers (protons + neutrons) for the stable isotopes of molybdenum range from 92 to 100. Therefore, the percent abundances of Mo-92 and Mo-100 cannot exceed 24% each. Since Mo-98 has 56 neutrons, it is possible for all of the remaining isotopes to have mass numbers less than 98, or less than 56 neutrons. For example if you assume that the percent abundances of Mo-92, Mo-98 and Mo-100 are all 24%, the sum of the percent abundances for remaining isotopes cannot be more than 28%. You can also then assume that Mo-99 is not one of these isotopes. This indicates that the average of the mass numbers of the four remaining isotopes must be about 94, which could be done with combinations of Mo-93, Mo-94, Mo-95, Mo-96, and Mo-97, all of which have fewer than 56 neutrons. Therefore, it is not required that Mo-99 is one of the seven stable naturally occurring isotopes of molybdenum.

3. A is correct. A beta-minus particle is the equivalent of an electron ejected from the nucleus. Beta-minus decay converts a neutron into a proton and an electron. Beta decay causes the number of protons in the nucleus to increase by one, resulting in the production of an element one position to the right in the periodic table, without a change in the mass number. Therefore, the product of beta decay of Tc-99 should be the element with one additional proton and the same mass number, which is ruthenium-99.

4. B is correct. As stated in the passage, the half-life of Mo-99 is 66 hours. The actual percentage can be calculated from the definition of half-life. A half-life is the time required for half the material to decay. After multiple half-lives (n), the fraction remaining will continue to be cut in half, as stated in the following equation $F = (\frac{1}{2})n$ where F is the fraction of the radioisotope remaining and n is the number of half-lives. In this case, the n = 24/66 = 0.36. The fraction remaining can be calculated as $(\frac{1}{2})0.36 = 0.78$ or 78%. Therefore 22% has decayed. To make the mental math easier, if you approximate n = 24/66 ~ 0.5. The square root of $\frac{1}{2}$ is approximately 0.7 ($0.7 \times 0.7 = 0.49 \sim 0.5$). If the fraction remaining is 0.7, then 70% remains, meaning that approximately 30% has decayed, which is closest to choice B.

5. D is correct. Nuclear radiation, sometimes known as ionizing radiation, can disrupt or break chemical bonds in important biological molecules, such as DNA. This can cause changes in genetic sequences that can cause abnormal mitosis and meiosis. A carcinogen is any substance that directly causes genetic changes that result in the formation of cancer. A mutagen is any substance that causes a genetic change and a teratogen is any substance that causes a malformation of an embryo. Therefore, unnecessary exposure to radioisotopes can cause all three effects.

6. D is correct. The test makers expect us to know the basics of how a mass spectrometer works. Sample particles are ionized, accelerated by a potential difference (voltage), and passed through a velocity selector such that all the particles that enter the uniform magnetic field will share the same velocity. Once inside the magnetic field, all of these charged, moving particles will experience Lorentz forces and begin to move in a circle, with the particles

path radii determined by their mass to charge ratio. In particular, their radius = mv/qB, where m = mass, q = charge, v = velocity inside the magnetic field, and B is the strength of the magnetic field.

7. C is correct. The question asks for the mass of decay product given off the Tc-99 sample. The sample will give off more and more beta-particles as it decays, but it cannot give off more particles once it has fully decayed. Thus, the plot will approach a finite amount of mass over time.
   A: This shows the mass of Tc-99 remaining as it decays, not the mass of the decay product.
   B, D: Exponential decay and growth do not show linear changes. Thus, the plots will not be straight.

Independent Questions

1. A student prepares the experimental setup depicted below. Ultraviolet light is incident on a metal plate connected to a voltage source. Under appropriate conditions, electrons are ejected from the metal plate and complete the circuit when they reach a detector. The circuit also includes an ammeter.

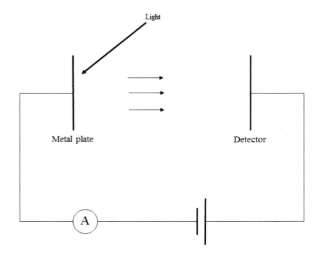

After the student identifies a particular wavelength of light sufficient to eject electrons, she increases the intensity of the light. Which of the following is the most likely result?
   A. Current flowing through the circuit will increase.
   B. Current flowing through the circuit will decrease, but will not reach zero.
   C. No current will flow through the circuit.
   D. Fewer electrons will be ejected from the metal plate.

2. Which of the following daughter nuclei is formed when tellurium-110 undergoes a single round of alpha decay?
   A. Tellurium-108
   B. Tellurium-106
   C. Tin-108
   D. Tin-106

3. Which of the following forces is the principle attractive force within the nucleus?
   A. Gravitational force
   B. Strong force
   C. Electrostatic force
   D. Electromagnetic force

4. If hydrogen gas is ionized and the light emitted by the gas is passed through a prism, which of the following will be true of the resultant emission spectrum?
   A. Since hydrogen only has one electron, only one band will appear.
   B. The spectrum will display bands at all wavelengths because of numerous electronic transitions.
   C. The spectrum will show discrete bands at certain wavelengths because energy states are quantized.
   D. The spectrum will be identical to that of lithium, which has an identical valence configuration.

5. Carbon-14 undergoes beta-decay to nitrogen-14 and has a half-life of approximately 6,000 years. Which of the following would be sufficient time for a given sample of carbon-14 to decay to 6% of its original amount?
   A. 28,000 years
   B. 24,000 years
   C. 22,000 years
   D. 18,000 years

6. A graph of the change in half-life of a given isotope over time is best described as:
   A. a logarithmic function.
   B. a linear function with a negative slope.
   C. a linear function with a slope of zero.
   D. an exponential function.

7. Which of the following types of radioactive decay LEAST changes the mass of the parent nucleus?
   A. Gamma decay
   B. Alpha decay
   C. β^- decay
   D. β^+ decay

8. The Heisenberg uncertainty relation can be written as $\Delta x \Delta p \geq \frac{h}{2\pi}$. Which expression describes the uncertainty in the position of an object with a mass of 10^{-9} kg whose velocity is known with an uncertainty of 10^{-12} m/s? (Note: $\Delta p = m\Delta v$)
   A. $\frac{h \times 10^{21}}{2\pi}$
   B. $\frac{h \times 10^{-21}}{2\pi}$
   C. $\frac{h \times 10^{12}}{2\pi}$
   D. $\frac{h \times 10^{-12}}{2\pi}$

Independent Question Explanations

1. A is correct. This experimental setup illustrates the photoelectric effect. Photoelectrons are only ejected from the metal plate when the frequency of the incident light corresponds to the energy required to overcome the work function for the metal. So long as light of the correct frequency is used, increasing the intensity of the light will increase the number of photons incident on the plate. Since each photon causes the ejection of a single electron, more electrons are ejected and more current will flow through the circuit.

2. D is correct. Alpha decay involves the ejection of an alpha particle, which is equivalent to a helium nucleus. The net result of a single round of alpha decay is the loss of two protons and two neutrons from the parent nucleus. The atomic number decreases by two, so we can see from the periodic table that the daughter nucleus must be an isotope of tin. Since four nucleons are lost, the mass number decreases by four, from 110 to 106.

3. B is correct. The gravitational force is negligible for objects with very small masses, such as subatomic particles. The electromagnetic force causes repulsion between protons in the nucleus, not attraction. The strong nuclear force is primarily responsible for holding the nucleus together.

4. C is correct. Electrons transition between discrete energy levels. Since the energy change associated with these transitions is quantized, the ionized gas emits photons with discrete, specific energy values. The resulting spectrum displays bands at wavelengths corresponding to the energies of these photons. Each electron in a single atom can undergo several different transitions (choice A is incorrect). The emitted photons are specific to each transition, not each electron. Emission spectra are unique to each atom (eliminate choice D).

5. A is correct. After four half-lives (24,000 years), 6.25% of the sample will remain. After five half-lives (30,000 years), 3.125% will remain. The only answer choice between 24,000 and 30,000 years is choice A.

6. C is correct. Half-life of a chemical isotope is constant over time. It depends only on the identity of the parent isotope.

7. A is correct. Alpha decay results in the loss of a helium nucleus, which contains two protons and two neutrons. Both classes of β decay result in the emission of a particle with a mass equivalent to that of an electron. However, gamma decay results in the release of gamma radiation, which is composed of high-energy photons. Photons are massless, making choice A the correct answer to this LEAST question.

8. A is correct. In the given equation, the uncertainty of position is represented as Δx. The uncertainty in momentum is given by $\Delta p = m\Delta v = (10^{-9}$ kg$)(10^{-12}$ m/s$) = 10^{-21}$ kg·m/s. The uncertainty in position is thus given by:

$$\Delta x = \frac{h}{2\pi \Delta p} = \frac{h}{2\pi \times 10^{-21}} = \frac{h \times 10^{21}}{2\pi}$$

IMAGE ATTRIBUTIONS

Chapter 3

Independent Q#4: https://commons.wikimedia.org/wiki/File:Two_nodes_as_mass_points_connected_by_parallel_circuit_of_spring_and_damper.svg by Adlange under CC-BY-SA 3.0

Chapter 4

Fig 1: https://commons.wikimedia.org/wiki/File:Diagram_Systems.png by Alkh.Alwa under CC-BY-SA 4.0

Fig 2: http://www.istockphoto.com/photo/chaotic-colorful-balls-and-organized-white-balls-order-and-chaos-gm520774802-91100925 by Artfoliophoto

Fig 3: https://commons.wikimedia.org/wiki/File:Kettle-convection-conduction-radiation.png by P.wormer under CC-BY-SA 3.0

Chapter 5

Fig 6: https://commons.wikimedia.org/wiki/File:Reading_the_meniscus.svg by Jleedev under CC-BY-SA 3.0

Chapter 6

Fig 1: https://commons.wikimedia.org/wiki/File:CoulombsLaw_scal.svg by Dna-Dennis under CC-BY-SA 3.0

Fig 2: https://commons.wikimedia.org/wiki/File:VFPt_plus_thumb.svg by Geek3 under CC-BY-SA 3.0

Fig 3: https://commons.wikimedia.org/wiki/File:VFPt_charges_plus_minus_thumb.svg by Geek 3 under CC BY-SA 3.0

Fig 4: https://commons.wikimedia.org/wiki/File:VFPt_charges_minus_minus.svg by Geek3 under CC BY-SA 3.0

Fig 5: https://commons.wikimedia.org/wiki/File:VFPt_capacitor.svg by Geek 3 under CC BY-SA 3.0

Fig 6: Adapted from https://commons.wikimedia.org/wiki/File:Dipole_polarization.JPG by Brews ohare under CC BY-SA 3.0

Chapter 7

Fig 5: https://commons.wikimedia.org/wiki/File:Capacitors_in_parallel.svg by Omegatron under CC BY-SA 3.0

Fig 5: https://commons.wikimedia.org/wiki/File:Capacitors_in_series.svg by Omegatron under CC BY-SA 3.0

Fig 6: https://commons.wikimedia.org/wiki/File:VFPt_cylindrical_magnet_big.svg by Geek3 CC BY-SA 4.0

Fig 7: https://en.wikipedia.org/wiki/File:Manoderecha.svg by Jfmelero CC BY-SA 4.0

Fig 8: https://commons.wikimedia.org/wiki/File:Regla_mano_derecha_Laplace.svg by Jfmelero under CC BY-SA 3.0

Chapter 8

Fig 7: https://commons.wikimedia.org/wiki/File:Allowed_and_forbidden_standing_waves.png by CK-12 Foundation under CC BY-SA 3.0

Fig 8: https://commons.wikimedia.org/wiki/File:StandingWaves.png by Guy vandegrift under CC BY-SA 3.0

Chapter 9

Fig 1: https://en.wikipedia.org/wiki/File:Onde_electromagnetique.svg by SuperManu under CC BY-SA 3.0

Fig 2: https://cnx.org/resources/ee3a03bb08982d5ee67583f9afd4f77601317ba4/Figure_28_08_05a.jpg CC-BY-4.0

Fig 4: https://commons.wikimedia.org/wiki/File:EM_spectrumrevised.png by Philip Ronan under CC BY-SA 3.0

Fig 5: https://en.wikipedia.org/wiki/File:Reflection_angles.svg by Arvelius under CC BY-SA 3.0

Fig 7: https://en.wikipedia.org/wiki/File:RefractionReflextion.svg by Josell7 under CC BY-SA 3.0

Fig 8: https://commons.wikimedia.org/wiki/File:Prism-rainbow.svg by Suidroot under CC-BY-SA 4.0

Fig 9: https://commons.wikimedia.org/wiki/File:Difraction.png by Bbkkk under CC BY-SA 4.0

Fig 11: https://commons.wikimedia.org/wiki/File:Single_Slit_Diffraction.svg by jkrieger under CC BY-SA 3.0

Fig 13: https://commons.wikimedia.org/wiki/File:Double-slit_experiment_results_Tanamura_four.jpg by Dr. Tonomura under CC-BY-SA 3.0

Fig 15: https://en.wikipedia.org/wiki/File:Thin_film_interference.svg by Nicoguaro under CC BY-4.0

Fig 16: From https://commons.wikimedia.org/wiki/File:Focal-length.svg by Henrik under CC BY-SA 3.0

Fig 18: From https://commons.wikimedia.org/wiki/File:Focal-length.svg by Henrik under CC BY-SA 3.0

Fig 19: https://en.wikipedia.org/wiki/File:Convexmirror_raydiagram.svg by Cronholm144 under CC BY-SA 3.0

Fig 20: https://en.wikipedia.org/wiki/File:Concavemirror_raydiagram_F.svg by Cronholm 144 under CC BY-SA 3.0

Fig 20: https://en.wikipedia.org/wiki/File:Concavemirror_raydiagram_2F.svg by Cronholm 144 under CC BY-SA 3.0

Fig 20: https://commons.wikimedia.org/wiki/File:Concavemirror_raydiagram_FE.svg by Cronholm 144 under CC BY-SA 3.0

Fig 21: https://en.wikipedia.org/wiki/File:Lens1.svg by Dr Bob under CC BY-SA 3.0

Fig 21: https://en.wikipedia.org/wiki/File:Lens1b.svg by Dr. Bob under CC BY-SA 3.0

Fig 23: https://en.wikipedia.org/wiki/File:Myopia_and_lens_correction.svg by Gumenyuk I.S. under CC BY-SA 4.0

Fig 24: https://en.wikipedia.org/wiki/File:Hypermetropia_color.svg under CC BY-SA 4.0

Chapter 10

Fig 1: https://commons.wikimedia.org/wiki/File:MODELO_AT%C3%93MICO_DE_BOHR.png by Thalia Inga under CC BY-SA 3.0

Fig 4: https://commons.wikimedia.org/wiki/File:Chlorophyll_ab_spectra-en.svg by Daniele Pugliesi under CC BY-SA 3.0

INDEX

This page left intentionally blank.